STOLEN
INNOCENCE

THE JAN BROBERG STORY

STOLEN
INNOCENCE

THE JAN BROBERG STORY

MARY ANN BROBERG

Disclaimer

All occurrences and conversations in the book are based on personal observations and recollections of the parties involved. In some instances, inner thoughts and dialogue have been recreated in order to effectively portray the events depicted in the book and are as close to exact as the memories of the sources permit. All of the main characters real names have been used in the book; however, some minor character names have been changed or omitted to protect the privacy of individuals connected to this story.

This book is dedicated to my incredible and supportive family who survived each crisis with dignity and perseverance.

Acknowledgments

I sincerely wish to thank those individuals who have given so much personal time and donated countless hours towards the development of this book. Great admiration and thanks to my husband, Bob, our children, Jan, Karen, and Susan, and sons-in-law, Matt and Larry, along with Jodie Jones, John Perry, and Mark Broberg. Each one has contributed to this project whether it be legal or professional advice, proof reading, editing, typesetting, leg work, or encouragement.

Too numerous to name are family members, friends and co-workers who read this story and insisted it be shared.

I acknowledge my editor, Darla Isackson, and offer thanks for her valuable suggestions and expertise which brought this story to its current status.

FOREWORD
by
Judge Charles D. Gill

It has been my experience as a Superior Court Judge for over twenty years that there exists for too many of our children not a childhood, but a "terrorhood." Most of these terrorized children's stories are never made public and are carried as lethal secrets throughout their lives. These children come from families of all races, religions and social standing. None are immune—not yours, not mine.

One impediment to stopping the terror is the public's inexperience in first recognizing and then dealing with the terrorist. This book is the encyclopedia of what adults should know about the particular terrorist called the pedophile. It is also a powerful handbook of all the things that loving and protective parents can do wrong when fate places them in these circumstances.

In fact, the loving parents in this case did everything absolutely wrong, while believing they were doing everything right.

During my first two years on the bench, I was faced with my first pedophile case. Perhaps like you, I did not know much about pedophilia and saw red at the very thought of an adult man having sex with an innocent child. The defendant in my case was a school teacher who the previous year had been named Teacher of the Year by his colleagues. Everyone liked him. He was kind, gentle, caring and trusted. He was also taking thousands of photos of children in their underwear and without. Thankfully, in his case, there were no allegations of physical sexual activity. He was a homosexual pedophile. That is to say his prey was always young boys. The pedophile in this book is a heterosexual pedophile.

While my case was pending, I attended a course in pedophilia at John Hopkins School of Medicine in Baltimore. It has a world-renowned clinic on sexual deviations. I wanted to know more about this once revered, now reviled teacher that I was about to sentence to prison. What made him tick? How does one know a person is a pedophile? What do they look like? How do they act? Was I in for a surprise!

Seated along with a few hundred physicians and psychologists, I watched four pedophiles take stage with Dr. Fred Berlin, maybe the most knowledgeable man in the world on the subject. The medical audience was as edgy as I. The four men identified themselves. The first was a married man with children. Other than being slightly obese, he looked like Joe average citizen. The second was a captain in the Marine Corps. The third, a reverend. The fourth was an unmarried construction worker.

No wonder the parents in this book had no clue from looks alone that their daughter was in danger from their terrorist friend. The Brobergs were and are a wonderful family with sound religious and ethical values. They instilled these values into their beloved daughter, Jan. They were very trusting and naïve. They were also an easy target for their "best friend," Robert Berchtold, a married heterosexual pedophile.

The Broberg and the Berchtold families were inseparable until Robert Berchtold kidnapped their precious twelve-year-old daughter one evening after a music lesson, then drugged, brainwashed and sexually assaulted her for months on end.

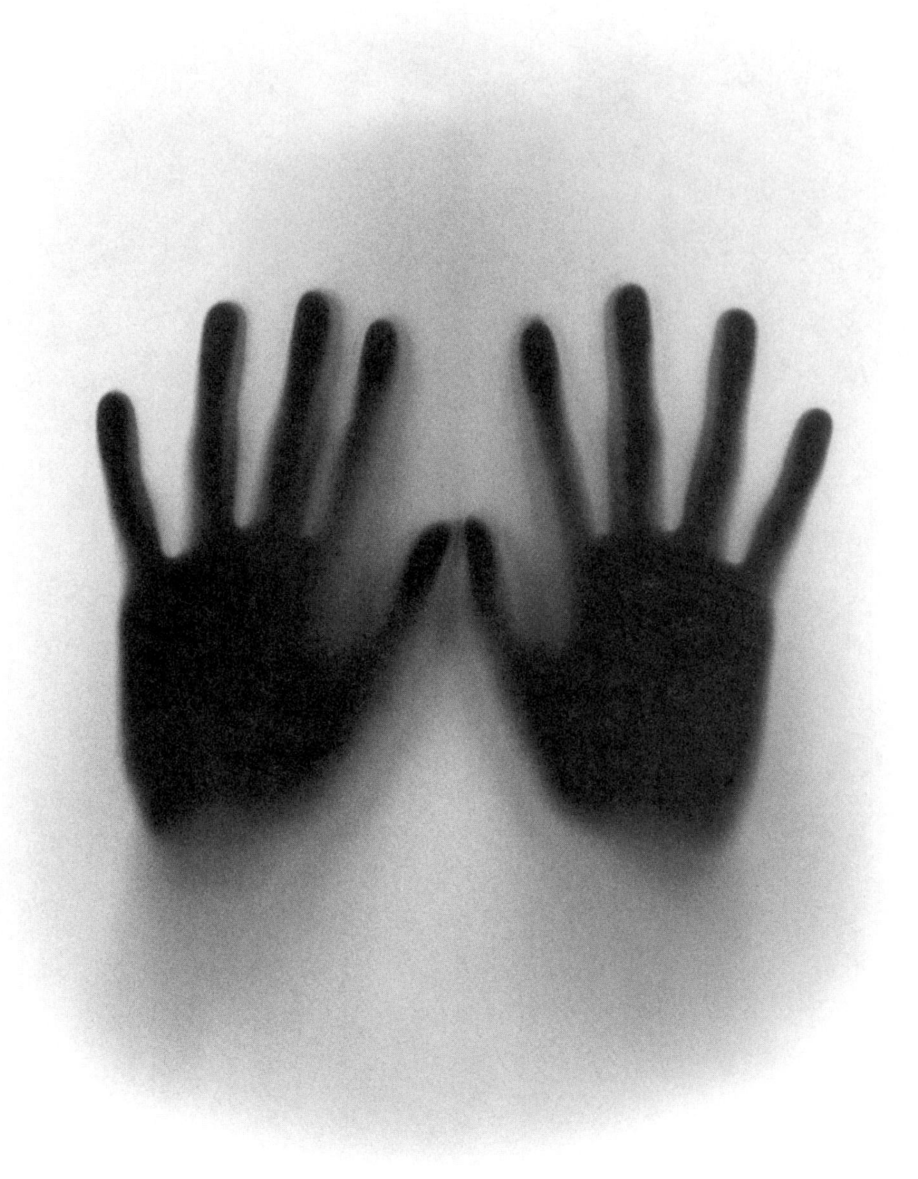

preface

There are many parts of Jan's story that may strike you as surreal. But everything you are about to read in this book is true and was well document- ed at the time it happened. Although more than twenty years have flown by since my daughter Jan was first abducted, I am not relying on my memory alone, and the terror of the experi- ence is easily reawakened. I walk into the room that used to be hers, sit down on her bed, and live again the questions that near- ly drove me mad when we realized Jan was missing: How could this happen to our nearly "ideal" family? How could I have given permission for Jan to go with Robert Berchtold—even for a few minutes? How could a man whose family had become our best friends, who had become like a brother to my husband, like a second father to my children, be a kidnapper? Was our trust in him completely misplaced? Where *was* Jan and what was hap- pening to her?

For nearly three years Robert Berchtold ("Brother B" or just "B" to our three girls) had said he loved our children like his own. Sure- ly he couldn't, wouldn't hurt Jan. But what kind of a man would disappear, taking his friend's twelve-year-old daughter with him? Was our best friend about to become our worst enemy?

I waited a painfully long time to even *begin* to find my answers. You, my readers, are lucky. You will walk, not only with me, but with my daughter through her bizarre, but absolutely real experiences from the first day, just as it happened. You will know up front what our daughter finally told us.

abducted!

October 17, 1974

That fateful morning I picked up the phone, and dialed the flower shop. When my husband Bob answered I said, "Robert wants to take Jan riding horses after school today. What do you think?"

"He already talked to me about it," Bob said. "He's visiting a customer in American Falls and the guy invited Robert to bring his kids to ride horses. The man has done some professional training, so Robert thinks he should see Jan's talent for riding, but I told him no."

"Why?" I asked.

"Mary Ann, it's time for him to back off. I know he's trying to help give our kids opportunities that I never could, but I'm still in charge of my family whether he likes it or not."

I was irritated. Bob's power struggle with Robert was starting to take its toll on their deep friendship.

When I picked Jan up from school, she excitedly talked about going horseback riding. "Your father said you couldn't go this time," I said.

"Why not?" she asked in surprise.

"I guess because you're so busy. You have a piano lesson today and there's so much going on." Jan quickly picked up that my feeble excuses were a cover-up for what I felt was simply her father's stubbornness.

"Dad needs to quit feeling guilty just because he can't do all the things Brother B knows how to do," she said. "I know Dad's allergic to horses, and if Brother B hadn't taken me out to Uncle Keith's, I still wouldn't know how to ride. Please, Mom, call Dad and ask him again."

My brother Keith owned several horses. For a long time we did not take advantage of his offer to teach the girls to ride. However, Robert's early life on the farm had given him familiarity with horses. With our permission, he had made arrangements with my brother to take our Jan and his son Jerry for their first riding experience. Keith was pleasantly surprised at Jan's ease at riding and encouraged her to come whenever she could. Riding became one more thing Jan excelled at and tried to squeeze into her already packed schedule. Robert was always happy to take her.

Before I had a chance to call Bob again, Robert popped in the back door and said enthusiastically, "Hi Jan! Are you ready to go?"

Jan looked at me, and I shook my head. "Robert, you know her dad said no. She has piano and what can I say?"

Robert protruded his lower lip and scowled, as if pouting. "Come on, let me do this for you. I have to go all the way out there anyway and this is a great opportunity for her." Quickly, he reversed his frown into a broad grin. "Besides, look at this gorgeous fall day. It's Jan's last chance to go since she will be training every day after school for gymnastics competition."

I shrugged and sighed.

Robert didn't let up. "I've made the appointment. It's already set. Let me drop her off at piano and pick her up when she's finished."

I protested again, but Robert interrupted. "Bob will be okay. It's his pride, you know. I need to quit ribbing him about his allergies to horses. Besides, having company will be nice. Don't you trust me?"

"Well, of course I do," I said.

Jan interlaced her fingers and shook them at me in a pleading way. "Please, Mom, please. I don't have any homework tonight. And I promise I'll practice piano when I get home." Eyes wide, head tilted, she waited for my response.

Weary of the coaxing, I heaved a defeated sigh. "Okay, you win, but I'm the one who has to explain to your father." Glaring at Robert, I asked, "How is it that you always get your way?"

"Must be my good looks," he said, chuckling. "Come on, Jan. Tell your teacher to make your lesson short because you have important things to do."

As Jan ran in to pick up her books off the piano, Robert hollered at her, "Hey, Jan! Have you had your vitamins today?"

Jan rolled her eyes and looked wistfully at me. I answered for her. "No, she hasn't."

Robert opened the door to the cupboard and reached up to the top shelf to retrieve a bottle of vitamins. The day he brought them, he put them in our cupboard and said, "Your girls are sick too much. These are better vitamins than those cheap Flintstones you buy. Try 'em. Do you ever see my kids sick?"

Grabbing a glass from the cupboard and filling it with water, he handed it to Jan. "Open wide," and popped the vitamin into her mouth. "Just what Dr. B ordered."

"Would you get out of here before you make Jan late for her lesson?"

Jan gave me a quick kiss and expressed thanks for letting her go, then dashed out of the house with piano books in hand.

Robert was trailing behind her. "Tell Bob I made you do it. Besides, I'll have Jan back by the time he gets home from work."

"Please do. We'll wait dinner for her." I stared after him as he dashed to his car.

"Don't worry. I'll take good care of her and she won't get hurt." He flashed a winning smile and saluted just before he jumped into the driver's seat.

Bob arrived home around six o'clock and I sheepishly related Robert's persuasiveness. Bob was irritated. "I'm not upset with you, honey. I know he can talk anybody into anything. How many times has he talked me into things I had no intention of doing? I just wish he would stop defying my stewardship."

Bob picked up the newspaper and headed for his La-Z-Boy as I finished preparing dinner.

The evening wore on, and Robert did not bring Jan home. Bob's frustration turned into concern. "Do you know the guy's name where they were going?"

I didn't. I had no details. "He just told me it was one of his better-heeled customers."

"Call Gail," he demanded.

I felt guilty for letting Jan go, and was growing increasingly edgy. I snapped back, "I've already called her twice. Robert told her that he and Jan were going to ride horses and he would be home before dark. Gail thought they were going to my brother's place. Surely they'll show up soon."

But they didn't. Where could they be?

■ ■ ■

When Robert dropped Jan off at her piano lesson he said, "I'll be back in half an hour. Then I'll take you riding." Jan tried keeping her mind on the piano pieces she had prepared for Mrs. Brink, but she kept looking at the clock. Mrs. Brink counted out the measures with exact precision while Jan repeated the drill over and over. Her lack of interest didn't deter Mrs. Brink's methodical instructions for the coming week as she urged Jan to spend more time on her piano studies. Jan peered around her teacher impatiently watching for Robert's car. Finally she spied it pulling up. Gathering up her books, she acknowledged her teacher's last minute advice, and issued a hasty goodbye. She bounced out the door and skipped down the front walk. Robert grinned happily as Jan opened the car door and jumped in.

"Whew! That lesson seemed to be extra long today. I don't know why, but I feel edgy."

"Oh, you're just excited," Robert replied.

Jan chatted exuberantly about school and the upcoming gymnastics meet. Soon the hum of the motor and the movement of the car had a tranquilizing effect, however, and she began fighting drowsiness.

"Wow! I don't know why I'm so tired," she remarked.

"It will be awhile before we get there. This ranch is past Massacre Rocks, about a half-hour drive. Just put your seat back and relax." Robert's voice was soothing. "You need to be refreshed to ride that stallion."

Jan moved the seat into a reclining position, took a deep breath, then stretched and yawned. She curled up on the seat and closed her eyes. Soon her small body relaxed, and she fell asleep.

When Jan awoke, she felt dazed and heavy, as though a great weight were crushing her body. Her eyes refused to focus; her thoughts were muddled, disjointed. She knew she had been riding in a car, and she could still feel motion, hear the hum of an engine, yet she seemed to be lying on a bed in a dark and unfamiliar room. Trying to gain control of her senses, she moved her body and was startled to find her hands strapped to something. Terrified, she tried to pull herself up only to find her feet restrained in the same manner. A scream stuck in her dry, parched throat.

A strange, high-pitched voice began speaking. "Fe.male com.pan.ion . . . Fe.male com.pan.ion." The phrase was repeated several times.

Horrified and overwhelmed by the eerie atmosphere Jan cautiously scanned the darkened room with wide eyes. Unable to find anyone attached to the mysterious voice, she gasped for air, thinking hysterically, What is going on?

She frantically tried to free herself from the restraints around her wrists and legs that confined her. A cold sweat engulfed her entire body as the realization sunk in: she was a prisoner!

The unearthly voice repeated, "Fe.male com.pan.ion . . . Fe.male com.pan.ion." Another shiver of fear shot through her. Still dazed, Jan felt out of touch with reality. Unable to fight consciousness, she slipped back into an unsettling sleep.

confusion!

Gail appeared at our house around nine o'clock that night admitting her concern. She was such a dear friend, and her concern for her husband was doubled by her concern for Jan. Bob was pacing the floor while I watched every passing car with anticipation. "Did the car break down? Why wouldn't they call from somewhere to let us know? Should we call the sheriff and have them start looking?"

Gail's face paled. She nervously fingered her car keys. "I don't know how to tell you this, but last week I went looking for Robert." Her long pause had our full attention. "I found him working on a motor home."

Bob bristled and stared at Gail. Attempting to understand what Gail was saying, he probed for more information. Gail dropped her eyes and drew a deep breath, exhaling slowly.

"For the last two weeks, Robert's been leaving home after dinner and hasn't returned until I'm asleep. He never explained where he was going, so I decided to follow him one night. He went to the storage unit where we keep our boat for winter." Gail swallowed, then raised her eyes. "I waited a few minutes then followed him in. The door to our storage unit was open and I could see him working on an orange motor home."

Apprehensive, Bob questioned. "Who does it belong to?"

Gail shook her head. "I have no idea. Probably a friend he's helping out."

Trying to absorb what Gail revealed, I remained silent, but new fears filled me. About six weeks ago, Robert told me he wanted to take a vacation, without Gail. I did not want to think about the rest of his conversation, but he was contemplating divorce. I suddenly felt a sharp jab in my stomach.

Bob's eyes narrowed as he waited, but Gail didn't say any more. I suggested, "Maybe we should drive out and see if the motor home is still there. Do you have a key to the storage unit?"

Gail thought for a minute. "I'm not sure. Maybe, it's on the key board."

Bob protested. "Let's just call the sheriff's office, give them a description of your car and they can find them."

Gail thrust the tip of her tongue to her lips and gasped. "No, please. Not yet. We need to go look."

Drawing in a deep breath, Bob released the air slowly. Gail handed him a slip of paper.

"Bob, I've been trying to call Robert's salesman, Jim, but he isn't home. If that guy with the ranch is a customer, Jim probably knows him. Here's his number. Maybe you could reach him while Mary Ann and I go check the storage unit."

Bob took the paper and laid it on the table. I could see the anxiety on his face and I felt responsible. I gave him a kiss, assured him we would hurry, then followed Gail out to her car. Ironically I still felt calm, assuring myself that my daughter was in safe hands. After all, wasn't Robert one of our best friends in the whole world?

As Gail and I began the trip across town, I tried to remain positive about Robert and Jan being late; surely there had to be a good reason for their delay. Conversing with Gail about the situation, she appeared upbeat. Her assurance that they would soon show up helped relieve my uneasiness.

"Maybe the motor home belongs to the rancher," I suggested.

Gail shrugged and remained silent for a few moments. I began to probe. "What do you think has caused Robert to be so happy lately? He sure hasn't been down on himself like he was for awhile."

Gail kept her eyes focused on the road and nodded. "You generally see Robert at his best. I see him at his worst. Strange thing, this manic depression."

"I don't know anything about it. There is so little said about depression or how to cure it. It's funny how people get so nervous when they hear about someone going to a shrink. Is Robert's depression anything like women get? You know, the baby blues?"

Gail said, "Maybe something like that."

"I wouldn't know about that either," I said. Nobody could wipe the smile off my face after I had a baby; it was such a pleasure to hold my babies in my arms after being so huge and miserable."

Gail forced a smile. "I hear what you're saying." A few moments later, she heaved a heavy sigh. "I'm so glad you guys haven't deserted us even though you know the worst of our problems. It's really been hard."

"Gail, we'd never do that," I said emphatically. "Does anyone have the perfect marriage? Don't even think that way. We love you."

"What on earth would I do if Robert left me and the kids?" Gail's voice quivered.

I had no answer for her. It was a thought I had entertained, but I didn't want to believe it could ever happen.

"I hate to sound stupid, but can you explain his problem to me?" I asked.

"You mean, manic depression?" Gail said. I nodded. "It's when a person either feels really great or very low. There's never any middle ground. Robert hides his problem well; he's afraid if people find out he's been going to a counselor, they'll think he's crazy."

"I wish he could feel better about himself. He has so much to offer," I said. "He is quite impulsive. How do you deal with that?"

"Oh, I ignore it most of the time," she said.

Nearing the storage units, Gail slowed the car. She stopped at the gate, got out, and after trying several keys, found one that fit the gate, unlocked it, then got back into the car.

My thoughts were still on their uncommunicative relationship. "I don't think I would handle a silent partner as well as you. How do you do it?"

"It's a big challenge. You know how he's been these past several months. He's either ignored, cursed, or blamed me for everything, and then expects me to know what's wrong."

Driving through the storage units, we strained our eyes to see if the motor home or Gail's new '74 Maverick station wagon was parked in the lot. Robert purchased the station wagon a few months ago after complaining that his kids were eating snacks in their Mark IV and he didn't want it messed up. Today, when he picked up Jan, he was driving the Maverick.

Gail found their unit, got out of the car, and tried each key on her ring but found no match. A new pang of fear pierced my stomach. Gail came back to the car and stared at me through the window. "What now?"

"Let's go home," I said quietly.

Gail slowly drove out of the lot. She took one final desperate look around hoping to see one of the vehicles. "I'll call in the morning and see if they will let me look in our unit."

Silence passed between us as we drove home. I wanted to say something comforting, but I had no words, no assurances. Finally, for the sake of conversation, I asked, "Is Robert really selling your business?"

Gail sighed deeply. "I don't know. He's never satisfied for very long."

"He told us he wants to open a sports business. Think he will?" I asked.

"I guess. Why not? Have you ever known anybody that can talk people into anything like he does? What a talent."

"I'm one of them," I said. "He has me wrapped around his finger."

"Me too. I guess that's why I married him. I fell in love with him the first time I met him. His charismatic charm hasn't changed one iota. He knows how to make everyone feel good." Gail smiled as she thought about Robert.

With Gail thinking positively about her husband, I remained quiet for a few minutes. When she finally turned to look at me, I asked, "What was his reason for going to Mexico last month?"

"Oh, one of his California counselors told him to get rid of the self-pity and look around at what he could do to make a difference for other people. You can't imagine how shocked I was getting that call from him saying he wanted to adopt a little Mexican girl. I had no idea."

"Did he explain?"

Gail nodded her head. "A little bit. I think the medicine they gave him has been a big help, but that treatment place said if he would focus his life on things that took his mind off his own problems, it would give him a new lease on life. Somehow this girl emerged. I guess his counselor knew about the family. Robert thought it was worth looking into. When he called me, he felt this would be something that would pull us together."

"I thought you'd lost your minds," I said.

Gail's voice was instantly warm and confident. "Mary Ann, when Robert called from Mexico, he was so excited. Here was somebody he could help. Call me crazy, but even I thought it might be the answer. The family lived in complete poverty with no father and several children. The mother knew there was no future for her daughter in Mexico and wanted her to have a chance. With us, she would get an education, food every day, and nice clothes—but her mamma wanted to meet me to make sure Maria had a good mother. So I went down there, we all signed the papers and Maria was ready to leave with us when the mother burst into tears. She couldn't let her go." Gail's voice cracked with emotion.

Tears brimming in Gail's eyes caused my own emotions to surface. In a whispering voice I said, "Oh Gail, no matter how little anyone has, a mother's love for her child is everything. I'd crawl the earth for one of mine."

Our eyes glistened in the passing of street lights. Only the hum of the engine broke the silence.

After gaining her composure, Gail reached her hand across the seat to pat my arm. I looked at her with tenderness. She remained silent, subdued. When she finally spoke, her voice was passionate. "Robert's a good man and a good father. I've been the biggest disappointment to him. Maybe I've tried too hard to make myself into what I perceived he wanted in a woman and a wife. Whatever I've done, it's all wrong."

I felt compassion for Gail. Robert knew the art of capturing the hearts of women, and Gail was aware of his magnetism. After all, she married him. She longed for his total devotion, but knew it had faded. Even I had felt exhilarated each time Robert told me I was extraordinary. His flattering remarks and complimentary words would swell my head, and tiny sensations would prickle my spine. I tried to shrug off his comments by telling him it was foolish talk and he was embarrassing me. Looking at Gail, I realized I must not contribute to my friend's pain.

When we arrived back home, Bob had called the highway police to inquire whether there was any report of a disabled vehicle in the area, giving a description of the Maverick station wagon. The answer was negative. Since he hadn't reached Robert's salesman, Gail called and Jim was home, but he didn't know where

Robert had gone and had no idea about the person he was going to see in American Falls.

Far into the night, we tried to put together conversations we each had with Robert recently. Why had he told me he wanted to take a vacation without his wife? Had he taken the motor home and gone to Sun Valley, or up to Jackson Hole? Was he trying to prove something? What was going on with his mind? Gail felt this was another of the impulsive behaviors she knew so well.

Jan would be fine. That was a fact we all agreed upon. He would never hurt her or any other child. His love for our children was an accepted fact. We just had to realize that maybe the car had broken down and he couldn't get to a phone. There was no need to get overwrought. We just needed to be patient. Nevertheless, I was restless all night. My mind would not let go of the agonizing question: where were they and what was happening?

■ ■ ■

Unaware of the passage of time, Jan stirred again and slowly opened her eyes. As she moved her tiny body, she became conscious of the reality that she was strapped to a bed. The room was dark and deathly quiet. Trying to gain a sense of why she would be there and what was happening, she tried to recall what the message was from the previous voice she heard earlier. Licking her dry lips and swallowing to moisten her mouth, she remembered leaving her piano lesson with Brother B, but was unable to recall anything after getting into his car. What happened after that? Was the voice real or did she imagine it?

A sliver of light flickered faintly around the edges of what appeared to be a door. In panic, Jan watched the door, waiting for her abductor to appear. But the ominous silence still hung heavy in the air.

Agonizing over her vulnerable position, Jan thought, Where's Brother B? Who was talking to me? It sounded like those guys on Star Trek. As she struggled to move, the silence was broken by the same high pitched, monotone voice that repeated words in a short abrupt manner. Alarmed, she listened to the weird utterance from this unidentified spokesman. "Fe.male com.pan.ion. Our peo.ple are dy.ing. You cho.sen to help us. You give us a child."

Moving her head toward the voice, she could see from the corner of her eye, a small ivory box situated near her head. The message was repeated several times before silence invaded the room. Terrorized by the message, unable to move, Jan felt as if she were being swallowed into a deep dark hole. Shuddering with fright, her agonizing thoughts continued. All the stories Robert had related about flying saucers, spaceships, and aliens came back to Jan in a frightening flurry. She tried denying that her present circumstances had any connection, but she reviewed the possibility over and over again in her mind.

Thoughts about her impending fate worked her into a frenzy. Her heart raced and her breathing was labored. She couldn't stop the tears from running off her face onto her shirt. Several minutes later a voice crackled again. "Fe.male com.pan.ion. You must help us. We need spe.cial child. You are cho.sen to have this child. Ve.ry im.por.tant to the fu.ture of our pla.net. Please save us. You can.not fail."

Jan's thoughts raced wildly and she was overcome with horror. Me? Why did they choose me? Save their planet? I don't understand what they want me to do. A special child?

The message was repeated over and over in that high, unearthly sta-catto voice. Sickened by the senseless petition and emphatic demand, Jan struggled to keep her emotions under control. Unable to bear the unbeliev-able request longer, she burst into pathetic sobs.

Jan felt sick to her stomach; she was afraid she was going to throw up, and felt extremely groggy. Unable to move from the uncomfortable posi-tion because of the restraints, Jan continued to struggle until she was exhausted; her nauseousness subsided. The darkness in the room made it impossible to distinguish between night and day. Hoping to shut out the voice proved impossible. She strained to cover her ears with her shoulders, but the restraints limited her mobility.

Over and over the messages repeated their haunting refrain. Several hours passed. Jan agonized, Why are they doing this? Exhausted, horrified, and longing for some comfort, she closed her eyes. Since she had awakened hours ago, she had been fighting an unnatural heavy feeling. Now she welcomed it as an escape from her unexplained circumstance. Finally, sleep comforted the little girl.

reality

The next morning, I awoke abruptly at dawn. *Jan's gone,* I frantically thought. *She's really gone.* Anxiety overwhelmed me and a hard, painful knot pierced my gut. Feeling smothered, I threw back warm sheets, slid from the bed, and rushed wildly into the living room. Crazy thoughts raced incoherently through my numb brain. *Where is Robert? Where did he go? What happened? Where is Jan? I have to know what is going on! Any minute now he'll drive up laughing his head off.* But a hard lump lodged in my throat and I couldn't swallow.

I dashed back to the bedroom and threw my exhausted body down beside my husband. "Oh, Bob. I can't stand this. I feel so helpless."

Bob threw his arms around me. "I've been praying all night, honey. I don't know what to do." Bob attempted to stifle his emotions, but the words choked in his throat. Sitting on the edge of the bed, we held each other and cried like babies.

"Oh Bob! Why did I let her go? Where are they?" My voice rose in volume.

Karen and Susan came running into the bedroom. "What's the

matter? Do you know where Jan is? What's happening, Mom . . . Dad?" They both jumped into the middle of our bed.

"Oh, girls. We're just trying to figure out where Jan is and having a little bawling session. Do you want to join us?" I attempted to smile through my tears at the two of them.

Bob questioned, "Do you have any ideas? Has Jerry or Jimmy said anything about their dad going somewhere? What do you think we should do?"

The girls shook their heads solemnly.

"Dad, you always tell me to pray when I'm sad," Karen replied.

Bob put his arm around Karen. "You're right. Let's kneel down right here and ask Heavenly Father to bless Jan and bring her home safe."

"And Brother B," Susan replied.

"Right, Susie Q." I choked back a sob, then muttered, "He better."

After an intense prayer, we shed more tears, then hugged each other, and retreated to the kitchen for breakfast. Eight-year-old Susan consumed her corn flakes and toast, then escaped to the family room for cartoon and puzzle enjoyment. Ten-year-old Karen stayed close by, listening intently to our conversation.

"We have to decide what to do," I said. "Do you have any ideas?"

"I've been thinking about driving to Brigham City. Robert talked a lot about places he used to go when he and Gail lived there. But first, I'm going to run to the store and get the crew going on some funeral flowers. I'll be home in a bit." (We owned a floral shop, and Bob had to keep things going.) Bob gave me a kiss and bent across the table to kiss Karen. Trying to be reassuring, he looked at Karen as he exited the back door. "I'm sure Jan is fine. Your job is to keep your Mom happy until I get back."

Clearing the table, I became absorbed with my own thoughts and ignored Karen's presence. After a matter of minutes she said, "Mom, it's really hard to think about Jan and not know where she is. Do you think Brother B will bring her home today?"

"I don't know, but we have to think he will." My statement expressed enough uncertainty that Karen looked at me with worried eyes.

"It might be hard for me at school when all Jan's friends ask where she is. I don't know what to tell them. Should I say she's sick? Don't you think Caroline should know what's happened?"

Caroline was Jan's best friend since first grade and the two of them were inseparable. Caroline spent more time at our home than any of Jan's other friends. Often, she was invited to share in family activities and trips. Realizing it would be a major concern, I nodded at Karen. "Karen, don't worry so much. If Caroline calls, let me talk to her mother and I'll explain. I hate to upset others since we know Robert will be coming back any moment."

I dialed the Berchtold home. "Any news, Gail?"

"No, not a word. I called the owner of the storage unit and he will be there at 8:00 A.M. I told him my husband was out of town and I needed to get something out of it," Gail said.

An hour later, Gail brought disappointing news. The motor home was gone. Only the boat remained in the unit. She begged us to have patience while she tried to locate Robert. "Let me call his family and see if they have talked to him."

Unfortunately, her contacts produced no information regarding his whereabouts, but she discovered Robert had purchased the motor home from a relative in Wyoming about a month previously. With this news, a wave of anxiety slithered through my body. *What is going on? Has he flipped out? Is he just trying to let Gail know their marriage is over? Did he have to put Jan in the middle of their conflict?* I thought.

Staring into space, I tried to put the details together. I was an emotional wreck and weary of trying to cope with the absurdity of what had taken place. The more I thought about it, the angrier I became. *How dare he do this? Who does he think he is? He needs to get back and face his problems like a man.*

Gail waited for Bob to come home from the store, but couldn't offer much help. She couldn't think of a reason why he would be in Brigham City. From all her phone calls to family members, she learned that none of them had seen or talked to Robert for weeks. Desperate to do *something*, Bob invited Karen to go with him and they took off for Utah.

I tried to do housework, but couldn't keep focused. I wandered aimlessly from one task to another, unable to concentrate. I went down and looked through Jan's room. Nothing was amiss; everything was in place. I thought how excited Jan and Karen were a few months ago to have their very own room when Robert offered to divide the large bedroom they occupied. It was a project we had planned for a couple of years, but had put on hold due to lack of funds.

"Let me do it," Robert said. "Bring the girls down to my store and let them pick out their own bedroom furniture. I'll get it for you wholesale and you buy the needed materials for the room. The labor is a freebie. Where could you get a better deal?"

The opening ceremonies began with a bang as Jan, Karen, Susan and Robert's three boys, Jerry, Jimmy and Joey, congregated in the hall with hammers in hand to make their mark where the new door would be installed to Jan's new room. They had a blast hammering down the wall. Each member of the family agreed to take assignments in order to get the rooms done within a two-week time span. Bob took the job of providing refreshments and giving out compliments, which he did profusely since he had no building skills. The girls ran errands to bring the right tools to Robert, handing him nails or boards, or doing whatever was needed while he meticulously measured, sawed, and hammered. My job was cleaning up, taping seams, or painting when I wasn't fixing meals and taking care of household duties.

Robert's patience was commendable and I often heard all of them laughing their heads off as he told stories and funny incidents from his life. Occasionally, he would stop to play a game or do tickle fights to break up the monotony.

Finally the construction was completed. Bob was enthusiastic as he thanked Robert for all he had done and insisted Robert needed compensation for his hard work and time. Robert firmly declared, "there are things one does in life for those you love and it comes without a price." He cherished our friendship and would do anything for us.

> <u>Jan's Diary, August 4, 1974:</u> Today Brother B called and said our furniture came. Mom's still painting, but we're getting the furniture tomorrow. Finally I get my own room. It's pretty. It has blue and white daisies on the wall. Brother B hung a love seat. But the cushion isn't done. Mom painted the shutters white and is making a bedspread to match the wallpaper. I practiced my lesson. At 5:30 I went to piano. Dad picked me up. On the way home we stopped at Freight Outlet and saw my furniture. It's beautiful. I went baby-sitting and she paid me a dollar. Brother B stopped in. We had a tickling fight.

Bringing myself back to the present, I thought, there is no reason for me to panic. He'll be back anytime with Jan. I needed to be patient and stop my worrying.

Hours later, Bob and Karen returned from their excursion with no answers. We called Gail; she came over and pleaded that we not call the police until she had exhausted every lead. "I know he'll show up soon. Just give me a little more time."

Gail's pathetic voice was desperate. I stared at Bob for an answer. "I don't know, Gail," he said. I think we should contact the law. There could have been an accident. Why haven't we heard?"

Gail began to cry. "I'm so concerned about my kids. What will they think? How can I explain it? I know he'll be back. He just does these off the wall things sometimes. If we get the law involved, he'll be angry. He has never done anything to get in trouble with the law before. You know he hasn't done this to hurt any of us. Please wait."

"But we can't go through another night not knowing. Something has happened and we need help," Bob said in desperation.

I put my arms around Gail's frail body and let her sob on my shoulder. Listening to her heart-wrenching wailing, Bob breathed deeply and his shoulders heaved heavily. He turned from the two of us and walked away.

It felt as if a golf ball had stuck in my throat. The only thing I seemed capable of doing was crying. Determined to keep my own emotions under control, I comforted Gail. I knew Robert would not hurt Jan. He always talked about our girls being like his own and he always treated them with extreme kindness. However, I had seen him act impulsively several times and this had to be another of those times.

Later in the day, I picked up the phone book and found the number of the local FBI. I dialed, but felt I was betraying Gail by making the call. As the phone rang, I frantically attempted to put my confused mind into sensible order. A recording relieved my dilemma by giving me a number to call in Butte, Montana, if the call was an emergency. The message stated the office would be open on Monday morning. I didn't call Butte. But how could I face another night of not knowing where Jan was?

■ ■ ■

Jan awoke to observe light filtering softly through a closed blind hang-ing at the window; yet the room was still dark, an engine still humming. Startled at her surroundings, she moved suddenly and discovered she was no longer confined by the straps at her ankles or wrists. She remained still, searched the room with her eyes, and was barely able to make out the out-

line of objects. A partition, which she previously imagined to be a door, blocked the view to anything beyond. She felt certain things had been rearranged from her earlier recollection, but there was more light than when she had first encountered her mysterious environment. Tucked high in the corner of the room, she spied the small ivory box. A door to her left was partially open; she could see it was a bathroom.

Dare she move? Would someone retaliate against her? Cautiously, Jan sat up. A sharp pain shot through her head and she felt dizzy. She groaned, cradling her head between her hands. Her limbs felt lifeless, and they tingled when she moved them. As she arose on unsteady legs she thought they might buckle under her. Jan squinted as her eyes became more accustomed to the dark. She moved carefully and quietly into the small bathroom compartment for relief. As she returned to her confined quarters, her solitude was abruptly interrupted with the same eerie high-pitched voice speaking again. Jan's worst nightmare was a reality. The sounds came from the little ivory box.

Apprehensively, she listened. "Fe.male com.pan.ion . . . Fe.male com.pan.ion. I am Zada. Listen to what I say!" Overwhelmed by the ghastly sound of the voice, Jan didn't move. "Fe.male com.pan.ion . . . Fe.male com.pan.ion. You do what I say or you will cease to ex.ist!"

The ivory box crackled and remained silent. Minutes ticked away. A wave of anxiety swept over her as she assessed her situation. What does that mean? Cease to exist? Jan sat motionless and felt sweaty. For hours, she had not uttered one word. She dared not speak to a faceless voice that delivered such weird, painful orders. This is awful. I just want to go home, she thought, her eyes brimming with tears.

For a long time, Jan cringed in fright on the bed and stared at the walls. As much as she hated the messenger's voice, the silence was worse. Finally she thought, If that person is watching me, why doesn't she say something?

Afraid to venture from her confinement, Jan watched the closed blind on the window sway; quick snatches of sunlight let her know that it was daytime. Minutes seemed like hours. Hours turned into excruciating agony.

After a lengthy period of silence, the repetitious messages again described the intended mission for the imprisoned youth. Listening to an inhuman voice demand unethical requests made the room into a torture chamber.

Jan couldn't understand why this was happening to her. She didn't know what to say or how to beg for mercy from the concealed person. She cried continually until she used the last of the toilet paper to blow her nose. She was convinced all her tears had been shed until she began hearing a new message, repeated again and again, of the devastating harm that would come to her family if she didn't do as she was instructed. The thought of Karen losing her eyesight, her dad dying, or Susan being taken by them if she failed to do what they told her, was incomprehensible. Why would they do that? Not my family, she thought.

Confined to the small room, Jan felt she was losing her mind. Nearing hysteria, she pondered what type of retribution she would face if she chose to go beyond the partition. Fear kept her a prisoner. Finally unable to stand her confinement any longer, Jan pushed against the partition, but was unable to move it. Determined, she pushed harder, pounding on the wall, crying desperately. She screamed in panic, "Help me! Somebody get me out! Help me! Help me!" No response. Where is my family? Will I ever see them again? Will they rescue me? In desperation, Jan slumped to the floor and cried despondently. Her agonizing mournful lamentations continued until her energy was completely wasted.

The tiny rays of sunlight Jan could see through the blind were fading, and Jan knew night was approaching. Not feeling strong enough to face another lonely, helpless night, she curled up into a ball and begged again. "Please, help me. I'll do what you ask, but don't hurt me." She burst into an agonizing wail and pulled the cover over her head. Compliance to the undisclosed stranger's charge had finally been accomplished.

"Fe.male com.pan.ion, your mis.sion very im.port.ant. Do not fail!" the voice demanded. Then, silence. Only Jan's tormented moan was heard. The mysterious voice didn't respond to her proclamation. By this point there was no doubt in the mind of this young victim that she had truly encountered persons from another world and that she had no choice but to comply with their requests.

Lying on the bed with the bedspread over her, Jan could hear nothing but the mournful hum of the engine. She lay there for hours awaiting the next blast of solicitations from the supernatural voice, but the box remained silent. Jan's mournful cries were the only sounds in the still silent darkness as she begged her captors to let her go.

Maybe I'm dying, she thought. She sobbed pitifully until she could cry no more. Her head throbbed as she fought to stay awake. Closing her eyes to ease the pain brought some relief. Exhausted and drained, she fell asleep.

■ ■ ■

October 20, 1974

Church on Sunday was strained. I was certain others would realize neither Jan nor Robert was there. As the day came to a close, we contacted family members to tell them about Jan's disappearance. We wanted them to know we would be contacting authorities in the morning; we had no choice.

Gail was devastated.

foul play?

October 21, 1974

All hell broke loose when the FBI answered their phone on Monday morning. The statement, "My daughter 's been kidnapped!" brought Peter Welsh, and a senior agent, Norm Probst, to our door within minutes of the call.

Mr. Welsh's first question was, "Why did you wait so long to contact us? This is considered an emergency."

Trying to answer that question took most of the morning as Bob and I related the close and endearing friendship we had with the Berchtold family. As the conversation went on and on, my mind went back to the first time I saw them in June of 1972. I was completely swept away by the memory; it was as though I were watching a movie of it.

Robert Berchtold was standing in the church foyer observing a group of teenage boys. He seemed annoyed by their boisterous laughter. His discomfort showed in his pursed lips and furrowed brows as the boys noisily exited the building into the warm summer air. He reminded me of a drill sergeant with his rigid posture and tightly folded arms. By his side stood a thin, willowy woman holding a baby; a toddler twisted himself around the woman's skirt.

As friendly members of the congregation stopped to introduce themselves, his stern look dissipated and his stance relaxed. He flashed a broad smile and vigorously returned handshakes while he and his wife pleasantly responded to the welcoming adults. Shortly, a group of children came running around a corner, shepherded by an older woman.

"I'm Robert Berchtold," the man said to the aging teacher, thrusting his hand forward to engage hers. "So, you've met my tribe of boys. Hope they didn't cause any problems. I warned them to be good, but I know what a handful Joey can be even at his best behavior."

The Sunday School teacher smiled and assured the gentleman his children behaved well. As the man turned to rejoin his family, a small group of chattering girls made their way down the steps.

Admiring the young girls, he smiled broadly, then remarked enthusiastically to the woman, "I finally got one."

Uncertain of his comment, the teacher said, "Excuse me?"

Mr. Berchtold replied, "Oh, I mean I finally got a girl. After four boys, our baby's a girl."

The teacher chuckled and nodded her head. "How nice," she stated.

My eavesdropping was unintentional. I was standing at the library window returning materials I had used for a lesson. As the new family headed out into the warm June morning, my friend Zola asked if I had met the Berchtolds.

Shaking my head, Zola exclaimed, "Oh, they're a nice family. I knew Robert Berchtold in college. Remember my twin sister, Zada? Well, Zada was engaged to Robert's roommate and we both double-dated with him. Isn't that something? Come and meet them." Grabbing my arm, Zola accompanied me out to the parking lot while my daughters rushed through the doors ahead of us. "They're practically your neighbors," she added.

The Berchtolds were walking toward their car when Zola shouted "yoo-hoo" and waved them down. Robert Berchtold was exuberant as introductions were made; he shook my hand jubilantly. "It's a pleasure to meet you. And you are a very impressive chorister. I've never heard 'Onward Christian Soldiers' sung with more conviction."

"Well, thank you very much," I said, flattered. His infectious grin and friendly personality were captivating. His wife, standing slightly in back of him, smiled pleasantly and affirmed his statement by nodding her head. Her response was reserved, even a bit shy. The baby she cuddled in her arms drew admiration from my three daughters.

"Robert and Gail opened a discount furniture store called Freight Outlet and bought a home two blocks from your house," Zola explained.

"Bring your family over and we'll give you a tour," Mr. Berchtold said. "We really like it, but the back yard needs lots of work. The terraced rock gardens would be beautiful if the weeds hadn't taken over."

Robert Berchtold, dressed in a white shirt and tie, tan sport coat and dark trousers, reminded me of Merle Haggard, the Country/Western singer. He was small in stature, probably no more than five feet eight inches tall, with a short pointed nose, wavy sandy-blonde hair, full bottom lip that protruded slightly, and glasses that covered blue-gray eyes which crinkled at the corners when he smiled. More impressive than his appearance was his friendliness and engaging personality.

Gail wore a red peasant blouse and colorful gathered skirt, somewhat wrinkled from wrestling a baby. Her thin body reminded me of Twiggy. Shoulder length brown hair and straight bangs made her long, angular face seem even longer. She looked freshly scrubbed, but I thought how a little makeup would pink-up her colorless cheeks and enhance her pretty blue eyes that were framed by dark-rimmed glasses.

Excusing myself, I motioned to my girls telling them we needed to go home. Mr. Berchtold's eyes danced with delight. "Wait, you can't go. We haven't met your beautiful daughters."

Zola pointed her finger at my oldest. "Well, this is Jan. She's nine and a great little actress. Last summer, Jan played Gretel in *The Sound of Music*. But you have to run fast to keep up with her. She's a real live wire."

Enjoying the notoriety, Jan's beaming smile reflected approval. "I'm almost ten and will be in the fifth grade," she added, fluttering long dark eyelashes that outlined her piercing blue eyes. A petite, strawberry blonde, whose tiny freckled nose crinkled when she flashed a grin, Jan was born with an overabundance of energy. She was an alive, spirited, people-pleaser child. Her unmerciful drive for stuffing more into life than humanly possible, was challenging, but an accepted fact.

Mr. Berchtold extended his hand and gripped hers. "Hello, Jan. I'm pleased to meet you." He bit down on his bottom lip and gave an approving nod.

Gail said softly, "Our oldest son is ten."

Jan nodded and turned to look at the boys. "Yeah, I met Jerry in Sunday School."

We watched Jerry, a handsome, sturdy-built brown-haired boy, wrestle a younger brother to the ground.

Zola continued her introductions as the parking lot emptied. "You haven't met Mary Ann's husband Bob yet, but take a good look at Karen. She looks just like her father. She's nearly eight, the same age as your Jimmy."

Feeling conspicuous, Karen looked down for a moment. Paternal genetics were well imprinted upon her. She had inherited a creamy-tan complexion, blonde hair, a short straight nose, and large, clear and penetrating sky-blue eyes. Karen was taller and statelier than her older sister, and claimed a quieter disposition. Content with less exhaustive projects, she nurtured with explicit kindness anything that purred, barked, chirped, or crawled.

"And this little cutie is Susan," Zola announced, pointing at my youngest. "She'll be a first grader this fall."

Susan blushed, and presented a less than enthusiastic smile. One could blame Susan's reserved nature on her young age, but her thoughtful study of situations was beginning to be recognized as part of her personality. Rarely did she give voice until she felt confident that her expressions would be taken seriously and without issue from her two older sisters. Susan was darkhaired like me, but fair-skinned, hazel-eyed with dark eyelashes and a perfect small button nose with one big freckle on it. I thought she was adorable.

"It's a genuine pleasure to meet such lovely young ladies," Mr. Berchtold said as he bent down and viewed each one intently, his eyes narrowing as he flashed a big smile. "You girls bring your parents and come over and visit."

They nodded their heads, and Susan pulled on my arm.

Grasping a last-minute opportunity, Mr. Berchtold asked," By the way, do you girls want a job weeding our flower beds?"

Looking at each other with mischievous grins on their faces, each waited for the other to answer. Mr. Berchtold added, "Oh, I'll pay. As much as I hate yard work, I'll be generous."

Sparing them a confession, I said, "It's not the pay. The last time they weeded my carrots, I don't know what happened, but we sure harvested great bunches of thistle. I've never figured out if it was an honest mistake or a plot to end yard duties."

Laughter erupted among the adults while the girls hurriedly dashed to our car. As I followed after them, Mr. Berchtold called out invitingly, "Remember, the invitation is wide open. I want to meet your husband."

"We'd love to come," I said, getting into my car. Driving away, I kept thinking that I never would have put Robert and his wife together as a couple.

We explained to the agents that within a matter of weeks, our children brought the Berchtold boys into their circle and we had all established a close relationship with their family. It was like no other friendship we had ever encountered. Devouring each segment of time with the Berchtolds became addictive as we planned trips, family activities and frequent outings. They were like family. Never had we imagined a relationship could enmesh us so immediately and consume our lives so completely. Robert frequently commented, "Your husband is just like a brother to me." And Jan had considered Jerry one of her best friends.

Picking up Jan's journal, I read them her entry from March 12, 1973:

> Today my parents are going out of town. We're staying at Berchtold's. I went down to Brother B's shop. Down there I answered the phone. We went on break too! For supper we fondued. It was fun. That night we showed films. Jerry held my hand and put his arm around me. It was good. It was a very fun day!

I pointed out to the agents, Jan's remarks about the Berchtold family from other journal entries such as:

> October 7, 1973: Our parents are out of town. We're staying at Berchtold's. Today is fast Sunday. I got up real early about 7:30. Brother B did my hair. In fast and testimony meeting I bore my testimony. I really had the spirit today. That night Brother B took us to the grocery store and said "anything that looks good, get it." We did. We got home and had a feast! We listened to Partridge Family music.

Brother B had a good talk with us and asked if we had to choose,
would we rather be deaf or blind. Karen didn't want to be blind. Yuk!
I don't want to be either one. Then Mom and Dad came.

The agents smiled and nodded. They were beginning to understand why we had not called them sooner. After they had gathered all the information they could from us, the two agents went to the Berchtold home. Later, they returned for more details. Gail's cooperation caused them to probe further and Mr. Welsh asked if Berchtold had ever given Jan drugs. We were surprised.

"No, only vitamins," I stated.

I presented the bottle of vitamins to the agent and told them about Robert making Jan taking a vitamin before she left for her piano lesson.

Mr. Welsh explained, "Mrs. Berchtold walked in on her husband and saw him dumping the contents of capsules into the toilet. When she asked what he was doing, he became angry and said it was none of her business. He flushed the toilet, gathered the empty capsules and left without any explanation. She thought they were vitamins, but didn't know why he was emptying them."

Hearing his comments made me flinch. I informed Mr. Welsh that earlier in the summer I had Jan checked by a doctor. Jan hadn't complained of being ill, only tired; she occasionally wandered the house listlessly. Sometimes her eyes appeared dilated. Then, seemingly energized, she tackled the day's activities with an over abundance of enthusiasm. The doctors reported her in excellent health following his examination. He had no answer to her intermittent lack of energy.

Mr. Welsh took the vitamins for testing at an FBI lab. Days later, he said, "These are vitamins, but that doesn't mean he didn't drug her."

He attempted to explain the next hurdle we would face: "Your daughter's abduction will be a big news story. You need to prepare yourselves, because your life will never be the same."

It was not what we wanted to hear. We didn't relish publicity or having our private lives disrupted. Mr. Welsh called the phone company and asked for the installation of a second phone line. It was important to keep our regular line open in case Jan or Robert should call. The agent went out to his car and brought back a large reel to reel tape recorder. "This will pick up every call. You can record every message. There's plenty of tape."

Agent Probst continued, "This recorder was used by a family in Montana whose daughter was missing for a very long time. They kept it in their home for over a year and a half before the person who abducted their daughter finally called. The call was traced, he was located, and eventually convicted."

"Over a year?" I responded in a discouraged tone of voice. "Did he murder the girl?"

The agent winced. "That was an abduction by a stranger. This guy's your friend," he said, raising his eyebrows while giving us a look of uncertainty about his statement.

Late that evening, my sister, Nadine, and her husband, Leonard, came to our home, their faces etched with worry. Leonard's brother-in-law was the Power County Sheriff. Trying to remain composed, Leonard said, "We have some news for you. Rulon called us. One of his officers found an abandoned green station wagon registered to Robert Berchtold near Massacre Rocks. He thought you should know."

"Does he have any idea why it was there? Or what happened?" Bob asked.

"There was a broken car window, but he didn't know much," Leonard said. Rulon called the FBI after he heard about Jan. The car has been impounded."

October 22, 1974

Tuesday morning, we pressed Mr. Welsh for information. He

carefully related the incident. "The car was found in a secluded spot twelve miles south of American Falls, near the Snake River. You're familiar with Massacre Rocks, aren't you?"

Surprised he knew, I nodded. Many times as a young girl, I worked in the potato fields around Massacre Rocks. Its name came from an Indian attack on a pioneer wagon train.

Agent Welsh continued, "The car is being transported to the Pocatello police station where a thorough investigation will be done. Right now, we have no answers. I've been out there with other law enforcement officers trying to piece things together."

"Any news about what happened to our daughter?" Bob asked with trepidation.

"No," Mr. Welsh paused as he viewed our questioning, alarmed faces. "But it's assumed Jan had been in the car. A multi-striped stocking cap that you said she was wearing was found on the seat. They also found a blue nylon jacket and two piano books that we're holding as evidence."

A lump lodged in my throat as I looked at Bob. Panic rushed through my weakened body. Bob quietly whispered, "Those are Jan's things."

"It appears that the day Berchtold disappeared, he left the store telling his sales clerk he was meeting a man who was giving him cash in exchange for some gold bars. The clerk reported Berchtold carried a large case out to his car which appeared to be quite heavy. He assumed it held the bars," said Welsh.

Bob and I looked at each other with surprise. It sounded rather eerie.

"There's one more thing you need to know," Mr. Welsh said.

Exchanging anxious glances, Bob and I stared at the agent. His words stunned us. "The left passenger car window was broken and had blood stains on it and a few other traces of blood were found inside the car. It hasn't been determined whose blood it is."

I gasped, "Do you think Jan is dead?"

Mr. Welsh cautioned us not to jump to conclusions, because they didn't have any answers. "Mrs. Berchtold had never heard about any gold bars her husband owned," he concluded.

With my voice quivering, I asked, "Mr. Welsh, do they think Jan and Robert are in the river?"

"I can't answer that." The agent paused while Bob and I absorbed the information. None of this made sense.

"There appeared to be only one set of footprints around the car," Mr. Welsh said. "A set of tire tracks nearby measured wider than a car—they could possibly have been made by a motor home."

"Right now, we don't have a lot of answers. We are still gathering information, but be assured all law enforcement agencies around this area are involved in the investigation. I know this is very difficult for you."

It wasn't possible that Jan's life had ended brutally. At least, I wasn't willing to accept it. Shaking my head, I said, "I know Jan isn't dead!"

There was nothing reassuring in a news report that stated, *"The Power County Sheriff's Office is engaged in a vigilant search along the banks of the Snake River in the disappearance of Jan Broberg and Robert Berchtold. Officers haven't determined whether foul play is a factor and their bodies dumped into the river."*

A new batch of worries surfaced. Had both Robert and Jan been abducted? Were they all right? Where was my little girl, and what had happened to her?

■ ■ ■

When Jan awoke, the heavy, dizzy feeling had lessened and a ray of light was beaming into the room, but the atmosphere was hot and stuffy. The partition was gone. Now what? she thought, alarmed. Nervously, she peered through the doorway. A motionless figure was lying lopsided on a couch with one arm hurled over the back of a cushion. Jan gulped and drew back, terrified.

Confused, Jan tried to make sense out of this unreasonable situation. Carefully peering into the room again, she studied the still form, then screamed in terror, "Brother B!" Her voice was hoarse. She felt as if a wad of cotton had been stuffed into her dry mouth. Hurriedly, she ran over to him.

When she saw his blood-smeared face and a bloody cut on his right hand, Jan began to bawl. "Brother B! Wake up!" Jan screamed. "Brother B!" She shook him and he began to move, moaning painfully.

Finally Robert opened his eyes and looked at her. "Jan? Oh, Jan! You're all right. Oh!" he groaned, grimacing as he attempted to sit up. "My head!" He grasped his hand and flinched, "Damn, I hope it isn't broken." He held it very carefully.

"Brother B! You're bleeding." Jan continued to wail. "What happened to—?"

He cut her off and blurted out, "Oh Dolly! You're alive!" Then he cried out, "These guys . . . they wanted you!" Robert grabbed Jan and hung onto her. "I thought they had taken you."

"Who, Brother B? What are you talking about?"

"Jan," he cried out, "they were aliens . . . from another planet. We had an encounter . . . with a space ship."

Jan, pale and shaken, looked at him wide eyed, nodding her head in agreement. Grabbing a dishrag off the counter, Jan dabbed at his bloody face and arm. Robert swallowed hard and quietly whispered, "It's so crazy. I can't believe what happened. Where are we?"

"I don't know? Where's your car?" Jan asked.

Robert pulled the shade back from the window. "Oh my hell! Look at this!" His voice was loud and excited.

Terrified, Jan looked out the window expecting to see another planet or that they were surrounded by aliens. Instead she observed a desolate, weed-covered desert. "Where are we?" she asked apprehensively, then began to whimper.

"I don't know, but I'm scared. I . . . I don't know what to think. I was driving to that ranch and got lost. It started getting dark. All of a sudden the car began doing strange, crazy things. I had no control. The instrument panel on the car went crazy and no matter what I did to steer it, I couldn't make the car go where I wanted it to. It was awful. I stopped the car and got out. That's when I saw them."

"Saw what?" Jan asked frantically.

"Lights. Several lights in a round circle hovering over the car. I was scared to death and tried to get back in the car, but I was overpowered," Robert said in a quivering voice.

"You're kidding!" Jan replied, stunned.

"I asked them what they wanted and they said you!" he blurted out desperately. "I tried to fight them off . . ." He choked on the words as tears glistened in his eyes. "This is what happened." He pointed to his bloodied hand and bruised face. "They pounded on me fiercely, but I couldn't stand the thought of them taking you." He snorted and cleared his throat.

Robert gathered Jan in his arms, his grip tightening as he held her close. "Oh Dolly, I'm so glad you're okay and here with me." His body was trembling as he held onto her. "If anything ever happened to you, I don't know what I would do." He choked back the words while resting his cheek on the top of Jan's head, his arms still wrapped securely around her. "You mean so much to me. I would die for you if I had to. I love you so much."

Jan was shaking her head thinking about the stories Robert had convincingly told about UFO's the past three years. Her mind raced furiously. At the time, she had sort of believed the stories might be true, but now, could there be any doubt? Jan asked, "But how did we get here? What's going to happen to us?"

Robert's answers were vague. "Dolly, I don't know where my car is. I think the best thing we can do is get out of here."

"Where are we going? Home?"

"We'll have to keep driving until they contact us again. They just told me I needed to drive South."

"Where did this motor home come from?" Jan asked.

Robert explained, "I bought it to take on buying trips. It was supposed to be . . . well . . . it was going to be a surprise for my family. But for the life of me, I don't know how it got out here. Hearing you scream brought me to. I guess I've been unconscious since I got beat up." He paused, staring off in space. "This is spooky."

Robert slowly released Jan from his hold, looked around, then moved up to the front of the motor home. Jan cautiously watched him, wondering what he had seen. She was relieved when he exclaimed, "Well, I'll be damned. The key's in the ignition. Who put it there?"

Jan started to cry, "Brother B, I'm scared. They tied me up and said lots of weird things."

"Oh Dolly, I know. They talked to me too. What did they say?"

"Oh different things. That I have a mission, but I don't understand what they mean. I don't want to talk about it. I'm just scared and want to get out of here," she said crying.

"Jan, be careful what you say. They might be close by, and I think they can hear everything," Robert cautioned. Hearing that announcement, Jan looked around nervously.

"Was it somebody with a funny sounding voice?" Robert asked.

"Yes, she said her name was Zethra or Zada, or something like that," Jan responded with fright. "I never saw them, but maybe we should go before they come back."

"Jan! Tell me what they said to you," Robert demanded. Walking over to her, he pulled her shoulders around toward him. "I can't believe what they told me, but we've got to be extremely careful. They said I'm to be the father of a special child and . . . well . . . they said you're to be the mother." Robert shook his head and looked bewildered.

Jan shrieked, "They told you that? Brother B, why did they say that?" Her voice quivered with emotion, "I don't want to!"

"I know. But it's not for now, Jan. Later, when you're older. But they warned me to complete my mission or I would . . ." He paused.

Jan waited for Robert to finish his sentence. Urging him on, she said, "Or what? What will happen?"

"*There are lots of people who want me dead. Even now I'm being hunted down and accused of terrible things. You have to believe in me, Jan. No matter what the cost, I want to live.*"

"*Why do they want you dead?*" she asked in alarm.

"*Because of the plan—the mission I've been given,*" Robert said.

"*But what about me?*" Jan asked bewildered.

"*They said you were chosen before this life because of your strong belief in God. You've remained pure and innocent and proven yourself. Before some young guy comes along and ruins it, your mission needs to be completed,*" Robert said.

"*It doesn't make sense,*" Jan cried.

"*A lot of things don't make any sense. If you think about Mary, the mother of Christ, it must have been very hard for her to hear what she had to do! But she listened to the angel and did what she was told. You're a very noble young lady. You've been chosen, and only God knows why.*"

"*Do you think they are real angels?*" Jan said tearfully. "*When will they come back?*" Tears rolled down her cheeks.

"*Oh, my precious Dolly.*" Robert reached for a tissue and dabbed at Jan's tearstained face. I know they were here and did this to me. He gripped his bloodied hand. "*These . . .*" Robert groped for a definition, "*people— aliens or whatever—really exist and we can't ignore them. We don't know for sure who they are; maybe they are angels. They meant no harm. I wouldn't have gotten hurt if I had listened to what they were trying to tell me. But I was so afraid you were going to be taken away, that I reacted and started fighting them. That was a crazy thing to do. They were trying to subdue me when I started swinging.*"

"*What did they look like—those people?*" Jan asked anxiously.

"*Just like us. They weren't strange or funny looking; in fact, they look just like regular people,*" Robert said. "*They kept telling me they were trying to save their world and they have to have a special child.*"

"*But we've got to tell someone!*"

"*No!*"

"*Why not?*"

"Can you imagine what people would do if we told them? We would be mocked and scorned," Robert said.

"I don't understand the mission, Brother B."

Robert shook his head. "I know, but they will tell you more, later. I can't believe this really happened. What about Gail . . . and my kids? I don't know what to think."

Perplexed, Robert sighed. Getting up, he went to the kitchen sink and turned the faucet. "Well, look at this. Water. I'm surprised. The last time I worked on this motor home, I couldn't get the water to pump."

Robert took a hand towel from under the cabinet and soaked it in the running water. He squeezed out the excess and then placed the towel on his face, wiping off the dried blood. When he blotted the bruise on his forehead, he shuddered. "Ouch! That's tender."

Looking over at Jan, who was still seated on the couch, he said, "Dolly, don't look so scared. This is something we both have to face, and for whatever reason, we'll have to make the best of it. In time, we'll understand it all."

He walked over to her, sat down, and took her hands in his. He held them to his lips and kissed them passionately. "Trust me, Jan, they will not hurt you. When they speak to you again, listen to them. They have a message we can't deny. I believe there are other worlds which are populated and much farther advanced than ours. They have greater power and knowledge than we do and they know our destiny. These people make visits to this planet in order to help us further our work, but there are so few that accept them or are in tune with what they have to say that they never get their message delivered. I know you are a special person who has a great mission . . . whatever it might be. Promise me that you will do everything they say. You have so much to give, and we have so much to live for."

Robert's solemn testimony left Jan contemplating the uninvited voices. The messages left her confused and frightened. No matter how she tried to ignore them, the hauntingly eerie words weighed heavily on her mind. Her only comfort was Robert; she knew his assignment was equally difficult, and that he completely understood her fear.

hide & seek

On the evening of October 22, the doorbell rang and a tall bearded man rushed into our living room, nervous and distraught. He introduced himself as Mr. King. He had just learned of our daughter's disappearance and requested a private audience with Mr. Welsh.

We later learned that the mysterious Mr. King had been Robert's counselor. He had referred Robert to the Clinic for Behavioral Therapy in Beverly Hills. After Mr. Welsh contacted California agents, they reported that the clinic was no longer in operation and had been closed down by the State due to questionable practices and the use of unethical methods of therapy. The FBI hadn't located personnel from the clinic to interview.

When Mr. King left, Agent Welsh presented us with a new word—"pedophile." Bob and I looked at each other, then asked, "What does that mean?"

Mr. Welsh asked, "Has Berchtold ever attempted anything sexual with any of your daughters?"

"Certainly not!" was my snappish reply. Never had our girls

ever indicated there was anything inappropriate in his attention toward them. No! We were certain this was not a possibility.

Realizing that we couldn't even pronounce the word, Mr. Welsh educated us on pedophiles and their warped obsession for young children. Although somewhat uninformed, we knew there were certain individuals who preyed on children for their own gratification, but we had never heard an offender called by that name. In the early 70s, television and radio talk show standards were highly regulated and I couldn't recall hearing any discussion regarding sexual abuse of children, nor was information published in the magazines or literature we read. How dare he even suggest such a thing. It had never crossed my mind, and I pushed the information right out of my head.

This is the fifth day since they left, I thought. I know they would call if they could and let us know where they are. Mr. King seemed quite concerned about Robert, worried about his conduct with Jan. But surely, surely, Robert is treating Jan with respect. We know he loves all our children like his own, just as we love his. Certainly Robert will realize we are worrying about him too. I'm praying hard they are both well and safe.

■ ■ ■

It seemed to Jan that Brother B drove for hours over hot desert country. The roads they traveled were narrow and graveled instead of paved. She seldom saw other cars or trucks pass them on the two-lane road. She was afraid to ask, but wondered if they would ever see stores and people, animals, farms, or just anything that looked like America. Brother B seemed very anxious as she watched his facial expressions. He didn't talk, which Jan thought was unusual.

When Robert realized Jan was growing restless, he turned and said, "They told me to go on this road, but it sure is long. I've been thinking about all that happened and can't believe what they did to you." He gave Jan a concerned look.

Jan shrugged her shoulders but made no comment. A few minutes later, she asked, "Brother B, do you know what day this is?"

Robert looked surprised. "Well, I'm not sure. I don't know how long I was knocked out. Probably Monday, maybe Tuesday. Why do you want to know?

"Oh, I was just wondering what everybody was doing at home," she said.

"I've been thinking the same thing. By the way, Are you getting hungry?"

Jan nodded. "And thirsty," she said. "Is it okay if I get a drink?"

"Oh, how thoughtless of me. Of course. Go back and see what's in the refrigerator. When did you last eat?" Robert asked.

"I don't know. They told me to get some food and I did, but after I ate I went back to sleep."

"Go back and find us something good. We can snack while I drive. I don't dare stop. Later, we'll get something more healthy."

It was late in the afternoon when they drove into a more populated area with better roads. Jan felt relieved as they passed homes, gas stations, and stores. Earlier she asked Brother B if he thought they were going to run out of gas. Robert said, "Zethra told me not to worry about it. If that becomes a problem, they will take care of it."

They continued to drive into the night before Jan saw blinking lights in the distant. Her first thought was that the lights might be coming from a space ship. She asked frantically, "What's that, Brother B?"

"I don't know for sure," he said. "Jan, go back and change your clothes. There are some things of Jerry's back there. And wear his ball cap. If we get stopped, I want them to think you are my son. Hurry!"

Jan rushed to the back and did as she was told. Her heart was beating rapidly as she threw on the Levis and sport shirt. Placing the cap on her head, she tucked her hair under the brim, swallowed hard, then waited for Brother B's next instructions.

"Now, come up here and sit down in the seat. It's the Mexican border patrol. They might ask who you are. Tell them you are Jerry Berchtold. Don't act nervous and we'll be okay."

Jan did as she was told and they passed through the patrol after Robert gave them some papers and told the officer that he and his son were there to vacation. Robert turned and winked at her. "Perfect, Dolly. They believed us."

■ ■ ■

When Cor and Elaine Hofman, lifetime friends and neighbors, heard the news of Jan's disappearance, they showed up at our door embracing, comforting, willing to help. It only took minutes for them to realize the phone was more than we could handle. Every morning, Elaine was at the house to handle the public and Cor was there each night to offer encouragement and walk his wife home.

Peter Welsh became our most welcome guest and a daily visitor who always appeared in a suit, tie, and beige trench coat. Mr. Welsh stood six feet four inches tall, and kept physically fit by playing tennis. At age thirty-five, he served as a part-time minister at the Methodist Church, which added to his expertise at providing empathy and understanding. We greatly appreciated his sensitivity to our highly stressful situation. His special interest in the case was a great source of comfort. Without his constant encouragement, it would have been difficult to endure the emotional burden. Growing weary of the formality, Mr. Welsh soon asked that we call him Pete.

Every day, when Pete stopped by, our spirits lifted. "I know you want to hear some positive news, but I don't have any. Don't get discouraged. Something is going to happen. Berchtold is a clever criminal and had every detail planned. But he'll do something to slip up and then we can make our move. It's going to happen, but I know that waiting is so difficult for you."

Lamenting over the bleak situation, our friend Cor felt compelled to conduct his own search and had the support of another good friend, Dale Kirkham, who had recently purchased his own private plane. With Mexico targeted as a likely place where Berchtold would be incognito, they focused on that area and talked of going there.

Pete Welsh felt the trip would be futile since we had no knowledge of Berchtold's direction.

Bob agreed. "Pete is the expert and we should listen to him."

With each passing day, however, I felt more desperate. Growing exasperated, I urged Cor and Dale to move ahead on whatever inspiration they felt. Bob tried to reason with Cor. "I hate to see you and Dale take off on a seemingly hopeless errand. None of us has any idea where they went, and going to Mexico is like a shot in the dark."

Cor was adamant about his decision. "And why wouldn't he go there after spending time there so recently trying to adopt a little girl? I think he was setting things up. A lot of people think that, including Pete Welsh. Every day that passes, I feel so useless and I can't stand to see what this is doing to you," Cor said. "At least I can have some peace of mind that I tried. Dale feels the same way. We have to help find her."

The day Bob was unable to get out of bed because of an emotional breakdown, Cor made his decision. Enlisting Dale's son as their Spanish interpreter, they prepared for the search. They had several flyers printed in Spanish which announced Jan's kidnapping and included pictures of the victim and her abductor. Dale piloted the trio across the border and landed at a small airport in Mexico. They both wore tacky clothes and a three-day stubble, hoping to blend in with the locals. They slung their sleeping bags over their backs as they hiked from one town to another.

One week later, weary and discouraged, they returned with no news or any sign of our daughter. They had nailed dozens of flyers to fences and telephone poles in small communities and placed hundreds into the hands of Mexican people and the police. Maybe from these efforts someone would recognize the pair. I had placed such hope in their trip, and felt extreme disappointment. Three weeks had passed with absolutely no word or sign of Jan. I felt the Lord had deserted me. Would we never hear from Jan? What terrible things could be happening to her?

■ ■ ■

The first few days in Mexico City were full of adventure. Since Jan had no clothes except what she had been wearing, their first priority was shopping. Robert insisted she buy a pretty dress fit for dancing because he was escorting her to a Cantina. It would be an "out of this world" event in the true atmosphere of authentic Mexico, he said.

Jan found the Mexican people delightful and interesting. She loved the little street vendors and the unique gifts they peddled. She loaded up a few small sacks with trinkets she found for herself and her sisters. When she asked Brother B if he was going to buy anything for his kids, he shook his head, then persuaded her to go down to the beach with him and run through the water along the seashore. There, they discovered a balloon ride that took them high into the sky whipping them over the ocean before they landed back on the sandy beach. These few days of fun helped Jan put behind her the traumatic experiences.

Her comfort was short lived; the voices from the box returned and the messages from Zada or Zethra never stopped for the duration of her stay in Mexico. When B heard the voices, he would go into a trance and act very strange. She knew he was bothered by their messages because after they stopped speaking to him, he would cringe and shake his fists in disgust. Too often, when the voices came, Jan was alone in the motor home; she found the messages terrifying.

One of her first specific assignments came shortly after their arrival in Mazatlán. Brother B left early in the morning to find a part for the motor home. Jan was awakened by one of the voices. She shuddered. Zada instructed Jan to find some books they had placed in a cabinet. She was only to study the first one and it would help prepare her to make the baby.

Jan located the books and took the first one out. Unaware of the contents, she opened the book. Gasping with shock, Jan felt her face flush as she stared at the first page. She quickly closed the book, as a shiver pulsed through her body. Jan was aghast at what she had just seen; she had never witnessed anything so revealing. Graphics, with printed directions about making love put a permanent marker on her brain.

When Brother B returned to the motor home, she breathlessly told him about the book and their instructions. B offered comfort. "I realize it has to be hard for you to see things like that, Dolly. You are so innocent. However, if there is anything you didn't understand, don't hesitate to confide in me and ask me whatever you'd like. It's my job to make you happy." Being obedient to Zada and Zethra's indoctrination, Jan finally found the courage to begin her study of the flagrant images.

Weeks later, Jan was instructed by the voices to take out a second book and look it over. Horrified, Jan swallowed hard as she observed pictures of naked children doing terrible things with other kids and men. Jan wondered, Am I going to have to do things like that?

The impressions of these images seared her mind. She would never forget them. They also increased her longing for home, for the carefree life she had known. Oh, what was happening to her family? *she wondered.* How were they getting along without her? Was Mom going crazy?

reassurance

November 3, 1974

Our stake conference (a biannual series of meetings of church members in our region) was held the third weekend of Jan's disappearance. Elder Gordon B. Hinckley, an Apostle in the leadership of The Church of Jesus Christ of Latter-day Saints, was visiting another stake in Pocatello that same weekend. Bob had attended to his responsibilities as a member of the stake presidency on Saturday afternoon, and had just returned home when the phone rang.

"Bob, Elder Hinckley has just learned about Jan. He would like to come to your home and meet with you. He asked me to call," President Clausen said.

Humbled by the gesture, Bob said, "We would be honored."

"If you would feel good about Gail Berchtold being there, Elder Hinckley thought she should be invited as well," President Clausen added.

"That's not a problem. I'll call her. I'm certain she will come."

A short time later, our prestigious guest arrived. Elder Hinckley said, "I can't understand why anyone would do this. What a

49

terrible thing to have happen." He spoke words of comfort, extending his love and sympathy to all of us. His presence was gratifying. We were invited to kneel in a circle around the living room while he pleaded to our Father in Heaven. He prayed for all concerned in this horrendous episode, including the law agencies. He called upon the Lord to protect our daughter and her abductor. His petition included peace, understanding, and wise decisions on behalf of those who were attempting to locate our daughter and Mr. Berchtold. He brought into our sinking hearts renewed strength and determination to meet the challenges that would be forthcoming. Every thought expressed was most gracious and kind. His presence was powerful. Elder Hinckley left us greatly humbled and subdued; his visit brought a renewal of hope.

Bob spoke in the morning session of Stake Conference the following day. His humble spirit and powerful message made an impression on the congregation. Letters and notes were generous from many who felt the humility of Bob's aching heart, but also his gratitude for a just and merciful God.

I seldom left the house for fear of missing a call from Jan or Robert. Gail visited our home regularly—either looking for support or giving it. Some visitors thought it strange that she came by so often, but they didn't understand our deep friendship and what we gleaned from each other. We mainly talked about the good times we had shared in the past and tried to avoid discussing the present circumstance of our loved ones.

Many people in our church considered Robert a sensitive religious man with strong convictions. His thoughts went deeper and beyond the usual chatter of religious matters. His fascination regarding the vast unknown mysteries of the universe crept into his conversations regularly. Lengthy discussions ensued over his belief that life existed on other planets, and what a spiritual life after death might be like in the great beyond. We had always listened respectfully to his opinions and methodical reasoning, but had never spent much time thinking about his theories.

One evening, Robert had stopped by the house waving a news article that reported the sightings of UFO's on the Nevada desert. He announced excitedly, "Dozens of people have reported seeing these objects flying around at night and are certain they are flying saucers, but the government is saying they are weather balloons because they don't want people to panic. It's a cover-up."

"Oh Robert. Whether they are real or not, I don't want you scaring my kids about all this talk of aliens and space ships," Bob said.

"Well, Broberg, I have my own thoughts about it all, but I would never frighten your girls. Besides, they're getting a big kick out of it," Robert said.

It was true that our girls talked a lot about the science fiction stories Robert shared with them. He was a master story teller and remembered every detail from the movie, *2001: A Space Odyssey*. He also had our girls hooked on *Lost in Space* and *Star Trek*, two poplar TV shows.

One evening at dinner, Jan asked, "Do we really believe there are other worlds like this one out there somewhere? Brother B said the Bible tells us that it's true and people just like us live on them."

Pleased to discuss a religious issue with her, Bob responded. "Well, yes. We know God has created other worlds, but we just don't know whether there are people on them just like us."

"Wow! Isn't that neat? Just think, somebody might be on another planet doing the same things I'm doing."

"Honey, don't spend a lot of time thinking about things like that," her father cautioned. "Those are mysteries we don't have the answers for right now."

As Jan danced off to practice the piano, Bob remarked, "Robert and his stories."

"Oh, Bob," I laughed. "It's all for fun. Robert means no harm."

As Gail and I reminisced, she admitted that her children had the same fascination with the idea of other worlds, and they were missing their father's wild tales. "Their questioning faces are more than I can take some days, Mary Ann. Being included in that prayer circle with Elder Hinckley has given me a new ray of hope," she said. "Wasn't his concern for Robert touching? I know Robert didn't do this knowingly. Something else was going on when he and Jan disappeared."

I nodded my head believing what she said was true. Where were Robert and Jan, I wondered? What would our lives be like when they were found?

I was fighting another emotional battle besides Jan's disappearance. For the past six months, my father had been gravely ill with emphysema. Since September, he had been clinging precariously to life. He detested hospitals, and begged my mother to let him remain at home.

Two days prior to his passing, I traveled to see him, knowing it would probably be our last visit. I set aside my personal problems and stood around his bedside with my six brothers and two sisters while feelings of his desperate struggle for life tugged deep inside me. He was curled into a fetal position, and as I watched him gasp for every breath, I prayed his release would come soon. He had suffered long enough.

At two o'clock in the morning, on November 10, 1974, our sleep was interrupted by the ringing of the telephone. Dad's life had ended. Relieved for him, but profoundly sad at the loss, I found comfort in my husband's loving arms.

No one thought Dad should be told about Jan's disappearance. He would have been appalled. Now, I thought, you'll know it all. Silently, in the darkness of the night, I prayed that my father's spirit could be with Jan, giving her comfort and peace. I felt strongly my Dad's presence . . . as if he were in the room with me. It was I who was comforted and blessed by his loving spirit. In a moment of heavenly peace I felt the Spirit of the Comforter blessing my life. In that brief encounter, I felt Jan would be fine. In a quiet whisper, I murmured, *"Thanks, Dad. I love you,"* and managed to sleep until dawn.

In the nights following his funeral services, when I couldn't sleep, I often stood at the window of the dining room, peering out into the dark, lonely night, emotional and weepy as I tried to visualize how Jan was feeling. Through my own wounded soul, I imagined her empty helplessness and deep longing for home and family. I wanted to reach out into the darkness and touch her cheek or hear the excitement in her youthful voice.

After a good cry, I would talk to myself. *Remember how you felt when Dad died—pray, pray, pray . . . tears won't bring her home . . . you need more faith, as Elder Hinckley said . . . he made some pretty poignant pleas to the Lord . . . you've always had a strong belief in prayer . . . and strong faith . . . don't give up . . . get some sleep . . . you need a clear head tomorrow.*

I'd been given sleeping medication from my doctor, but never took it. Amazingly, I slept about six hours a night, which seemed adequate, but food lost its appeal. With a persistent knot in the pit of my stomach, I had no appetite.

A few days after my father's funeral, my brother was returning to Kansas with his family when his car broke down in Red Desert, Wyoming. The family stayed overnight at a motel while repairs were made. Early the next morning, Lynn walked into a coffee shop and chose a seat next to a State Patrolman. Lynn talked about Jan's kidnapping, probing the officer for information. Stirring a cup of coffee, the officer replied, "I saw an orange motor home cross those railroad tracks just a few days before the APB was received. Damn, if we had known about the abduction sooner, we could have nailed that guy. Who knows which way he was headed?"

■ ■ ■

Brother B stayed in each city only a few days. Weary of traveling from town to town, Jan asked all too often where they were going and when they would be there. Brother B's common response was, "I don't know. They will tell me when to stop and tell me when it is time to move on. We have no choice." There was no TV to watch, no American movies to go see, no books to read in English, and only Mexican music. Growing bored with nothing to do, Jan found enjoyment checking out street vendors and seeing their wares. Annoyed by her begging, Robert would give into her pleading until he could no longer tolerate the shops. Trying to be diplomatic, he would entice her to the beach with rented snorkeling gear or surf boards where she found contentment.

Robert didn't take Jan to tourist attractions and told her it was because it wasn't safe. The voices told Jan that her male companion's life was in danger. If she was to complete her mission, it was critical that he remain with her. She was to be loyal to him because he had been chosen by the councils of the universe to father her special child. The warning of her "evaporating" if she failed weighed heavily on her mind.

Every day, Brother B gave Jan a vitamin pill in the morning and a relaxing pill at night to help her sleep. Most of the time, the voices awakened her during the night. Thinking they might not come if she was already awake, she resisted sleeping. Brother B worried about her health and offered his pills so she could rest. Jan always felt threatened by the inhumane messages. Gradually, she came to accept them as a part of her life and wearily submitted to their requests.

Their travels took them to Mazatlán where Brother B found a pretty trailer park with trees and nice trailer homes. They parked next to an elderly couple, Judith and Henry, who wintered yearly at the resort. After weeks of moving around Mexico, Jan was eager for a normal association and took readily to Judith, a kindly woman. Judith and Henry were a cheerful couple who loved to visit and liked to play cards. After Jan gained the approval from Zada to be with Judith because she was not male and therefore safe, Jan made daily visits. It was a good change since Judith taught Jan to play Cribbage, Rummy, and Solitaire. Judith complimented Jan often, telling her she was very smart because she could remember the cards so well; she bolstered Jan's damaged ego.

As one day followed another, Jan became more and more restless. She began pestering Robert for information: "What was happening at home? What had he heard? Were Zada and Zethra going to make her stay here forever? When could they go back?"

tightening the web

November 19, 1974

We were into the fifth week of Jan's abduction. A psychic who had worked with law enforcement on locating children in Utah had contacted Bob's uncle and told him she wanted to offer her services. She needed a piece of Jan's unwashed clothing and a personal object before she could give her impression regarding Jan's whereabouts. Whether it was desperation on our part or a gesture to appease the uncle's request, we gave him the requested items. The lady concluded that Jan had traveled through Wyoming and was possibly in Canada. It was easy for us to dismiss her conclusion, but the uncle persisted. Reluctantly, Bob left early with his uncle for a trip into Wyoming. Bob strongly opposed the "cockeyed trip." His uncle insisted and felt even if they were grasping at straws, Bob needed to get out of the house for the day. The drive would be good for him.

I often felt comforted by reading thoughts Jan had recorded in her journal. It gave me a sense of closeness to her. I tried to find the criminal intent that law enforcement consistently relayed to us, but from all our dealings with Robert, we couldn't imagine that he had taken Jan because he wanted to hurt her or us. The following entry seemed to verify my feelings.

July 25, 1973: The Berchtold family are so close to me. Sister B and Brother B are just like second parents and the kids are just great. I made Sister B a little present and made a card saying how much I loved her. She cried and said that was special. Neat!

It was past six o'clock in the evening when I received a phone call from Robert's brother who worked at a car dealership in Ogden, Utah. When he announced who he was, I felt a surge of adrenaline shiver through my veins. "I had a phone call from Robert today," he reported.

My heart leaped with anticipation. Just hearing that Robert had called caused a wave of anxiety and a tingling sensation down my spine. With a lump in my throat, I asked, "Where are they? How is Jan? Is she all right?"

Joe Berchtold said, "He didn't tell me where they were, but he said Jan is fine and driving him crazy. All I know is that he's far away and unless you do what he wants, he isn't coming back. If you don't cooperate, you will never see either of them again."

My ability to think sensibly suddenly disappeared. His words sounded threatening. "Okay," I said trying to stay calm. "What does he want? I'll do anything to get my daughter home."

"He's refusing to come home if he's going to jail. He claims it's all your fault and that you've made it impossible for him to come back."

"What does he mean?" I asked, bewildered.

Joe was a bit snappy as he explained, "He'd have been back weeks ago, but you called the FBI and charged him with kidnapping. He's been trying to figure out how to come back and not end up in prison for the rest of his life."

My voice began to tremble as I blurted out, "What were we supposed to do? Does he have any idea what he's done? What in the hell was he thinking? All we want is Jan home."

"Okay, this is his proposal. Just listen and don't freak out," Joe said firmly. "He wants you and Bob to give him permission to marry Jan."

I gasped as my hand shot up to cover my mouth. His statement was shocking. I was stunned; my mind in total confusion. Marry my twelve-year-old daughter? There was no logic to what he was saying. "Is he crazy?" I asked.

"I know it sounds bizarre, but he said he needs protection from prosecution. I'm to tell you he means every word he says because he's not spending the rest of his life in the slammer. He insists it's your only choice, if you want to see Jan again."

My heart was pounding so furiously I patted my chest gently in an effort to calm it. Attempting to assemble the staggering news into some kind of sense and deal with the impact, I mumbled, "He wants to marry Jan?"

"That's what he said." Joe's message was direct and blunt.

Did this man realize the torture of these past weeks? Did he have any compassion for us or our daughter? I perceived him to be a heartless rebel while he continued delivering the message from his brother.

"He said if you won't give him permission to marry her, then make him Jan's legal guardian. It's the only way he can come back without being charged with kidnapping. You really made it hard for him."

"What a gutless idiot," I retorted. "Does he have any conscience?"

Hearing the anger in my voice caused Joe to soften his approach. "Don't get upset at me. I'm just the messenger. I suggest you find a lawyer who can draw up some kind of legal paper, if you decide to go through with this."

"Then what?"

"Robert's calling me back in a couple of days. Will you let me know what you're going to do?"

Searching for words, I couldn't put things together. "We'll have to do something."

"I told Robert your phone was probably bugged." Joe waited for my response, but I didn't answer. Cautiously, he asked, "Is there any way you can keep this from the FBI?"

"Go to hell!"

"I really am sorry about this. It's so stupid of him." This was his first hint of compassion.

"I can't give you an answer until I talk to Bob," I said, still shaken from the disconcerting news.

My thoughts ran rampant. *Maybe it is the only way to get her home, but how utterly disgusting. Marry her? Ugh! Let him be her legal guardian? I don't know. I know I'd do about anything to get her back. Oh, hurry up, Bob, and get home. We need to talk.*

Two days before the call, Pete had gone to FBI Headquarters in Washington, D.C., for a week of training. Pete tried talking his way out of going, but was unable to convince higher authorities that our case was more important than this training. One of his last comments before he departed was about the chance that something significant could happen while he was gone. With a lump in my throat, I called the FBI office and left a message. Agent McDaniel's response was immediate. As soon as he arrived at our home, he rewound the tape, and replayed Joe's call. Then he put the tape in a leather satchel and left.

I stood at the kitchen window impatiently, watching every car that went up and down the street. It was nearly eight o'clock when Bob arrived home. His day had been uneventful, the scenery beautiful, but hopelessness weighed heavily. Relating Joe's phone call and the disturbing blackmail demands, I became emotional and Bob became angry. Not knowing what was behind Robert's strategy, we hoped it was as he said—a desperate effort on his part to return without facing the inevitable prosecution. Regardless, it was news—news that filled our hearts with new questions. What was happening to Jan, and when would we see her again?

■ ■ ■

The first "touching" experience happened about three weeks after they arrived in Mexico. Robert exposed himself as he was showering, then laughed, explaining he had nothing to hide if they were going to get married. Jan remembered how she turned away, her cheeks flushed.

There was only one available bed. They shared it. As he moved his hands over her small body, she felt guilty and dirty. How could she make him stop?

She suddenly remembered the night that summer before when all the kids slept out on the trampoline at Berchtold's in their sleeping bags . . . Karen, Jerry, Jimmy, Susan, Joey and Jan. They lay on the trampoline looking up at the stars while Robert told stories about flying saucers, other worlds, planets, and people who lived there . . . aliens. Everybody squealed with fright. It was so scary.

Sometime during the night, Jan was awakened by something moving around her. Startled, she opened her eyes and saw Brother B next to her. The way he was looking at her was strange—-different.

"What are you doing?" she cried out.

"Just tucking you in . . ."

Jan lay still for a moment, realizing something was wrong. She felt uncovered, bare, and discovered her underpants were at her feet.

She screamed again, "What are you doing?" and bounded from the bag. She dashed in the basement door scared and nervous, and ran up the stairs. Gail, awakened by the sound of a door opening, heard frantic feet on the stairs. She leaped out of her bed and saw Jan, who began to bawl as Gail approached her. Jan tried to explain what had happened, but couldn't. "Brother B was— my panties— I don't know what happened," she sobbed as Robert darted into the room behind her.

Attempting to redeem himself, Robert explained to Gail, "I didn't do anything. I was watching the kids from the bedroom window and Jan seemed to be very restless. I wondered what was wrong so I went down to see—and while I was tucking her in, she woke up. I think she must have worked off her undies from thrashing around so much. I didn't touch you, I promise Jan. I would never do anything to hurt you. Please believe me."

Jan had scrunched next to Gail and remained silent. Gail quietly said, "Jan, why don't you come in and sleep with me? I think Robert's scary stories have caused you a real upset." Glaring at her husband, Gail icily remarked, "I wish you would quit telling those horrible nightmare tales. Don't you think you should go down and sleep in one of the boy's beds?"

Jan's memory of that encounter remained vivid in her mind. She wanted to believe Brother B hadn't taken her panties off—that he would never do anything to her that she didn't feel good about. She hadn't been able to tell her parents, or Karen about the incident. Even Caroline didn't know.

Now, far away from home, in a country where she didn't even speak the language, there was no one to turn to, nowhere to go to get away from the bad feelings. And there was no way to hide from it—no way to pretend anymore that Brother B would never do anything she didn't feel good about. Still, ironically, her thoughts kept turning the finger of blame back to herself. It was my fault these things happened, *she thought.* If only I would get sick and die or be killed in a car accident. But what would that solve?

Oh please, somebody, help me!

■ ■ ■

November 23, 1974

Efficient and highly motivated, Richard McDaniel moved quickly. FBI agents in Utah installed a recording system at the auto dealership and moved in. Every message Joe received would be recorded. Agents from the area were prepared to stay for a very long time if necessary to intercept the promised call. Joe was coached to keep his brother on the line for as long as possible.

Nearing the noon hour on Saturday, an apprehensive Joe answered the phone and heard his brother's voice. Joe had been told to tell Robert that we were getting the papers ready but he didn't have them yet.

"What are they doing? Giving their consent for marriage?" Robert asked.

"I don't know. Mary Ann called and said they would either do that or give you guardianship," Joe lied. "They want Jan home."

Joe asked for an address where he could send the papers. Robert refused to give him any information. Instead, he would call Joe back again and give instructions when he knew the papers were in Joe's hands.

Robert demanded, "Call Brobergs and tell them to send the papers immediately. I have to know exactly what they say before I'll come back."

At the urging of the agents, Joe tried to extend the conversation. He asked about the weather and Jan, but received only guarded information. Robert revealed nothing which would lead to his location.

Growing nervous, Robert told his brother he had to get off the phone. "I'll talk to you next week. Just tell the Brobergs to hurry up."

For the next hour, telephone personnel were under great pressure. From carefully planned strategy, the phone lines were left open while trying to trace the call. If one operator closed the exchange, the call would be lost. After connecting with several toll exchanges, they finally secured what they supposed to be the originating location: Mazatlán, Mexico. The call was placed from a hotel.

As soon as McDaniel had received information from his counterparts in Utah, he shared the details. Trying to remain calm was out of the question. Even though we were relieved that the long nightmarish experience was nearly over, there were still too many unknowns.

Preparing us for unforeseen situations, McDaniel told us the current plan of action was now being orchestrated in Mazatlán. "The FBI are moving cautiously and have contacted the American Embassy in Mazatlán. They spoke with the American Ambassador and have explained the uncertain circumstances. The problem now is locating Mr. Berchtold and your daughter. Mazatlán is a large resort city and the agents are discussing a plan with the local Mexican police on how to proceed in finding them and detaining Berchtold without violence. The FBI are demanding that certain precautions be taken to protect your daughter. No one knows Berchtold's present state of mind; he could become desperate or violent, and perhaps hold Jan hostage for his own protection. We know he has a handgun, and they fear Mexican police might react if they feel threatened. Anything could happen at this point, so it's not over."

With that said, movie scenes of bloody shoot-outs between lawmen and criminals flashed through my mind. I had to think positively, and I dismissed the gruesome thoughts. Wait, worry, and pray seemed to be the only conclusions from this frantic day.

safe, but not sound

Finally, in the early evening hours, the long-awaited news arrived. "Both the kidnapper and girl are in custody at a Mexican jail." It had taken hours for the Mexican police to locate the motor home, but they reported that Berchtold surrendered peacefully.

We were overcome with gratitude, weeping tears of joy and shouting jubilant words of praise and thanksgiving to a loving Heavenly Father. The prayers of hundreds had been answered. Jan was safe.

Gail had been in and out of our home throughout the day and had suffered intensely. On one hand, she expressed gratitude that the ordeal was reaching a conclusion, but on the other, realized what the end result would mean for Robert and her family. Needless to say, she was visibly upset when the news came about the arrest of her husband. With tears streaming down all of our faces, Bob and I embraced her.

I whispered, "I'm so sorry, Gail."

She responded, "So am I." She exited our home, her face a study of worry, despair, and extreme hurt from her weeks of hellish endurance.

Agent McDaniel gave us the phone number to the Mexican jail. After two desperate attempts, a male voice answered. He spoke no English, but realized the call was for the *señorita Americana*. With the four of us clustered around the phone, the sound of Jan saying hello brought shrieks of emotion and tears.

Jan's desperate, shaky voice trembled as she stated, "Come and get me! I'm scared and don't know what to do."

While we were trying to console her, the emotional outburst by each one of us was unnerving. Karen and Susan were ecstatic. Tears ran down their cheeks while they were telling Jan to come home.

"Be patient, Jan," her father stated emphatically. "We love you and will be there as soon as we can make flight arrangements.

All we could hear were her sobs, saying, "Please, hurry!"

I could hardly contain myself as concern over the welfare of my child overflowed; I wanted to give her immediate comfort, immediate relief. "Jan, are they treating you okay?""

Her reply was choked between sobs, but we heard, "Uh-huh! They're nice, but I can't understand them."

"Have you had anything to eat?"

"Huh?" she asked.

"Food," I said again. "Have you eaten?"

"Not since breakfast. I don't think they're going to feed me." Jan's voice was full of emotion.

"Well, you have to eat!" Bob declared.

Karen and Susan seemed to have the most calming effect on their sister. When it appeared Jan had her emotions under control, Bob told her we needed to hang up. It was difficult saying good-bye, but after we had expressed our love over and over, there was little else to say. Finally, we ended the call with our assurance that we would come as soon as we could make arrangements.

Thoughts of my little girl alone in a Mexican jail were tough to handle. Strong maternal instincts insisted that she needed comfort—

now! Within minutes, Bob blurted out, "Missionaries! If we could locate the mission president, I'll bet he would send some Elders to check on her." It seemed an answer to my anxiety.

After several calls, Bob was able to contact the current mission president in Mazatlán who promised to send two missionaries to the jail and see what support they could offer Jan. My mind was eased, at least for the moment.

McDaniel told us to get visas, make plane reservations, and take Jan's birth certificate. How could we get visas on a Saturday night? I thought there was little chance until Monday. However, the Hofmans were personally acquainted with the county clerk and made arrangements for us to meet him within the hour.

My adrenaline was running rampant as I pulled the metal security box off the shelf to gather the needed documents. I opened the folder, and thumbed through the papers. I couldn't find Jan's birth certificate! I looked again. Panicked, I screamed at Bob as I frantically searched a third time. "Jan's birth certificate isn't here! I found Karen's, but Susan's is gone too." Thinking hard about the last time I saw them, my mind flashed back to a scene last summer.

When Robert approached us about becoming the guardians of their children should anything ever happen to him and Gail, we told him we would consider it, but asked him if he shouldn't turn to his family, or Gail's family first.

"There isn't one member of my family I like well enough to entrust the care of my children. And Gail's only sibling is a lesbian. We have no other resources," he replied.

Bob answered. "Well, if you feel so strongly about us taking that huge responsibility, Mary Ann would have to have the final say." Raising his eyebrows, his blue eyes met mine for an answer. This was a big favor, even for his best friend to ask.

I turned to Robert and asked, "First I want to know what Gail thinks about this? And your kids?"

"Gail worships you both and thinks you have the ideal home. You certainly don't have any reservations about the way our kids feel about you, do you? They are here more than at their own home."

Without any hesitation, I exclaimed, "Well, sure. Why not?"

Astounded at my willingness, Bob looked at me wide-eyed, then turned to Robert. With humor in his voice, Bob pointedly looked into Robert's eyes and said, "Just be sure to leave your fortune to us."

Robert laughed, "Sure, you can have every penny of that $5.00 I hid in my top drawer. Now what about your girls? Can we return the favor?"

Bob thought for a moment. "Being an identical twin has its advantages. My brother Dick and I agreed to raise each other's children if something ever happened to us." Smiling, Bob added, "Our kids would never know the difference."

"I don't believe that for one minute," Robert said, chuckling. "Did you and Dick draw up any legal papers that I can look at?"

"No. Why go to all that work? We told our wives and since they didn't protest, we didn't think it was necessary. Am I right?" Bob's eyes met mine, seeking approval.

I nodded in agreement with him. Looking at Robert, I said, "Well, I have a will. My sister and brother-in-law entrusted us as legal guardians of their three children and gave me a copy of their will. I know they wouldn't care if you looked at it."

After Robert left, Bob and I joked over the enlarged family we could possibly inherit and wondered what we were using for brains.

A couple of days later, Robert stopped by and asked to look at my sister's will. He followed me back to our office where I took the metal box down from a shelf and began searching for the will.

While going through the papers, Robert spied our girls' birth certificates. Admiring the tiny footprints, he remarked, "Look at these little feet. Aren't they about the cutest things you've ever seen?"

I was amused at his sensitivity over matters of the heart.

That day, several months ago, when Robert admired their birth certificates, was suddenly all too clear in my mind. I looked helplessly at Bob. "Oh no! Robert!"

"What makes you think he took them? What good would they do him?" Bob questioned.

"Who knows. He knew they were here." I felt frantic. "What should we do?"

"Have you looked through everything?" I nodded. "Then you'll have to take her blessing and baptism records. We need to go."

News of Jan's discovery traveled fast. Friends and family members stopped to express gratitude and love, give tender embraces, and wish us well on our journey. Phone calls were numerous. One call was from Las Vegas relatives who heard about Jan's recovery at a basketball game between Idaho State and Las Vegas. During half-time, the Pocatello sportscaster said he had a special announcement for Idaho fans. "Tonight, twelve-year-old Jan Broberg has been found safe and well in Mexico."

"You can't imagine the fury that announcement caused," our aunt exclaimed. "The crowd from Idaho went wild."

Bob's uncle added, "And the LV fans thought we had lost our minds because we stood and cheered louder than we had all evening. It was the most exciting part of the entire game."

Finally, the house was growing quiet and I was able to throw a few items together for our departure. From the corner of my eye, I caught a glimpse of Karen standing away from the confusion. Susan was asleep on the couch.

At that moment, the realization of Karen's emotional struggles smacked my overburdened brain. Karen and Susan had not been ignored intentionally, but because of our chaotic life for the last five weeks, they had received little attention. Although they deserved much more, their patient, calm personalities had allowed us to put all our energy into this painful crisis.

Karen watched quietly as I put some clothes into a suitcase. Without a word, her wishes were revealed by the look on her face.

I laid the clothes aside and turned to her. "Oh Karen, this has been so hard for you and Susan. I know you would like to go, but we don't know what we'll have to face when we get there. We'll be back as soon as possible."

Karen remained silent. Bob tried to cheer her up by telling her of the fun she would have with Uncle Dick and her cousins. When that didn't work, he gave her a big kiss on her forehead. "We'll call after we get there and let you know everything."

With tears brimming her eyes, Karen looked longingly at me. "Can't I stay with Jimmy, instead?" she asked.

Bob's eyes widened as he raised his eyebrows waiting for me to respond. "Oh, Karen. Gail has so much to worry about, it would be better not to have you there right now," I said, putting my arm around her and directing her to our bed. Sitting next to her, I continued, "You've suffered so much and I'm sorry that you and Sue haven't had more attention. Can you be patient with us for a few more days? We'll improve. I promise."

Embracing her, I watched huge tears fall from her beautiful blue eyes. Reluctantly, she resigned herself to the fact that she would not be going, but wanted to be awakened before we left so she could say goodbye.

How ironic that all three of my girls had seen Gail and Robert's home as a safe haven, as the place they would most like to be next to home. How could we explain how all that had changed?

By the time I laid my weary body down to sleep, my brain

wouldn't turn off. Over and over, thoughts emerged. *Finally, the worst is over. Jan's alive. And safe. Who ever imagined this could happen to us. Thirty-nine horrid days. Now, getting through all the crap will be hard. What's going to happen to Robert and Gail, their kids? Oh, dear. Jan will be back home and that's what counts. I wonder what she has been doing all this time? Does she know what Robert wanted us to do? What did he tell her? Certainly, nothing bad happened to her. Oh, where in the world is she sleeping tonight? Maybe there are beds. Oh, I hope she got something to eat.*

I kept telling myself to go to sleep. There was nothing I could do about it right now. Although I tried to convince myself that everything was okay, my emotions wouldn't allow me to believe it. I found myself in tears and consumed with thoughts and fears I didn't have the ability to turn off.

Bob finally asked if I were ever going to stop tossing and go to sleep. I apologized, but began listing my concerns. As I lamented about all the uncertainties, Bob sighed deeply and uttered his favorite oft-stated phrase, *"And this too shall pass!"*

Somehow, I didn't find that particularly comforting. What about now? What about Jan NOW?

■ ■ ■

November 24, 1974: Last night, was the worst night of my life. The Mexican police broke down the door to the motorhome while Brother B and me were sleeping. I started bawling because they had guns and they hit B and knocked him down. I think there were about ten policemen that were hollering and waving their guns around. When they pushed us out the door and shoved us into that little car and all of them got in, I was squished in the middle of those three policeman who put me on the hump in the front seat. They kept talking in Spanish and every time Brother B tried to say anything to me, that one guy would hit him. I just kept thinking that I didn't want B to talk anymore and get punched again. I just kept bawling because I was so scared. When they put him in jail, I stayed in a dirty room that only had a broken-down chair. I had to tuck my feet under me so the mice wouldn't get on me. I wonder if the policemen are going to feed me? I'm about starved.

I'm really glad Mom and Dad are coming to get me. I can't wait to get home. I'm really homesick for everybody. It's been boring here with nothing to do. I wish my parents hadn't called the police. It isn't B's fault. If something happens to him, I'll get another male companion. Sometimes, I get real scared because I think Zada and Zethra might come and take me. What if I evaporate like they said?

reunions!

The world seemed to reward our inexpressible joy by providing us a quiet, reverent morning on our early Sunday drive to Salt Lake. Blessing-counting was abundant in our conversation. At the airport, we left our coats in the car and boarded Western Airlines, changing flights in Denver to Mexicana Air.

Suddenly the anticipation of seeing Jan, along with my confusing thoughts about her condition, brought me back to reality. A wave of anxiety swept over me, bringing tears to my eyes. When I stepped off the plane, the warm humidity of the Mexican coastline enveloped me. Panic set in: Where do we go? How will we get there? How will we communicate when no one speaks English?

An airline hostess gave us information about procedures and told us our first stop should be at the Foreign Exchange booth for Mexican money. Bob attempted to communicate with gate personnel and became frustrated. Finally, someone appeared who spoke broken English. We followed him to the baggage area to pick up our luggage. He waited for us to exchange our American dollars, then took us to waiting taxicabs. He hollered in Spanish to one of the drivers who immediately broke into a big grin and said, *"¿Como está? ¿Habla Español?"*

Bob replied, *"Nei venn er, amigos."* Turning to me with a grin on his face, he remarked, "He doesn't understand Norwegian either."

The cab driver stood nodding his head, still smiling. We smiled back shaking our heads. "No speak Spanish."

Our escort again spoke to the driver and told him where we needed to go. The driver sat in his taxi waiting for us to get in. Bob slipped a few pesos to the courteous escort, thanking him profusely. We loaded our luggage into the back seat, climbed into the cab, and didn't even have the door closed before the enthusiastic driver put the car in motion.

Our driver was anything but cautious. I found myself bracing each time he pulled behind a vehicle, then swerved around it, honking his horn at animals or people wandering across the road. He rarely used his brakes and had one speed—fast. He sped over the bumpy road taking corners and curves without slowing down, throwing us from one side of the seat to the other. He seemed to hit every pothole on the road with no concern for his passengers' comfort.

As dusk fell I centered my mind on the unfamiliar surroundings to alleviate concern regarding our driver's poor driving skills. The homes we passed were small and in need of repair, the automobiles, old. We passed several beat-up pickup trucks on the bumpy unpaved road, their cargo beds loaded with passengers of various ages. I peered through open doorways into small, antiquated shacks. Black and white TV's were blaring in nearly every one. I wondered if they had seen the kind of sharp colored pictures we had on our sets and if their fuzzy reception bothered them. I also wondered how they survived the hot sultry night air in their confined cramped quarters. I felt a twinge of guilt for taking for granted my comfortable surroundings at home.

The driver stopped at the entrance of the town square, let us out of the cab, and pointed toward the jail. As we took our belongings from the cab, our eyes locked on the gray sandstone wall. With suitcases in hand, we walked into a courtyard. A mariachi band was playing loud Mexican music; hoards of people were clapping hands to its rhythm while others danced wildly. Firecrackers were popping and smoke filled the sky. Looking into the sea of brown faces, we felt out of place. Suddenly, a familiar shriek penetrated above all the confusion. Hurriedly, we rushed toward the voice which continued to scream at us. When we saw Jan, her jumping was so intense she appeared airborne. As we ran towards her, she darted forward, leaping into our outstretched arms. We unashamedly wept and laughed and hugged while curious onlookers chattered. After the weeks of anxiety and anticipation, we deserved these moments.

Police officers encircled us. They kept repeating, *"La Mamá! El Papá! La Mamá! El Papá!"* The officer in charge thumped his chest, and smiling broadly said, *"Yo soy papá!"* indicating his own role as a father. I gathered he was relating to our joy at being reunited with our daughter.

We were escorted by four officers into a shabby room containing a few broken-down wooden chairs. The unpainted walls were cracked; loose plaster hung around the gaps.

Anxious to take Jan and leave, Bob said, "Let's get you out of here." However, conversing with the Mexican officers was difficult. Our attempts to explain that we wanted to take our daughter with us to a hotel turned into a comical charade. Laughter seemed to be the best solution when no one knew what the other was saying.

Jan said, pointing, "This is my father and this is my mother. I love them and I want to go with them." Her animated gestures brought rounds of laughter from the men. They nodded their heads, which we thought was giving us permission. However, as we began to leave, one officer frowned and shook his head "no."

Jan repeated her words again with the same results. Finally, Bob understood they wanted some proof that we were Jan's parents. Bob took the legal documents from the manila envelope he carried and the officer escorted him into a cubical around the corner. Jan and I remained in the outer room with three other policemen.

While we waited, we watched a hungry mouse run back and forth searching for a morsel of food. I tried to ignore it, but Jan said, "There's more than one in here. I watched them all night." Jan hadn't slept since the police brought her to the jail, and she looked haggard.

When I asked, "Where's Brother B?" Jan pointed to a large beat-up wooden door behind us. Looking at the door, I saw a crudely fashioned wooden latch on the outside of the door which could be opened easily by a flip of the hand. I couldn't imagine how they kept the prisoners locked in.

I felt an immediate surge of uneasiness knowing Robert was so close. There was a sizable gap along the side of the door which made me feel unsettled. I thought, *he is probably looking at us. I'm sure he hates us because of what has happened, but he deserves this.*

Jan sat rigid on the tipsy chair; her eyes widened and a shadow passed over her face. "Brother B is in there and we have to get him out. They are really mean to him and he's scared they are going to kill him. We've got to take him with us." Her shoulders sagged against the back of her chair. " I'm afraid something's going to happen to him."

"I'm sorry Jan, but we can't get him out. The FBI will have to do that."

Jan raised her head, eyes narrowed, and questioned. "Why did you tell the FBI that I was kidnapped?" Her words were sharp. "It made things so hard. Brother B said if we went back, he would be sent to prison for a long, long time."

"Jan, we had no choice. We didn't know what had happened to either of you."

"Mom, you know Brother B loves me. He wouldn't let anything bad happen. We've just been having fun. I wanted to come home a long time ago, but B said we couldn't. He was afraid something would happen to me." Jan picked at the hangnails on her fingers nervously.

I looked at her intently. "To you? You haven't done anything wrong. He shouldn't have taken you in the first place."

Jan sat mute. Her silence bothered me.

Wanting answers, I continued to probe. "Tell me what happened the day you left with Brother B? Where did you go after your piano lesson?"

"To ride horses, but he got lost and couldn't find the guy's ranch. I got tired and fell asleep. I don't remember."

"Well, it must have taken a very long time to drive here," I said. "Do you remember crossing the border into Mexico?"

"No."

"Well, what did Brother B tell you when you found out you were in Mexico?"

"That it was a vacation." Jan turned, stared at me with innocent eyes, seeking assurance. "You said I could come."

I shook my head. "No, Jan. That is not true. I only said you could go horseback riding for awhile."

Jan grew uneasy and looked down at the dirty floor. "I don't want to talk about it anymore." She kept her eyes on the wooden door as she continued to bite her fingernails. Her next comment brought an escape from my interrogation. "I'm really starving. I haven't eaten anything since last night."

"Oh, you did get to eat last night. What a relief."

"Some missionaries brought me a hamburger and orange pop. Did it ever taste good!"

A lump lodged in my throat. "Oh, really? Wow, your Dad called the mission president and he said he would send some missionaries by. What did they say?"

"Not much. They were really nice and just asked how I was doing. They said they might come back today, but they didn't come."

She paused, her eyebrows raised and eyes open wide. I waited to hear more. A sad look crossed her face, then, shaking her head gently, she explained, "I was going to save some for Brother B, but I didn't see him."

I was taken by surprise and asked, "Have you seen him since you've been here?"

"Yeah, today. Before you came." She looked at the officers that were standing in the outer doorway. Quietly she leaned forward and said, "He had to give one of the policemen his wedding ring so he could talk to me."

"What did he say?" I prompted.

Jan dropped her voice to a whisper as if she were afraid the officers would hear. "He was worrying about me, but told me not to worry about him. He said that he would die for me if he had to and I should go home with you guys."

Growing fidgety, Jan shifted from one position to another. Her bottom lip quivered. "They already beat him up and he's afraid they'll kill him when we leave."

Jan clenched her hands together and drew them to her lips. Seconds passed before she spoke. "He told me they won't do anything bad to him while I'm here, but he doesn't care if he dies because everything good in his life is over and he's going to prison for a long time."

The rage I felt toward Robert raced through me like a bullet. How could a mature man put such a heavy weight on my daughter. I held my temper, but remarked coldly, "He isn't going to die, Jan. He's trying to scare you and make you feel sorry for him."

Jan sat sullen and didn't respond. Looking nervously at the door separating Robert from us, she asked, "Can we get out of here?"

"I hope so. I wonder if your Dad's convinced them yet?"

Jan moved off the battered chair and peered around the corner into the small office where her father had disappeared. "What's going on, Dad?"

"I guess I'm about through," he said. "The police officer has taken our visas and knows we can't leave Mexico without them. He kept saying *mañana*, so we will come back tomorrow." Bob grimaced, put the remaining papers back into the envelope, and stuffed his drivers license into his wallet. "Let's get out of here."

Waving goodbye and smiling broadly, the three of us took leave of the office. The friendly, smiling officers shouted phrases that sounded encouraging.

Entering the courtyard, Bob shrugged his shoulders and sighed deeply. "What if someone steals our visas? That guy just stuck them in his desk."

I could see the anxiety in his face.

We hailed a taxi and the driver took us to a hotel. Pleased there was air-conditioning, we inspected the room to check its cleanliness and agreed to stay the night. There was no restaurant in the hotel, so we ventured a few blocks down the street and found a small, scary-looking food establishment. Timidly, we ordered items that sounded somewhat familiar and found the food quite tasty. Jan chatted cheerfully, expressing her relief at our arrival, and giving us a few details about her adventures in Mazatlán.

Returning to the hotel, we made the promised call to Karen and Susan. "When are you guys coming home?" Karen asked.

"Pray we can get our visas back and we'll be on our way tomorrow," Bob said.

Jan's conversation with her sisters seemed normal. There were no empty words or avoidance of feelings. Her dialogue focused on her sisters, friends, and school. This was a time of rejoicing.

When she got off the phone we shared the news of her grandfather's death. She seemed void of emotion and her only response was, "Oh, I'm sorry. How's Grandma?"

She had little concept of the legal implications—what she would face upon her return. She chattered about one experience after the other. Concerned about the confiscated visas, Bob paid little attention to her chatter, until she asked, "Why did you tell the FBI that B kidnapped me? He can't go to prison. He loves me and would never let anybody hurt me. We have to get him out of jail. Tomorrow, you have to tell the police that he didn't do anything wrong and he has to go back with us."

I swallowed and glanced at Bob knowing he was having a hard time with Jan's present mind set. Bob said, "It's late, honey. Let's talk about it tomorrow. What's important is the fact that you are safe and well. We are so blessed."

It was unfair to expect Jan to know what we had suffered. And what about her? Certainly Robert's arrest and her night in the jail had been traumatizing, yet she brushed it all aside. Was avoidance a way of coping with her own anguish?

■ ■ ■

While Jan dressed in her familiar nightgown from home, she thought about her unbelievable day. She didn't want to remember being in the jail with no food, no one to talk to, watching the mice run around, but she couldn't keep the thoughts out of her mind. It was like watching a movie in her mind. She saw herself going to the front door again and again, looking out at the people in the courtyard. Every time a policemen had waved her back. She tried to tell them she was just looking for her parents.

What a relief when one of the guards opened the door to where they had thrown B. She saw him standing with a bunch of Mexican prisoners who were pointing at her and talking very fast. The cell was dark and dirty, with hanging plaster and small barred windows near the ceiling where light filtered in. The guard had motioned her to go in. Timidly, she walked past the other prisoners and stood close to Brother B. The guard waved his gun at the others, yelling at them in Spanish, and they all moved back.

Jan began crying. "I'm sorry, Brother B. Are you okay?"

"Oh, I'm a bit battered and bruised. One of the guards beat the crap out of me this morning. I'm afraid they might kill me if I have to stay in here very long."

His words only made Jan feel worse and she began sobbing. "What can we do? You can't stay here. When Dad gets here, I'll tell him that you can't stay."

The guard looked at the sobbing girl and moved his weapon. Robert said, "Dolly, please don't cry or they might make you leave. I gave that guard my wedding ring so he would let you come in and see me. I don't know how much longer he will let you stay so you have to listen and remember to do everything I tell you."

Blinking her eyes, Jan tried hard to push her emotions away. Swallowing hard, Jan nodded as a few teardrops trickled down her face.

Robert said, "Do you remember what Zada and Zethra told you never to talk about?

Jan said, "I think so. They've said a lot of things to me."

"Well, Dolly, there are only four things you have to remember. Number one is that we can't tell anybody about them. Nobody can ever know who they are. Number two is the mission. You can't tell about the baby that will save their planet. Three, never mention the pills I give you to sleep, and four, you can't tell anybody about you and me touching each other. No one will understand it's part of the plan for you to learn about making a baby. Do you understand? Will you promise me?"

Jan nodded as she sniffled and fought back tears.

"Tell me what I just said," Robert remarked in an authoritarian voice.

Jan related the four rules that had been drilled into her head over the last five weeks. Robert squeezed her hand gently and said, "You've got it down perfect. I know there will be some who will want you to tell them that I took you. But you know how it all happened."

"I know I can't tell anybody about Zada and Zethra, Brother B, or I won't have a spirit, whatever that means. And Susie, they will take Susie!" Her eyes welled up with tears again as she bit her lip and wept silently.

"You'll be able to do this, Dolly. You're a strong spirit that's been given wonderful gifts. I just want to live so I can fulfill my part. Pray for me, Dolly. I need your faith to help me get through this. Trust in the Lord with all your heart and he will answer our prayers."

"You have to get out of here," Jan declared. "I don't want another male companion."

Robert stroked Jan's hair, then wiped away the tears that continued to emerge from her sad blue eyes. "Be strong. You're my only reason for living. Pray that I will live to see you again."

Jan finally slipped into a fitful sleep, but Brother B darted in and out of her dark dreams—and she kept waking up wondering what would happen to him.

■ ■ ■

Bob was up early the following morning. He complained of having a restless night, blaming it on the uncomfortable atmosphere of the room. Mixing air-conditioning with the humidity had created an unfamiliar dampness. Little sleep only added more discomfort to our suspenseful visit.

"I can't stand this place," Bob said as he fumbled around in his wallet and pulled out a piece of paper from McDaniel. "Conrado Batiz Canessi is the American consulate. Maybe he can recover our visas."

Jan and I dressed while Bob went downstairs to find someone who spoke English. On his return, he beamed. He had information regarding a reputable eating establishment and had learned that the ambassador's office was nearby. Bob called and made an appointment.

It was midmorning when we located Señor Canessi's office. The American Embassy was an impressive Spanish building with wide marble staircases and decorative wrought iron railings around the mezzanine. We were given directions by a lovely Mexican woman, who spoke broken English.

Señor Canessi greeted us cordially. He spoke English well, but had a strong accent. He was large in stature, with a bushy mustache, thick black hair slicked back. I noticed that his cotton jacket needed pressing. After a few minutes of conversation, he asked to speak with Bob alone. Jan and I waited in the receptionist area. She asked, "Is Dad going to tell that man that Brother B didn't kidnap me and he needs to get out of jail?"

I told her I didn't know.

We walked around looking at pictures on the wall and other artifacts on display. I wondered why it was taking so long. Finally, the door opened. Bob looked pale and extremely shaken. He thanked the Señor, stating we would be back in two hours. He rushed us down the marble staircase, out the door, and into the street without saying a word.

"Are you all right?" I asked. "What's the matter?"

"We have to come back and get our visas. He called the Police Chief while I was there and told him to bring the visas to his office."

"Was there anything else? You were in there a very long time."

"I just can't talk about it." He choked back a sob.

We walked without any direction while Bob tried to get hold of his emotions. Finally, we found a small park, stopped, and sat down.

I waited for Bob to speak. He groped for words that would not come. Silent tears rolled down his cheeks. It took several minutes before he blurted out in a painful cry, "Jan and Robert are married!"

I was stunned. He addressed his next remarks to Jan. "The Ambassador said it looks to him like you and Robert were living as man and wife."

Bob's cries were pitiful.

Jan revolted. She stood facing her father with her feet spread slightly, eyes locked on his accusing face. "That's a lie! I never married B! That man is not telling you the truth!" The flush left her cheeks and her face turned white. She put both hands over her face and covered a sob.

Bob pulled a document out of his shirt pocket that looked very much like a marriage certificate. It didn't bear Jan or Robert's signature, but had their names on it as husband and wife. It looked very legal. Jan was visibly upset. She continued to deny it.

I tried to calm Jan and comfort Bob. It was excruciating. Finally we all lapsed into a silence that was unnerving. Jan never asked again about Robert's plight or what was going to happen to him. Bob remained mute.

Returning to the Ambassador's office, we retrieved our passports with great relief. We took a taxi to the airport and were able to book a flight leaving Mazatlán in a matter of hours.

On the airplane, Jan and I took seats next to a chatty lady who had been in Mazatlán on vacation. She asked if we had a good vacation too.

"No, this hasn't been a vacation," I said. "Our daughter was kidnapped and found in Mazatlán. We are taking her home."

"Oh, my hell!" she shrieked. The conversation ended as she eyed Jan suspiciously.

Jan looked at me with hurt in her eyes. "Don't tell people that," she whispered. She crouched in her seat and pulled her blue brimmed hat over her eyes. I realized that my remarks, no matter how true, had been extremely insensitive to Jan.

When we changed flights in Los Angeles, Bob telephoned his brother, Dick, and told him we would be arriving at the Salt Lake Airport around six o'clock. Dick promised to bring Karen and Susan to meet us there.

Jan's excitement began to mount as we neared our destination. Informed about Jan's abduction, the airline personnel extended the red carpet for us. Bob told them we were emotionally drained and would appreciate it very much if they would keep our arrival private. Television and newspaper reporters all over the Intermountain West had requested an arrival time, but fortunately, the airline crew honored our privacy.

After we landed, we were invited to wait for our family in the private room where pilots and flight crew wait before departure. The suspense and anticipation were getting the best of Jan; she repeatedly opened the door to peek out.

It seemed a long time before she finally spied her siblings walking across the rotunda of the terminal with Uncle Dick. Jan shrieked ecstatically, "Karen! Susan!" It was a repeat performance from the previous night—they ran to each other, embracing and screaming with delight. The hugging, kissing, sobbing, and jubilant rejoicing made a glorious scene. We were a complete family again.

conflicting voices

November 26, 1974

Jan's homecoming couldn't have been more gratifying. Cards, letters, phone calls and personal vis-
its all contributed to our joyous celebration—until Gail came to see
Jan and broke into sobs. Our warm hugs and expressions of sympathy must have appeared meaningless to her as she felt the excitement of our home and contrasted it with her own. Certainly Robert
would be convicted of kidnapping, which meant a prison term.
With such a grim future ahead, my heart ached for Gail.

The following day, Jan was seen by a gynecologist. Jan vocal-
ized her dismay openly even though the doctor did his best not
to traumatize her. His report that there was no evidence of sexual abuse brought us huge relief. It was gratifying to know that
our earlier conviction regarding Robert seemed to be true. He
didn't do anything to hurt her and we could push all those dis-
tasteful thoughts out of our minds.

Jan's refusal to discuss her kidnapping was most distressful to
us. She denied being abducted and told everyone, "I wasn't kidnapped." Thinking she needed time, we didn't try to convince her

otherwise. Restoring normality to her life seemed the best solution. The trouble was, we didn't have any idea what was really going on in Jan's mind. She just wouldn't tell us.

■ ■ ■

Dear Brother B,

I'm writing even though I don't know where you are. I'm really scared for you and hate thinking about you in that yucky jail. Mom and Dad have been talking to a guy from the FBI. His name is Pete. Nobody knows about "you know what" and I won't tell them. Know how much I love you and hope you can come home really soon. Until then, be good. I'm hiding this in my blue cushion you made for my love seat. I'll mail it when I find out where you are.

Love, Dolly

Dear B,

I haven't talked to Sister B, but she came over and talked to Mom. I heard mom say you were okay. Sister B said they moved you to the states. I was happy for you and hope things are going better. I'm glad you didn't die. Remember I love you.

Love, your Dolly

■ ■ ■

Jan had returned to school with her bubbly personality seemingly intact. Since she approached her life with exuberance and we could see no evidence of distress or withdrawal, Bob and I didn't feel any urgency to get her into a counselor.

A trip to the grocery store that first week she was home tied my stomach in knots. An acquaintance sought details about the abduction, saying, "I understand Jan and 'that man' were married. Is that true? What did he do to her?"

I fled the store unable to cope with the woman's insensitivity.

Church members rallied around us and the Berchtold family. However, we soon became very confused. Some ecclesiastical leaders were quite emphatic that justice should prevail and Brother Berchtold should be prosecuted to the maximum. Others begged us to be forgiving and show mercy for Robert and his family saying his children deserved to have their father at home, not locked up.

The Berchtolds were well-liked and Robert had earned the confidence of many church members. One sister pled with us to be kind since he had suffered a mental breakdown. Another recognized him as a wonderful, understanding man who wouldn't harm anyone. "He needs your love and sympathy. He's been so good to me through my husband's illness."

It was a constant dilemma. Our religion taught *man is to forgive all* and *only God is to judge*. How could we justify that principle in this type of crime? What would the Lord have us do? As our anger subsided; confusion prevailed. We didn't know how to feel anymore.

We met with a Federal District Attorney from Boise in December. He was in the midst of preparing for the preliminary hearing scheduled for the 3rd of January. As we discussed the supposed marriage between Jan and Robert, the attorney recognized it was a tough situation for us, but this was an important piece of evidence to present at the trial. "I need the marriage certificate."

"But I don't have it," Bob replied.

"What? Where is it?" Mr. Elliot asked.

"I sent it to a Mexican lawyer asking him to annul the marriage. Señor Canessi gave me the name of a reputable lawyer and told me what I needed to do," Bob explained.

"You're kidding! You already sent it?" Mr. Elliot asked, his voice rising in volume. "Does Pete have a copy?"

"I showed it to Pete, but he didn't take it. How would I have copied it?" Bob asked, defensively. "Run my pen over it with carbon paper? It's not likely a mimeograph machine would do the job."

Pete was stunned when approached by Mr. Elliot. Yes, he had looked it over, but didn't realize Bob would send it off before the trial. The marriage certificate was to be a key piece of evidence against Robert.

Robert had been moved from his confinement in Mexico to a federal facility in Nogales, New Mexico, three days after we returned home. He remained there until he was transported to the Pocatello County Jail, a few days before Christmas. On Christmas Eve, Gail posted bail.

Jan's Diary, December 21, 1974: Brother B got back to Pocatello. I'm so happy, even if he is in jail. I bet his family is happy too. I don't know when I'll get to see him.

Pete forewarned us about keeping our distance with the Berchtolds. "I know you'll see them at church and school, but keeping Berchtold out of prison is their first priority. Gail is a nice lady, but she is still married to him."

Bob said, "I hope I never have to see or talk to Robert again."

"You'll have to see him at the hearing, but you don't have to talk to him," Pete said.

"I hate the thoughts of a trial."

"I know, but you're going to have to face it," Pete stated. "The judge will decide after the hearing if there's enough evidence for a trial. Just remember what he did to you, in fact, to this entire community. I feel sorry for his wife and children, but this guy needs to pay for what he did."

We greeted Christmas day with enthusiasm and gratitude. However, when we returned home after a visit to Grandma's house, we realized something was wrong as soon as we walked through the door. The air was nippy and I thought the furnace had gone out. I followed the girls into the hallway to hang up our coats and peered at the thermostat. It was only 63 degrees. I felt a cold gust of air coming from the end of the hall.

Bob continued down the hall and into the den and yelled, "I think there's been a thief in the house. A window is wide open in here." The girls looked worried as they dashed into the den. As he shut the window, their father warned, "Don't go downstairs until we explore the house."

Bob and I went from room to room, checking to see if anything was missing. Everything appeared to be in place except for two drawers askew in Bob's dresser. Searching the drawers, Bob found money still concealed in his secret hiding place. The only missing item was a cherished ring that had belonged to his father. A search of the house revealed no intruder. Since the doors were still locked, the open window perplexed us. It was twelve feet from the ground. Newly fallen snow from the previous day covered the back yard. There were no footprints.

Our suspicions weren't discussed until our daughters had gone to the family room. Bob's eyes were inflamed, his voice snappish. "I know it was Robert. He probably wants that incriminating marriage certificate. Wait until he hears that I sent it back to Mexico."

I rolled my eyes and shook my head in disbelief. "He still has a key to our house. How could he be so bold? We better get new locks for our doors."

Jan's Diary, December 26, 1974: Whew! When we got home last night, someone had been in the house and I thought it was Z. I heard Dad say it was probably Brother B, but there's no footprints outside. I know they are watching me, but I haven't told anybody anything. I don't want to go to court and I'm scared. If I tell them that nothing happened, I should be okay.

A few days after Christmas, Gail called and asked to visit with Bob alone. Although reluctant, Bob gave in to her pleadings.

Gail was sullen when she arrived. For one hour Bob and Gail conversed privately. When the meeting ended, Gail walked to the front door wiping her eyes with a Kleenex. She left without speaking a word to me.

Bob was subdued. "Her husband sent her over to do his dirty work. She has asked us to drop charges against him. If we don't, he's going to do everything he can to prove us unfit parents."

"What's he talking about?"

"Oh, don't you know? We contributed to his mental problems because we knew he was under treatment, yet we encouraged him to come over and spend time with our girls." Bob's ears were crimson, his jaw set. Quiet fury was pulsing through his body. "He claims instead of us protecting Jan, we literally threw her at him."

"Oh, that's a good one," I said shaking my head. "What else?"

"Gail wants us to help save her family and asked that we not press charges. Sending him to prison will solve nothing."

"Sure. He dug himself into a hole and wants us to get him out."

I slumped onto the couch, wanting the anxiousness to dissipate. We vacillated back and forth about the grueling future and what this decision meant to all of us. How could we escape a humiliating trial? My frustrations began to accelerate. Desperate, I recoiled and blurted out, "I hate the thoughts of going to court. I hate seeing a family torn apart. I hate everything that's happened. I want to forget it all."

Bob stared blankly at me, then rubbed his brow nervously. "We have to go through with this. He broke the law. I hate what he did and it was wrong, Mary Ann."

"I know, but if we had just waited a little longer, he would have brought her back and we wouldn't be in this mess." Putting a hand over my mouth, I felt hopeless, hurt, and sad. Quietly, I whispered, "Then, he wouldn't have married her." Tears welled up in my eyes and began trickling down my cheek.

"No, honey," Bob said, clenching his fist. "He didn't have to marry her. Besides, I want to believe Jan, that it's all a lie. We did the right thing by bringing the law into it."

"But think about Jan." My voice was full of emotion. Tears continued to fall onto my sweater as I tried to brush them away. "People all over this town will be talking, asking questions like Mrs. Johnson did at the grocery store. I don't want to put up with it anymore."

"You feel pretty confident that Robert didn't do anything to her, don't you?" Bob asked.

"According to the doctor and Jan, he didn't," I said.

"Pete thinks differently and believes Jan just isn't telling. He's the expert about these kind of things," Bob said.

"Jan acts normal and is very happy. I think she would tell us if he did anything to her," I replied.

"You're right. I don't believe anything happened, either," Bob said confidently. Leaning forward, he placed his hand on my shoulder. "Honey, we need to stay focused on what happened. My biggest concern is the same as yours, and that is Jan. It's so unfair to her."

Preserving Jan from public humiliation was our first goal. Having our daughter marked by society with a questionable reputation was most repugnant. Would she gain the respect from peers that a twelve-year-old deserved? The unexplained marriage was so ghastly. Whatever the cost, could we stop it from becoming public knowledge?

A late afternoon phone call from Berchtold's lawyer took us by surprise. She asked, would we be interested in meeting with her and discussing a proposal that might save us from an unwanted trial?

If so, she would be at her office with details. After a few hours of deliberating, we decided to find out what she had in mind.

Her plan was plain and simple. If we would agree to drop the kidnapping charge and sign affidavits that stated "we believed Jan was unharmed while in the company of Mr. Berchtold, and that he thought he had our permission to take her," we could go back to raising our children and put all of this behind us. She left us alone to make the decision.

Bob and I read and reread the affidavits while struggling with our own sense of justice and fretting about the impact it would have on so many people. We finally concluded that this ugly situation was our problem and we were the ones being affected. Feeling desperate, we signed the papers and went home to lick our wounds, realizing there would be repercussions. It was a long, dismal New Years.

By Monday, Berchtold's attorney had contacted her legal peers to announce our willingness to sign affidavits.

Within a matter of hours, an explosive federal attorney called us from Boise. "What have you done? How could you make such a statement and let this criminal off? This is a disgrace to the law profession. Why did you go see her? Why didn't you call me? Don't you know you never make a deal with the criminal's attorney? That's my job. I do the negotiating." His voice shook with rage.

Bob listened, then replied. "We are sick and tired of this entire mess and want to put it behind us. We can't take anymore. We want to get on with our lives."

"That will not happen until we get through the trial." Working to control his anger, Mr. Elliot's voice softened. "And whether you like it or not, there is going to be a hearing. I will not let this jerk off. Meanwhile, stay away from his attorney and any other person associated with the Berchtold family."

When Pete came by, he was bewildered. Instead of hitting us with another lecture regarding our stupidity, he sympathized with our arduous ordeal. "I understand why you signed the affidavits. Berchtold has a tough attorney. It's her job to get her client off and if anyone could win, it would be her. You can be assured, she will tear the prosecution apart."

Bob and I looked at each other with dismay. It was most embarrassing to realize how naïve we were to the legal system. Pete waved his hand back and forth. "What is done, is done. The newspaper has your affidavits and it will be blasted to the public. For your sake, you need to call the prosecutor's office and let them help you write a statement to the news media."

Leaning back on the sofa, Pete rubbed his neck, looking first at me, then Bob, gently nodding his head. "You know, this is everyday business for us." Pete paused, pursing his lips, with the hint of a smile lighting his face. "Can I ask you a question?" We both nodded, still dazed from our ignoramus decision. "Have either of you ever been in court before this?"

Bob shook his head while I confessed to going to traffic court once for a speeding ticket. Pete grinned. "That doesn't count. It's our fault for not preparing you to face the legal aspects of a heavy duty trial. You need to toughen up and prepare for the worst. You are good people. Don't let anyone tell you different, okay?"

The reaction to the news article infuriated some people in the community. Several anonymous phone calls flooded our home telling us we were *chicken! stupid! disgraceful liars!* for not wanting to prosecute. How could we let a kidnapper off, making the community unsafe for children? It was our obligation to put him away for the sake of society.

Two days following the published affidavit, our statement appeared:

BROBERGS EXPLAIN FEELINGS . . .
BERCHTOLD BOUND OVER FOR TRIAL
Robert E. Berchtold, 38, was bound over Wednesday

afternoon to Sixth District Court for trial, following Magistrate Dell W. Smith's denial of a defense motion for dismissal of the case on the grounds of insufficient grounds for prosecution.

Berchtold has been charged by the state with kidnapping in connection with the Oct. 17 disappearance of 12-year-old Jan Broberg, Pocatello, reportedly later found unharmed with Berchtold in Mexico.

In an attempt to provide an explanation for affidavits filed in the Federal and Sixth District courts, the Broberg family released the following statement late Wednesday afternoon through Deputy Bannock County Prosecutor Howard L. Armstrong, Jr.

Statement from Robert and Mary Ann Broberg:

"Due to the statements that have been made and due to the possible misinterpretations and misunderstandings that might have been placed upon our affidavits, we wish to make the following comment:

"Because of our anxiety and the traumatic experience that we and our daughter, Jan, have gone through during the past few months, we feel that this is a period in our lives that we would like to forget and certainly wish had never happened.

"With this in mind, and being grateful for all of the help that we have received, and for the fact that our daughter has been restored to us unharmed and just as pure as when she left, we felt that the easiest way for us to pick up the threads of our lives was to have all connections with the last few months severed as soon as possible.

"We now realize that this was foolish and that there is nothing that we can do or say that will alter the things that have happened since October 17, 1974. We are now prepared to go forward with whatever testimony we have and tell the truth and will sincerely trust in the law enforcement officials, the courts, and all concerned to see that justice is done."

January 3, 1975

The morning of the hearing was a cold, snowy day. The Federal Attorney's decision not to appear at the hearing was not discussed with us. The county's prosecuting attorney, Bart Petersen, and his deputy prosecutor, Howard Armstrong, would handle the hearing. Pete Welsh would represent the Federal Government. Mr. Petersen, a neatly dressed, middle-aged man who had a warm, fatherly presence, asked us to come to his office an hour early so he could brief us on the proceedings of the hearing. In previous visits, his mild manner and reassurance allowed me to feel relaxed and talk freely about our family's relationship with the Berchtold family. However, today's circumstances didn't warrant any warm fuzzy feelings. It was his intent to prepare us for the defense since our last confrontation had been so devastating. Nervously, Jan bit her fingernails while waiting for the interview. Bob sighed deeply as Mr. Petersen stressed we only needed to answer the questions truthfully. "Don't be alarmed. You're good people and have been victimized by Berchtold. I'm not going to let his attorney tear you apart."

Jan was emotionally unprepared. Seeing Robert for the first time since her Mexican fiasco caused her to turn pale. I thought she might pass out. After opening statements were made, the judge decided to close the hearing to the public and have each of us face Berchtold and his attorney independently. Jan was the first to give testimony while Bob and I waited our turn in an outside hall. When Pete accompanied her from the court room, Jan's color had returned and she seemed relieved.

Bob asked, "Well, how was it?"

Jan replied, "It went good."

Pete responded, "Her denial of being kidnapped wasn't the best news of the day. We'll talk about it later."

As I took the witness stand, I tried not to look at Robert because his sad, pleading eyes could be very persuasive. I thought how right it would be for me to despise him, but instead I felt pain as I answered questions by the prosecutor and defense lawyer.

I found his attorney's questioning difficult and intimidating. It appeared she was leading me towards admitting I was an unfit mother who hadn't protected my child from Mr. Berchtold. I denied her charges since I believed I had always been an attentive, loving mother who cared deeply for my children.

The course changed when I was asked about Berchtold's depression and my knowledge of it. She asked how many times I had talked to him when he was depressed. I couldn't give her a definite answer.

"Why would you allow your daughter to go with him alone when you knew he was emotionally unstable?"

Trying to preserve my dignity, I answered quietly, "I didn't think he would take my daughter." I felt flushed and was certain my hot cheeks would be taken as an admission of guilt. Would I be regarded as a negligent mother? It was uncomfortable having my judgment questioned.

I easily answered the questions regarding my relationship with Robert, explaining the close friendship we enjoyed with his whole family. I thought of him like a brother, a trusted and devoted friend who would do anything for our family. Nothing could have surprised us more than for Robert to take off with our daughter.

As more questions emerged, I became frustrated and felt that everything I said was being misconstrued. My fingernails dug into the palms of my hands as I attempted to explain personal feelings.

Yes, I knew there were marital problems between him and his wife; Yes, I care a great deal for Mr. Berchtold and his family; Yes,

I knew he suffered from depression, but didn't realize the extent of it; Yes, I felt it was a tragedy that our child was taken by Mr. Berchtold; Yes, he did talk about wanting to take a vacation without his wife; No, I never gave Mr. Berchtold permission to take my daughter; Yes, I believed Jan *was not* sexually molested by Robert Berchtold.

The grueling testimony left me exhausted.

With the hearing over, the prosecutors and Pete felt confident there was just cause to bind Berchtold over for trial. However, they felt Jan and I both needed to take a harder stand against his heinous crime. If we didn't, it would be hard to convince a jury. We had to leave our feelings in regard to our prior friendship behind us.

■ ■ ■

January 12, 1975

Robert was standing by the door when Jan came out of Sunday School class. He told her she was perfect in court and not to worry. Things were going to be okay. He had heard from Zethra, but the bishop was coming down the hall, so he couldn't finish telling her. Robert ducked into the Sunday School class and hustled Jerry out. As Robert passed Jan, he whispered, "You'll be hearing from them soon."

Since Jan's departure from Mexico, the voices had not bothered her. It had been a huge relief since she was trying to put them out of her mind. Everybody at the hearing wanted her to say that Robert kidnapped her, but she couldn't lie. It was them—the people from that planet that did it and she would never tell. The fear of her ceasing to exist weighed heavily.

■ ■ ■

Having the hearing over was a great relief, but there would be a trial. Berchtold's lawyers didn't win their case they had based on our affidavits and Jan's insistence that she was not kidnapped. For now, Jan could return to school and hopefully, we could all resume a bit of normality.

It was awkward seeing the Berchtolds at church, in the grocery store, going and coming from school and other familiar places. Trying to ignore them was impossible. Jan and Jerry remained good friends and shared classes in Junior High while Karen and Jimmy were in the same fifth grade class. Sunday School classes offered the same scenario which kept their camaraderie intact. None of them would let adult legal problems interfere with their strong friendship.

Bob demanded we maintain our distance. How could we go to trial and be fair with the prosecutor if our family was still entertaining a relationship with the Berchtolds? The Berchtold and Broberg kids had been inseparable for years. They didn't understand Bob's request, especially when a mysterious illness struck Jerry. He was hospitalized and his delirium raged for several days, leaving his legs partially paralyzed. Our daily prayers included him. Jan put together a care package full of encouraging notes and surprises intending to present her "basket of love" when he arrived home from the hospital. I agreed with my daughters that we should visit him.

Bob was unbending about his decision. He sat down at the kitchen table as I cleaned up the dishes and said, "It's not okay to visit Jerry. Others are attending to the family and he is getting plenty of attention."

"How do we cut off our feelings for them when we rub shoulders everywhere we go?" I asked, while wiping off the counter. "Maybe the girls need to go to a different school, or stop going to church."

"Don't be foolish," Bob remarked while drumming his fingers on the table. "But we can't continue to be friends. I know that sounds terrible, but we have no other option."

What he said made sense, but my heart wouldn't allow me to

agree. "I don't expect us to be best friends ever again. However, showing Jerry some compassion is our Christian duty, don't . . ."

Bob interrupted. "Have you forgotten what Robert did, or was it some kind of nightmare that only I remember?"

There was silence between us as I thought about his comments.

Hoping to get his point across, Bob asked, "Honey, when do we stop this overwhelming compassion and just face the fact that Robert has a problem bigger than us. I hold no malice for Gail or the kids, but the door has to close between us forever."

Stubbornly, I hung on. "Why should the rest of the Berchtold family be punished for what Robert did?"

"You can't be loving to the kids without including Robert," Bob said. "They're a family, Mary Ann."

I threw the dishcloth into the sink, then turned to Bob. "And they've been in our children's lives for the past three years," I said, defensively. "Everyone we talk to has an opinion. On one hand, we're told to be understanding and forgiving, then others want us to spit in their faces and nail Robert to the wall! I'm fed up with it."

Unable to handle my attitude, Bob removed himself from the kitchen and retreated to his easy chair and the newspaper. Discord was growing more intense between us with each encounter involving the Berchtolds. Convinced there was a way to work through all the muck, I refused to be persuaded otherwise.

A few days later, Gail and I were brought together working on a quilt at a church gathering. Lighthearted and unrestrained conversation took place among the group of women busily hand stitching an elegant floral pattern. It seemed good to have positive feelings return.

After the meeting, Gail and I talked privately in the parking lot. We realized things would never be the same, but somehow, if we could remain friends, it would ease the hurt. We eventually hugged and went our separate ways. Within hours, Robert called, gushing over the possibility that the past could be mended and our old friendship restored.

My cheeks flushed as I listened to the excitement in his voice. Putting on a strong front, I said, "I don't think so. We have a trial to go through, Robert. Bob's feelings run deep for what you did."

"Oh, this will all be resolved in time. Why are you guys so stressed out?" Robert asked. "Relax, and stop your worrying."

Determined to make him understand, I remained strong. "There are too many scars, Robert. I know you will never get through our door again."

The agitation in Robert's voice was noticeable. "Didn't Jan come back just fine? Has she said that I did anything awful to her?"

"I can't talk about any of this with you," I said, thinking about the trial.

There was a deep sigh on the other end of the phone. In an apologetic manner, Robert spoke quietly, "Mary Ann, I'm so sorry for hurting you. I didn't mean to. Please, believe me."

Unable to respond to his statement, I remained mute. Several quiet moments passed before he continued, his voice shifting to a gentle tone. "I guess it was desperation and I just cracked. By all means, it was not intentional. I'd been off my medication and don't know what happened. You and Bob probably don't realize how much I've depended on you. I can't even count the times I thought life wasn't worth living. You guys gave me a reason."

Feeling a twinge of compassion, I swallowed hard.

Robert's voice trembled, "As I sat in that horrid Mexican jail and saw you and Jan through a crack in the door, I wanted to die. You looked terrible—like you'd lost a lot of weight."

The memory of that fitful day flashed through me like a lightning rod. My shoulders sagged as I slumped into a chair. "You'll never know," I said, shuddering at the thought.

"Since I've been home, I've wanted to tell you and Bob how awful I feel." Robert's voice was full of emotion as he began to cry. "Can you ever forgive me?"

"I can't right now," I said, insulted by his offer. "Day after day, I cried. Susan and Karen cried, and Bob nearly had a nervous breakdown. If you really want to know, it was like a knife piercing my heart!"

Robert sobs were heard clearly while he tried to express remorse. "Mary Ann, how can I ever make this up to you and Bob? Tell Bob I'm sorry. He was so upset at the hearing. It kills me to know how much he hates me."

"Bob doesn't hate you, Robert," I said, resolutely, "but you'll have to tell him yourself."

"He said he never wants to talk to me again," Robert blubbered.

Listening to Robert's pathetic whimpering caused me to wonder if it was fair to totally blame him, knowing he was unable to reason normally.

He blew his nose, then cleared his throat before continuing his apology. "Bob knows Jan is like my own daughter. I would have died for her before I let anything happen to her."

Pangs of anxiety shot through me. How could I excuse what he did? "Robert, I need to go," I said, anxiously.

"I'm not through. I have more to tell you," he said.

Without hesitating, I said, "Sorry, but I have to go."

Hanging up the receiver, I burst into tears. Getting a grip on myself, I set about doing my household chores, but throughout the remainder of the day I was preoccupied with the call. My battered emotions shifted from one episode to another—the great times we had together, the boating, the family dinners, the long talks on the patio. Those days were gone. Now I was remembering the weeks of torment, the jail, the marriage, those disgusting affidavits, the hearing, and waiting for the trial. One of our primary worries had been whether Robert had molested Jan, but apparently he didn't, and we were relieved. There had to be a better explanation for that marriage license. Whatever possessed him?

Shortly after the court hearing ended, Robert finished liquidating his business and was granted permission from the court to move to Utah where he obtained employment. His weekend visits brought him to church with his family where his winsome personality was conveyed to church members as he shook hands, smiled, joked, and was positive and polite. Frequently, he would glance over where we sat and acknowledge us with a friendly nod and smiling face. His presence irritated Bob beyond words.

■ ■ ■

Later in the week after Robert left Pocatello Jan again heard the dreaded high pitched voice quietly calling her, "Fe.male com.pan.ion." She awoke startled. The familiar feelings of panic swept over her as she carefully looked around her darkened bedroom. Sitting on the dresser across from her bed was the ivory box. Glaring at the object, her heart rate accelerated as she listened to the message which warned what would happen to her should she talk about her mission to anyone. Overcome with fear, she trembled and obediently nodded her head. She was reminded to stay close to her male companion. It was important they work on the plan together. Again, she was warned about her impending demise. Afraid someone would hear the message and her life would abruptly end, Jan listened intently for footsteps on the upper floor. There were no sounds. Ordered by the voice to close her eyes and go back to sleep, Jan obeyed, pretending to sleep, but the panic that engulfed her would not allow it. She did not dare move a muscle, and hoped the visitor would assume she was sleeping and leave. After what seemed an extreme length of time, Jan cracked her eyelids slightly and peered toward the dresser. The box was gone! Where did it go? Its disappearance was a mystery. Afraid to get out of bed, she tossed restlessly until dawn. Creeping out of bed, Jan looked on the floor, under her bed, in dresser drawers, and opened the closet, but the box was nowhere to be found. Certainly the power of her visitors was not of this world.

11 # gone, but not forgotten

With Robert gone from the neighborhood, the relationship between our children became more acceptable to Bob. It was apparent we could not convince our girls to stay away from them. Eventually, visits to the Berchtold home were permitted with an understanding that they were not to be there anytime Robert was there.

Gail and I visited occasionally, but the previous intensity we knew before Jan's disappearance diminished considerably. Whenever she stopped by our house, her visits were short. She knew Bob's feelings were quite tender and she didn't want to add more salt to his wounds.

Summer arrived and the trial was delayed again which only added to Bob's anxiety. The longer the delay, the more complacent I became in my thinking about the outcome. I hadn't let go of personal feelings for Robert, and Bob knew it.

"Perhaps there will never be a trial," I said. "Robert didn't abuse Jan and he's making great strides. Everybody at church says he's doing just fine. Sister Bird thinks we should just forgive and forget. After all, are any of us perfect?"

Bob said, "I believe in forgiveness, but forget? Quite un-likely. I know Robert is not a dangerous criminal, but I just can't trust him. It's too bad things ended up like they have and all our lives are a mess. If he will take care of his own family and leave mine alone, there's a chance we could be good neighbors and friends again. However, he has to prove that before I will give him any of my time again."

It seemed to be a fair response. Bob was void of vindictiveness and made an effort to acknowledge Robert when they were at Church. Otherwise, they maintained their distance. Robert made one feeble attempt to make amends; he called Bob, but their con-versation ended when Robert expressed his dismay that we called the FBI and didn't give him a chance to bring Jan back.

Oliver, the community's summer musical, held auditions and Jan was cast as Oliver Twist; Susan was also in the cast. Rehearsals were held nightly for six weeks and tension in our home subsided. The day the show opened, Gail brought a copy of the classic novel and presented it to our girls with a sincere sentiment written on the inside. The girls were touched by her thoughtfulness. Bob approved of her kindness and told her so. On opening night, Karen came to claim her seat next to us after checking in with Susan and Jan. She reported the cast was talking about a dozen red roses that were delivered to the green room for Jan. Scribbled on the card were the words, *Love you forever, B.*

Bob was furious. "So, you don't think Robert has designs on Jan? How do you explain this, Mary Ann?"

The following day, Bob walked to the Berchtold home and faced his foe. "Leave my family alone! Stay away from them! Get out of their lives forever! All I want is my family without you inter-fering," he said in a sure, steady voice.

"Broberg, give up. You want them all to hate me, but you can't change love, so stop fighting it," Robert said.

Bob's temper flared. "No, I don't want them to hate you, but believe me, I will never give up trying to convince them what you really are." He poked Robert in the chest with his finger. "Before you lose your own family, wake up!" Bob turned and walked away, confident he had made his point.

After Bob's confrontation Robert's hostility toward Bob began to surface. Friends indicated he was quite upset with Bob for not being more understanding towards him and their predicament. Jimmy told Karen that there was a handgun hanging on the steering wheel of his Dad's new motor home and his father declared it was his security to protect him from his enemies since he now had a lot of them.

■ ■ ■

August 1975

Having more freedom through the summer months for bike rides and spending time with friends also allowed Jan to meet secretly with Brother B. She had been instructed to call him collect every week to discuss where they would meet and she had to work out a time when her parents wouldn't be suspicious. B heard from Zethra and found out there were other people assigned to help them. If she got notes or phone calls from strangers, she was told not to panic, just do what she was told, and destroy the notes. He had a number for her to call later that day. Before dropping her off one day, he gave her a supply of pocket change to use in pay phones when making her required calls.

Jan called the number and immediately knew it was Zethra. Her message was alarming. If B goes to jail, Jan might be assigned a new male companion. Jan feverishly thought about another stranger coming into her life. I'm so scared. I don't want anybody but B. Zethra said it isn't time for the mission, but she will tell me when it is. What if they come and get me?

Jan called B and told him she was scared. He said as long as she did what they told her, everything would be okay. He warned her to stay away from all males. Jan thought, my friends think I'm weird. They all like guys and wonder why I don't.

■ ■ ■

Late one Saturday evening, we received a phone call from a woman who needed funeral flowers for her father. He had passed away and the family had forgotten to order them. The viewing was on Sunday evening in Logan, Utah. Could she pick the flowers up Sunday morning around eight o'clock? Bob was agreeable to her request.

Wanting to have the flowers ready when the lady arrived, Bob left home at six o'clock that morning. In less than an hour, the phone rang and awakened me.

It was Bob. His voice was strained. "Mary Ann, I just had a weird experience. This morning when I pulled into the back of the store, a man and a woman were sitting in a car all cuddled up. It seemed a little peculiar, but I parked and went in the back door of the shop and watched them for a few minutes through the back window. After I pulled the flowers out of the ice box, I looked again and they were gone. I opened the back door, like I usually do, to enjoy the morning air and listen to the birds. I was busy getting the casket piece started when the strangest feeling come over me and I felt impressed to close the door. I went back to tape the oasis onto the casket frame when I heard someone trying to get in the back door. I about passed out, but fortunately, I had locked the door. After getting my bearings, I called the police and asked them to come over."

"Maybe it was the lady wanting her flowers," I said.

"I don't know. I didn't see anyone outside. I gave the police a description of the car I'd seen earlier and one of the officers left, hoping to find it. The other policeman stayed with me, in case the lady came for her funeral piece. I called Hall's Mortuary and told them the man's name, but there were no services scheduled. We've decided it was all a hoax to get me down here alone."

A spine-tingling chill raced through my body. Immediately, Robert flashed through my mind. *Why would I think he had anything to do with this?* I dismissed the thought, but didn't like the crawly feeling prickling my skin.

Bob sounded assured. "I think it might have been someone trying to rob the store. When that lady called last night, there was loud music in the background and I thought she was probably drowning her sorrow at a bar."

"Just get yourself home," I said impatiently.

Following that incident, Bob couldn't decide if Robert had anything to do with it, but became more cautious demanding that all association with the Berchtolds should stop. He didn't give the girls a reason, but was definite with his feelings. "Stay away from places where the Berchtolds go, including Bonneville Park. I'm sorry, but it has to be this way."

The girls felt like prisoners without an explanation. Robert was furious and began a blitz of phone calls to our home. "What's wrong with Bob? Why is he putting up this front and not letting our kids see each other? Doesn't he know what he's doing to them? If it has to do with me, tell him not to take it out on the kids."

With summer coming to a close, Gail made a major decision to move closer to Robert's work, although they would not be living together. It was obvious Gail needed help with her family and she was hopeful the move would bring some kind of resolution to her and Robert's fragile marriage. Bob was elated, the rest of us cried.

Gail and I and our children exchanged letters and phone calls after the family moved to Utah, and invitations to visit were numerous. Gail finally persuaded me to bring the girls for an overnight visit and I accepted. Disgusted and angry, Bob put his foot down and demanded the relationship end. He could not tolerate it any longer. Intense anger disrupted between us and I accused him of forcing me to give up a friendship I cherished.

"Until this trial is past and Robert and Gail are divorced, you cannot continue to be a part of their lives. I will not and cannot put my girls in harm's way any longer. Our children have always been your first priority. What's going on? You need to stop encouraging their feelings and get over yours as well," he said.

I retaliated and struck back. "Where's your heart, Bob? Gail needs a friend and I intend to be one."

"This is not about Gail. You are still mesmerized by Robert. You need to decide who is most important here, me or Robert," he declared.

I denied it, but part of me still carried a banner of knowing, caring and wondering about Robert. It had become a major problem and I better figure it out because my marriage was in jeopardy. *What has happened to our "ideal" family?* I wondered. *Will we ever resolve these differences?*

The impending trial was postponed for a third time after Berchtold fired another attorney and hired a new one. Even after the Berchtold family moved, Robert was seen in the community often as he made preparations for the trial.

After three trial dates had been set and rescheduled, another was announced. We heard little from the prosecutors office about what was expected from us. It was rumored that Berchtold's attorney had been working to settle the case out of court. Bob and I had high hopes that would happen.

Nearing the end of March 1976, I answered the phone at midday to hear an anxious voice. It was Robert. He and his attorney were discussing a plea bargain with Federal Prosecutors which could eliminate a trial.

Trying to stay calm, I took a deep breath and exhaled slowly.

"Oh, this is quite a surprise. It certainly has to be a big decision for you. What has to happen to settle it?" I asked.

"There's some conditions attached and I want you and Jan to hear them before I decide if I will agree to plea bargain. Meet me at the top of Buckskin Road when Jan is out of school," he demanded.

"I can't bring Jan," I said.

"Jan has to be there! It's very important," he responded defensively.

Realizing they were still bargaining, I approached him cautiously. "What do you want to discuss with her? Is this another situation like the affidavits?"

Robert struck out vindictively. "Oh, for hell's sake! It's nothing like that. I already told you, Mary Ann, I won't agree to their conditions without knowing what Jan thinks."

"And how will any of that concern her?" I asked.

"Do you want to go to trial?" Robert's irritation with me was apparent in his voice. "I thought this is what we've all wanted. Either you bring Jan or there will be no plea agreement."

"I don't know if we will be there or not," I said.

"Three o'clock, with Jan!" were his final words as he banged down the receiver.

I agonized. Bob's tolerance with me had worn thin and our marriage had suffered acutely through this difficult year. He let me know, in no uncertain terms, that he would do anything to see Robert behind bars. Bob had said, "His goal is to destroy anyone or everything that stands in his way. He only thinks about himself."

Bob's anger toward "this home wrecker" was clear. "I don't want any of my girls around that man and will do whatever is necessary to protect them from him. If you won't see to that, I'll have you removed from this house."

Those words echoed in my ears as I made a hasty decision and picked the girls up from school. Driving home, I explained that I had to run an errand with Jan, and dropped Karen and Susan at home. When we were alone, I told Jan where we going and the reason. She looked at me apprehensively and scowled. "Mom, you know what Dad said. We're not supposed to talk to Brother B."

I nodded and raised my eyebrows. "Oh Jan, if Robert will work this out so we don't have to have a trial, your Dad and I will be so happy."

Robert was off to the side of the road, waiting. The minute he saw us, he jumped out and came over to our car, scooting into the front seat next to Jan.

"You're late. I thought you weren't coming," he said.

"Sorry, but I had to take Karen and Susan home."

He flashed a forced smile. "I'm glad you came. This is very important and I didn't want to make a decision until I told you about the deal."

Instead of relating the plan, he asked Jan questions about school while I apprehensively squirmed. Pangs of anxiety were fluttering through my stomach as I attempted patience. Finally, when I felt he had wasted enough time, I asked, "What's the plan, Robert? We have to get home."

"Oh, relax. You need to lighten up."

Recognizing Jan was nervously biting her fingernails, Robert finished his neurotic chattering. Softly moaning, his eyebrows arched and he stared intently at Jan. After a few moments, he turned and glared directly at me. "This has been a very hard day. The Feds aren't going to let me go free. Either I plead guilty and receive a reduced sentence, or go to trial and drag us all through the mud."

Jan eyes widened as she looked at Robert, then turned to me, expecting a reaction. I made certain my eyes didn't reveal how I felt, but inside, I thought my gut would burst. *Could we be so lucky,* I thought, *that he would plead guilty and get this over with?*

"My lawyer thinks by going to trial I could get off, but that would cost us plenty." Robert slowly exhaled, his shoulders dropped, with his face downcast. He did not move or speak for several moments. There was a slight jerk of Robert's head as his mouth tightened. "Jan, I'm only thinking of you. If there was a trial, you are the one who would suffer the most."

I thought, *Oh, you are so clever. Playing the "good guy" role for Jan. What a manipulator. You took her. You are the guilty one.*

For the sake of cajoling Robert to plea bargain, I commented graciously, "Thank you, Robert. We haven't wanted Jan involved in a trial either, and it appears you are the key to stopping it. I know it's a lot to ask, but for her sake, there doesn't seem to be an alternative."

Robert's eyes narrowed, his jaw set firmly. Turning to Jan, he asked, "What do you think I should do, Dolly?"

Jan reacted by throwing her hands up and shrugged. Uncertain, she replied, "Uh, I don't know. I don't want you to go to jail."

"Well, it's either that or dragging you through a whole lot of crap." Robert looked at her with pleading eyes and asked, "Think you could love a jail bird?"

Disturbed by his remark, I said, "We've got to go."

"So do I," he said. "I have to go back and let my attorney know. The Feds want my answer today."

I stared at him unemotionally. Jan said nothing as she searched Robert's face curiously.

"Well, you two aren't much comfort. What I'm doing is for you, Jan," Robert remarked.

I wondered what he expected us to do. Cry? Beg him to change his mind? The news was such a relief, but I only dared rejoice inwardly.

Robert continued, "If I knew you wouldn't be hurt, I'd fight like hell, but you know the truth and so do I. In time, everyone will know."

He stared at Jan for an unusual length of time. His strange, transfixed look was something I hadn't seen before; I felt extremely uneasy. What did he mean by that remark?

With the corner of his mouth curling into a smirk, he winked at Jan. "Don't you worry, Dolly. It's going to work out just fine. No one is going to hurt you. Trust me." He paused, smacking his lips with the smirk on his face unchanged.

I looked at Jan and saw her eyes grow large and anxious. As I glanced at Robert and then back at Jan, I immediately knew something was wrong. The color drained from her face while little beads of perspiration dotted her forehead. Jan crossed her arms over her stomach and began swallowing hard.

"Honey, are you okay? Are you sick?" I asked, alarmed.

Jan put a hand to her mouth and slumped down in the seat while waving at me to leave her alone. I watched Robert grimace as he opened the car door and got out. A minute later, Jan forced a slight smile, shrugged her shoulders and said, "I'm okay. I was kind of sick. I think it was my lunch."

At that moment, the blood rushed out of my head and I felt stunned. It was a moment of truth. *Something has happened. She isn't okay. What has he done to her?* Feeling extremely anxious, I tapped the steering wheel impatiently. As if I'd been hit over the head with a bat, my sensibilities were quickened.

"Well, I better go," Robert remarked. Jan nodded when he asked if she was okay. He hurriedly kissed her forehead, smiled and said, "Thanks for coming. I'll let you know what happens."

Once again, turning back, he reached into the car, patting Jan's arm. Cocking his head to the side, he stated, "Remember, you're my special angel, Dolly. Don't worry about one thing. I promise, everything will work out the way it's supposed to."

Driving back home, I tried to converse with Jan, but it was impossible. Laying her head back on the seat, she closed her eyes, seeming very disturbed. I knew from her reaction to Robert's brief words, that his remarks were very upsetting. But it was the unspoken exchange that was eerie. *What is going on?* I wondered.

Robert called to report a plea bargain had been worked out. He would be serving jail time with details forthcoming after a federal judge considered the agreement.

Bob didn't say a word when he came into the house, but I could read the message on his face. "I guess you know Robert was in town today," I said.

"Yes, he called the store, but luckily I wasn't there." Bob's voice was cold and unfeeling.

"Did you know he is pleading guilty? They've worked out a plea bargain and there won't be a trial," I said with a healthy amount of enthusiasm.

"That's nice," Bob remarked sarcastically. "Is that what you decided was best?"

"Don't you think so? It's what we wanted to happen. He *is* guilty."

"What I think doesn't matter anymore," Bob said in disgust. "Why did you take Jan? I don't want him near her or any of my girls! I thought I made that perfectly clear."

"Did you have your spies watching me? It doesn't matter what I do; it's never right," I exclaimed.

"And it never will be as long as he is in the picture. I'm sorry, Mary Ann. Very, very sorry! I can't take any more."

The atmosphere was frigid. We didn't speak to each other the rest of the evening. That night I couldn't sleep, and lay staring into the dark void. I knew Bob had reached his limit. I also knew he was right. My thoughts ran rampant through most of the night. *Robert frightens me. What he said about needing Jan's approval bothered me. Then, that look. It hit the very core of my soul. What has he done? And what if something happened to Bob? What would I do?* Knowing I had allowed myself to be a victim of deception was a hard pill to swallow. Why hadn't I seen it before now? I permitted Robert to confuse me about what was most important—my husband and children.

The next day, Bob and I had a bitter exchange after the girls left for school. Refusing to listen to anything I had to say, he complained that I was jeopardizing the safety of our girls, and he couldn't allow that any longer. During the confrontation, I impulsively packed a few clothes and drove to my mother's home in Utah.

After the impact subsided, I began thinking more sensibly. Analyzing my predicament brought the first recognition; *I've been a complete fool, but that is beside the point. Bob has to know what I felt. He probably won't listen. Why should he? Bob may never want me back. How could I be so stupid? I'm so passive, it's sickening. Jan needs protection from Robert. Something's wrong. I can't put my finger on it, but I just know.* Anxious and confused, I needed time to think how to bring things together.

My mother adored my husband and knew he was not to blame. She couldn't imagine how I had created so much chaos. Her advice was to "get home and fix it."

Receiving little sympathy from her, I visited my little sister and cried on her shoulder. Eileen said, "I've had my share of tough times, but this is the first time *you've* ever asked for *my* advice."

"It shows what a self-centered idiot I am," I responded through my tears. "I've always had the right answers before—or thought I did, but Bob won't even talk to me. It's been icicle city for way too long."

"My perfect sister," Eileen said, with a touch of sarcasm.

"Ha! Well, now it's 'idiot' sister," I responded. "How could I be so brainless? I've let so much die between Bob and me. Everything's a mess."

"Since Jan's kidnapping, your lives have been anything but calm. You both need to get past your anger and face the issues that are tearing you apart. There is a solution."

Shaking my head, I mumbled, "Oh, I don't know. Probably divorce."

"Oh, pooh," Eileen said. "This isn't like Bob at all. I think all the stress has pushed him over the edge."

I cast my head down and nodded. "No doubt about it. It's been a tough year and a half."

Watching me struggle, Eileen muttered, "I grew up thinking people like you were unreal. It's kind of nice knowing you're human."

We both chuckled.

Throwing my arms around her, I hugged her. "Well, I don't know how I'm going to do it, but I better get it right."

"Just get in your car and go home. I'm calling Bob," Eileen said.

My arrival home was full of emotion. Bob's demeanor was subdued. I had prepared several speeches on my drive home, but now I had forgotten all of them. We stood looking at each other for a few desperate moments hoping the other would be the first to speak. Finally, I said, "I'm so sorry. Will you let me come back?"

Sobbing, I fell into Bob's open arms as he lovingly patted my back.

Whispering in my ear, he said, "Welcome home."

Greeting my daughters, I apologized for my departure and not saying goodbye. Each one affectionately expressed how happy they were to have me back home. Regretfully, Bob and I knew we had created a difficult home environment. It became a precious time of commitment as we spoke with our children and promised to work out any contention in our home, assuring them that our marriage was secure.

As our discussion evolved, the Berchtolds came into the conversation. Each daughter expressed their desire to remain friends and hoped to see the Berchtolds whenever possible.

Karen said, "It was wrong that Brother B took Jan, but she came back okay, so what's the big deal?"

"Besides, Brother B is going to jail, so the kids could still do things together and he wouldn't be around," Susan said, thoughtfully.

As Jan listened to the conversation, she became very agitated and threw the book she was reading across the room. Jumping up from the couch and waving her arms, she darted across the room and stormed out yelling, "I wish everybody would stop blaming him. It's not his fault. Maybe someday you'll all understand."

Should I expect the girls to feel any different than I did a week ago? I thought. However, this gut feeling has not changed since I saw Jan's reaction this past week when talking with Robert. I know something is wrong and Bob knows it. How are we going to find out what it is?

escalating tension

Our year had been full of anger, distrust, and uncontrollable emotion; personal bitterness was destroying us. Saying "I'm sorry" was not enough. Removing the wedge between us would take concentrated effort, but we recognized it was time to stop blaming each other and revitalize our relationship.

Willing to tackle our fragmented emotions, we squeezed time together into every available minute of our busy schedules and discussed all factors that had led to the fragile condition of our marriage. We admitted personal failings, deeply reflected on our individual strengths and weaknesses. Determined to keep our marriage intact, we vowed to remain loyal, true, and completely honest with one another as we fought our way through this difficult evaluation and readjustment.

We agreed that eliminating Berchtold from our lives was crucial to our survival. It was painful to see the truth, but we realized Berchtold had carefully noted our "Achilles' heel" and took advantage. While undoing emotional damage from the past was a major goal, keeping our children safe in the present was the more acute problem. Through subtly maneuvering his way into our lives and winning our complete trust, Robert was home free with our children. Any continued accessibility to Jan had come through me, and he greatly resented Bob's interference. He knew that the easiest way to remove Bob from his position as protector and father would be divorce. Since we were not going to let that happen, Robert was crippled, but not finished. How should I prepare for his next intrusion?

■ ■ ■

Spring 1976

The next invasion of Jan's privacy occurred one night in the spring. Zada's shrill voice uttered the same repetitive messages as in the past, but added that her male companion had been found pleasing before the councils of the universe. He was worthy to continue the mission with her and the time was nearing for her to be with him. It was important for her to follow her male companion. Jan was so shaken at hearing the unexpected piercing voice, her body tightened as if she were paralyzed. Moments later, she rushed into Karen's room extremely distraught, her voice shaking as she whispered, "Karen?" Karen only grunted as Jan trembled in fear and crowded herself next to her sister's sleeping body. Karen mumbled, "What're ya' doin'?" as she moved over to make room and fell back to sleep. Unable to sleep, Jan listened intently to every creak and eerie sound originating in the dark, silent night.

The next morning, Karen probed, but Jan dared not expose the reason why she invaded her sister's bed. She made up a story about getting spooked because she heard a scratching sound outside the window.

After that experience, Jan found it difficult to sleep in her room. She often slipped into the family room at night or talked Karen into sleeping in her bed while she rolled up in a blanket and occupied the blue velvet hanging bench.

Following this intrusion, Jan began receiving specific instructions from several strangers. The first was delivered to her at school. She had never seen the guy before, but he walked up to her, called her by name, smiled and nodded knowingly, then handed her a note. His grungy appearance startled her. He looked about twenty and wore a grease-smudged tee shirt and dirty Levi's that were torn on the upper thigh, exposing flesh. His unkempt hair was long and straggly. She watched him casually walk across the beaten-down grassy trail toward Buckskin Road, never looking back. Her heart pounded as she read the brief note that was written on a torn piece of lined paper:

> It's time. A way has been opened. Don't put it off.
> Remember your mission. Call 555-6918.
> Do as instructed.

She destroyed the note.

A male voice answered the phone and told her to ride her bike to the Anderson Trailer Park on Saturday morning. Someone would be there to talk with her. It was raining on Saturday and Jan knew her mom wouldn't want her to ride in the rain. Jan was busy dusting the family room trying to find an excuse to leave when her mom called downstairs and said she was going grocery shopping. Relieved, Jan jumped on her bicycle and peddled furiously to her appointment.

The small trailer court was junky looking. All the trailers were old and in need of repairs. There was no grass around, just weeds. As she stopped and got off her bike, the door to a trailer opened and a man with a short brown beard hollered, "Over here." Fearing for her safety, Jan stood in the pouring rain looking at him. Another figure looked over the man's shoulder and Jan recognized Brother B. With a huge sigh of relief, she hurried up the wooden steps and into the trailer. The place was dirty, foul smelling, and unkempt. Another male was sitting at a kitchen table with a cigarette in his fingers. The male door greeter took a seat at the table and poured coffee into mugs.

Brother B smiled and gave Jan a hug. "You made it. I was beginning to worry. Sorry it had to rain, but you are amazing. Take off that wet jacket and let it dry off." Jan followed him to a couch where they sat down as he continued to explain. "I didn't dare come anywhere near your house because I'm being followed. We have to be extra careful with everything from now on. Now that the mission is so close to being worked out, my life is in danger."

Wide eyed, Jan nodded as she watched the two strangers out of the corner of her eyes. They appeared uninterested in what was taking place.

"Did you get the message from Zada?" he asked in a quiet voice.

Jan nodded.

"I did too, so I've been working on a plan. I'm going to open up a game center in Jackson Hole this summer and you have to come. I'll be getting a divorce and will work out a way for us to get married. It's going to be hard, but what else can I do? Your parents will be the hardest to convince, so we better start now thinking how to get you there."

Robert looked anxiously at his watch. Seeing Jan shiver, he motioned with his finger and said, "Come with me." She followed him and they left the trailer. He walked her around the back of the lot and guided her into his parked car. After turning on the engine, he adjusted the heater letting warm air blow on Jan's trembling body. "Damn, I hope you don't get sick again. I'm not around every day to make sure you take your vitamins. I know you don't have much time before you have to get home, but I need a little time alone with you before you take off. So, tell me what you think about this summer?" he asked.

"It would be fun, but I don't think my parents will let me go," Jan replied.

"Let me worry about that," Robert said pulling her close and throwing his jacket over her. "It has to work out, even if Bob and Mary Ann refuse to let you come, I'll figure out a way."

Other messages followed. With each delivery, Jan's anxiety increased. Instructions to meet unknown persons in unfamiliar places frightened her, but she dared not ignore their warnings. Fearful for her own existence, she obediently obliged. Occasionally, she received a brief message over the phone, but most disturbing were the whispering voices in the middle of the *night reminding her that B was her chosen "male companion" and she must complete her mission. The box would appear out of nowhere and be gone just as mysteriously.*

Disheartened, Jan thought, One of them told me that I'm supposed to have this special child before I'm sixteen. If B's in jail, or gets killed, what then? I don't want another male companion. Things are getting bad. I'd like to forget about everything that's happened. If only I could. *Despondent, Jan closed her eyes and wept.*

■ ■ ■

Each time the phone rang, I hesitated to answer, knowing it could be Robert. When he did call, I responded politely, but briefly.

Bob was more direct. "Robert, we are doing fine and don't need any interference. Your stewardship is Gail and your family. Please don't call here again. Goodbye."

A few days before Memorial Day, I picked up the receiver and heard a jubilant voice. "Hi! Where have you been? Or have you just been ignoring my phone calls?"

"I've been busy, working at the store," I replied anxiously.

"How are things going between you two?"

"Wonderful!" Bracing myself, I took a deep breath, then exhaled. "Robert, you have to quit calling."

Robert sighed. "Be assured I'm out of your lives. I think it's great you're working things out." His voice had a pleasant, cheerful ring.

"Good," I replied, relieved. "I have to go. Bob's expecting me at the shop."

"Okay, sure. I'm just passing through, but thought you'd like to know that Jerry and me are on our way to Jackson Hole to open up a game center."

Surprised, I said, "Wow. That's a change from the car business. Hope you do well."

"Oh, it's going to be fun. You guys will have to come up," he said.

I thought, *oh brother. Doesn't he get it? No matter what he's told, he won't give up.* "I really need to go. Good luck," I said.

"Has Jan told you that she wants to come and work for me this summer?"

Stunned, my mouth dropped open in utter disbelief. "What did you say?" My voice had raised a decibel or two. "What are you thinking?"

"It's not my idea, it's Jan's."

Unable to control my fury, I pounced on him. "Get out of her life and stop meddling in our family."

I slammed the receiver down. *Who does he think he is?* The audacity of his thinking we would let her go! Gathering what was left of my senses, I drove to the shop and reported his disturbing call.

School closed for summer vacation on a good note since Jan was chosen drill team leader for the next school year. It seemed a great opportunity to celebrate and take a summer vacation to California. Excitement mounted as we put our plans in motion. However, Jan's anxiety began to surface as the week progressed. Finding enough courage to approach me, she set the stage carefully, not wanting to be misunderstood. In a nonchalant manner, she said, "I need a job, but I don't want to baby-sit."

I nodded my head and smiled. "Oh good. Your dad has wanted you to work at the shop and get some experience."

Jan frowned and ignored the proposal. "Did you know Brother B is opening a Family Fun Center in Jackson Hole?"

My stomach dropped. Taking a deep breath, I said, "Yes, I heard about it. How did you find out?"

"From Jerry. He's already up there working." With a sizable amount of enthusiasm, Jan related what she knew. "It's really going to be neat. They've got all these fun machines and games and it's for kids only. Adults aren't allowed. I could buy my own school clothes and drill team stuff and, well, you know all the other things I need. What do you think Dad will say?"

"I can tell you right now, the answer is no. Parents don't let kids your age go away to work for the summer. You can talk to your dad, but I can tell you already he won't approve."

"Yeah, he *hates* B!"

"Your father doesn't hate B, but he doesn't want you around him," I said. "He still hasn't served time for his kidnapping charge. Robert doesn't use good sense, Jan."

Jan's eyes narrowed, her nostrils flared and she blurted out. "How many times do I have to say it? He didn't kidnap me! We couldn't come home because you guys called the law. And now you're going to ruin this too."

Stunned at her outburst, I defended my position. "Well, you are not going, so just get it out of your head."

Jan stood with her hands on her hips with her head wagging back and forth. "I want to get out of this town. Do you know how people look at me? I can't stand to stay here because you blew a little thing all out of proportion. Now everyone treats me funny. I'm not a normal kid anymore because of what you did."

Tears were running down her face, her voice too high, too loud. She turned and ran from the room.

I opened my mouth to speak, then closed it. *What could I say that would make a difference? Wow! I didn't know she felt like this. I wonder how long Robert has been plotting this out. She's dealing with a lot of emotions right now. This will all blow over in a few days.*

Bob's arrival from work brought the issue to the surface. Jan explained that Brother B had found a place for her to live with some good people. Jerry would be there and she could make $4.00 an hour.

Bob didn't sugarcoat his feelings and gave his opinion without mincing words. "No, Jan. You're not going. Don't even think about it. Robert can't be trusted. Furthermore, I don't want you talking to him on the phone at all."

Jan's eyes welled up with tears and a wave of disappointment swept over her face, but not a sound came out of her pursed lips.

Vacation plans were moved ahead of schedule. It was decided to invite Caroline to go with us, hoping this gesture would appease Jan's disappointment.

A few days passed before Robert called our home. The first words he spoke were, "Jan's going to run away."

"What?" That sounded incredulous.

"Jan called and told me her dad won't let her come."

"Did you really think he would? What planet are you on, Robert."

"I actually thought he would have better sense. You guys think I'm behind this, but Jan's been the one pushing this pretty hard. If you don't let her come, she's going to run away."

"You liar! Leave her alone!"

"Ha! You don't think she'll do it? Well, don't say I didn't warn you."

Berchtold was in town on June 8, 1976, to receive sentencing which amounted to five years in prison with all but forty-five days suspended. He would serve that time in the Bannock County Jail in September. The thirty days he spent in jail before being released on bond would be counted toward his serving time. It was shocking to realize he would serve a total of *fifteen days!*

With Robert in town, I watched Jan like a hawk. I didn't want her to leave the house in case he had a plan that included her. Our trust level was at ground zero knowing his influence was powerful and anything possible.

Jan nervously announced, "I think I'll go on a bike ride over to Caroline's."

My response was immediate. "I'll drive you."

Instead, she practiced the piano.

With Caroline along, our family left on a two-week vacation during the month of June. It was wonderful to be away from the pressures of life, and comforting to know we were far away from Berchtold and his phone calls. It was a great time to give our girls undivided attention and recapture unity as a family.

Realizing the hold Berchtold had on Jan, Bob and I seriously discussed selling our business and moving. One of Bob's employees was interested in buying our shop, and we discussed possibilities on the purchase. As they began looking for financing, Bob and I began exploring other business opportunities in Utah.

After a weekend trip, we returned home, hopelessly discouraged. Neither one of us felt it was what we wanted to do. Within a couple of weeks, the financial picture soured for the buyers, and the plans never reached fruition.

Instead of selling, Bob decided to remodel and expand the shop. He threw himself into an extensive remodeling plan, secured a bank loan, and laid out his ideas with a building contractor. New excitement emerged.

During July, calls from Berchtold were numerous as he claimed Jan would not listen to him about staying home. She was determined about coming to Jackson Hole.

"Jan has been told not to call you. Quit talking to her. Make it easy and tell her not to call you anymore."

Robert moaned. "I'm trying to tell her she can't come, but she won't listen."

"Well, try harder. She isn't coming and that's final."

Robert sounded worried. "She keeps saying she will run away if you don't let her come."

"I know my daughter, and that is the last thing she would ever do." I felt confident saying that and knew Robert would never persuade me otherwise.

"Why don't you let her come for just a few days? She'll find out it isn't that great and will be begging to go back home."

Exasperated, I raised my voice. "Do you know what 'no' means? Forget it, leave her alone, and quit calling. Bob and I are tired of your persistent interference."

Robert's anger escalated. "Believe me, Mary Ann, I will not give up what I've fought so hard to get no matter what I have to do! I've paid too high a price to let go."

His voice was determined, threatening.

In a fit of rage, I struck back. "You're a sick man! Don't ever call here again!"

Robert's voice screamed back violently. "You'll be sorry. If I have to, I'll take her to the jungles of Africa or South America, and you will never see her again."

I slammed the receiver down, trembling. I had no doubt he meant every word. Shaken and distressed, I drove to the store to consult with Bob. He offered comfort and calmed me.

"When I get home, I'll talk to Jan."

Jan's restlessness was disconcerting. When we explained our fears she didn't respond. She avoided looking at us while she wiped away tears. We asked her to explain Robert's accusations about her running away, but Jan, always a willing communicator, now refused to talk. Her demeanor deeply troubled us.

"Jan, what's going on? Talk to us. Can't you see what he's doing to you?"

Jan shook her head. "Just let me go to Jackson and everything will be all right."

"I can't let you do that, honey. I love you too much," Bob said.

Looking at her father, she begged, "If you loved me you would let me go. It's not B's fault."

"No, honey. It is his fault because he is trying to persuade you against our wishes. Even if this doesn't make sense to you, it has to be this way."

Jan didn't respond. She sat sullen and stared. Bob and I were sick about the change in her over the last few weeks. She had become quiet, moody, and easily agitated.

Over the next few days, Jan steadily voiced her plan. She was going to Jackson and no one could keep her from going. It was alarming to see her insistent behavior, something we had never before witnessed. Her sisters had no insight either. Karen invited Caroline over, hoping Jan would confide in her best friend. It didn't happen.

Returning home from running an errand, I found Susan crying and holding her arm from a bike wreck. Jan had been thoughtful enough to tie a makeshift dishtowel sling around Susan's neck to support the battered arm.

"Where's Jan?" I inquired while inspecting her arm.

Through Susan's wailing, she said, "Gone."

Stunned, I felt the adrenaline drain from my body. "Gone where?"

Her howling continued, but she managed to answer my question. "To Jackson Hole."

The weight of her words caused my shoulders to sag. My fingers dug into Susan's flesh and she let out a yelp. I apologized and released my grip to avoid putting more pressure on her injured arm. Groping for words I asked, "How did she go?"

Whimpering, Susan replied. "A taxi came. She was going to the airport."

"No!" I cried out, panicked. "When? How long ago?"

"I don't know. Fifteen minutes, I think," Susan replied.

I frantically looked at the time. "When was the plane leaving?" I asked anxiously.

Susan moved her arm and the pain brought on another round of howling. "I don't know," she cried.

"Susie, get in the car. We have to get Jan."

I grabbed the keys and opened the door for Susan. She crawled into the back seat of the car and laid down, cradling her bruised arm. Attempting to comfort her, I babbled about getting her to the doctor and seeing what was wrong while I wildly sped onto the highway and headed to the airport.

With my heart pounding furiously, I grasped the steering wheel so tightly my knuckles turned white. Listening to Susan's mournful cry gave no relief to my anxiety. My stomach churned unrestrained. I thought, *Jan didn't have money for a plane ticket. This is ridiculous. I've got to talk to her. She can't go see Robert.*

Assuring Susan it would only take a few minutes, I parked at the curb of the terminal and rushed in. Jan was standing at the Western Airlines counter paying for her ticket with a roll of bills. I was astounded at the cash she had. Trying to be calm and not cause a scene, I quietly said, "Jan, you are not going to Jackson. Come on, you're going home with me."

A few passengers standing in line stared at the two of us as the agent handed Jan her ticket. I struggled to be composed. Jan seemed so rehearsed. "Oh, Mom. I'm a big girl. Don't worry. Everything is going to be fine. I'll be home soon."

"So! Do you know what you're doing? You're making a terrible choice," I said. "Robert took you once and he'll take you again. Don't let him ruin your life. He's nearly ruined mine."

"Mom, it's okay," Jan said, quietly. "I'm just going to be there for a couple of weeks to earn some school money. Drill team stuff costs a lot and I want to help earn it myself."

Jan had a small bag in her hands and began walking towards the aircraft. I raced after her. "Jan you know this isn't right. Your Dad is going to explode."

My words fell on deaf ears.

"Mom, tell Dad I love him, but I have to do this. There's a letter for him on the kitchen table."

I grabbed her elbow and tried to pull her back. She jerked away. "I'm going," she hissed under her breath, her eyes set and her face clearly warning that she would make a scene.

I stared at her walking faster now. She had distanced herself from me as a group of passengers crowded in.

Calmly tossing her head back, she said, "Oh yeah, I'm going to be living with an attorney. I'll call and give you guys a number where you can call me. Everything is worked out."

I went completely numb. My weakened body felt like all the life had been drained from it. Here was my thirteen-year-old child in command, and I felt helpless.

Just before Jan walked confidently through the door, she turned back and hollered, "Mom, I love you."

I watched her board the plane and felt like vomiting. I couldn't believe I was powerless. Feeling nauseated, I dashed out the door, and ran to the car with tears running down my face. I looked at Susan still in pain and I bawled uncontrollably. I kept telling myself this was better than Robert taking her. I would know where she was and she wouldn't stay long. Drill team practice started the first of August and school at the end of the month. Jerry was there and he'd look after her. He was a good kid.

By the time we arrived home, Susan was asleep. I awoke her and ushered her to the living room where she laid down on the couch. Mentally, the long-term emotional battering had caused its damage. I felt like a zombie; unfeeling, uncaring, unable to cope with life around me.

I was sitting at the kitchen table when Bob drove into the garage. Showing no emotion, I handed Jan's letter to him as he walked through the door and inquired "what's going on?" Too weak and beaten down to care, I sat unresponsive as he opened the envelope and read Jan's note:

Dear Dad,

I'm sorry that things didn't work out the way you wanted. But I know down deep that this is what I truelly want. This is a very unique situation and I hope that you can understand. I know

I haven't been the *best* daughter in the world but I hope that someday we can have the kind of relationship a father and daughter should have. I love all of you and I'm sorry if I've hurt any of you. But life goes on and we have to live our lives the way that we see fit. Maybe I'm selfish and blind but I'm trying. I care about all of you. Thanks for understanding. I guess I'm pretty lucky.

Love, Jan

Unable to give sensible details of the events surrounding Jan's departure, my thoughts were incoherent. Bob sensed my state of mind and approached me cautiously. Fearful I was on the brink of a nervous breakdown, he gently reassured me it wasn't my fault and apologized profusely for my overwhelming assignment.

He was furious at Berchtold. "I have never wanted to kill anyone in my life except him. Do you think the Lord would forgive me?"

I felt defeated and an inept failure, even more so after Susan's sleepless night. Her arm was so swollen the next morning she was unable to move it. X-rays showed a fracture. The emergency room doctor put her arm in a cast. I was devastated that I hadn't taken her in immediately, and extremely despondent.

When we returned home, Bob went to the medicine cabinet and brought me a sleeping pill. I'd never used them when Jan was missing, but at this moment, exhausted and traumatized, I didn't protest. He pulled the covers back on the bed, closed the blinds, and told me he would take care of things while I slept.

A new day brought me to my senses. *What should we do to get Jan back?* I thought. *Jan needed to be deprogramed from Berchtold. He had brainwashed her beyond belief.*

■ ■ ■

July 27, 1976

In her mind, Jan tried justifying the way she left home. It was not her intention to hurt her parents, but until she had filled her mission to have the child she couldn't explain anything to them. In time, they would understand. Brother B told her it was up to her to either get on with her mission, or fail. Was she ready to endure the consequences?

Robert met her at the airport and squealed with delight. "You're going to love it up here," he remarked. "There's lots of planning we have to do in a short amount of time. I've got you scheduled for a doctor's appointment tomorrow and tonight we're going to the Pink Garter to see a play. This would be a good place for us to live when everything settles down."

Asking why she had to see a doctor, Robert explained that it was an allergy clinic. "You are sick too often and I think it's allergies. In all these years since your mom had you tested, she never bought you medication. I want to make sure you are healthy and in good physical condition when you become a mother yourself."

Jackson Hole was buzzing with tourists and Jan found the Fun Center a busy place with lots of kids in and out all day. She thought parents weren't allowed, but that wasn't true. Some of the adults had more fun than their kids. Jerry and Jan worked together providing customers with tickets, change, and keeping the Center clean. Cast members from the playhouse came to chat and told Jan to come over and they would show her around the theater. Jan was ecstatic. Her ambition in life was to be an actress. Shopkeepers in the plaza would ask Robert if Jan was his daughter and he would laugh, roll his eyes at Jan and say, "well, something like that."

Before she had time to make much money, Brother B told her about a phone call from his attorney. It was not good news. Jan had to return home because her parents were ruining everything. If she didn't go back, they were going to have him put in jail. Frustrated, Robert said he would talk with other people who were part of the plan. She needed to do whatever it took to make the plan work. Her parents wouldn't like it, but they had backed both he and Jan into a corner and they would have to fight like hell to get out of it alive. Promising Brother B she would follow the

*plan, Jan gathered her belongings while B loaded his car with gifts for her
fourteenth birthday.*

■ ■ ■

Our plan of action was to hire a lawyer and proceed with a civil
lawsuit against Berchtold.

I called Berchtold's attorney and informed him of what had
taken place. "Berchtold's enticement is more than we can handle.
We are filing a law suit against him. We want our daughter home
and out of his clutches. In fact, we want him out of our lives forever."

The attorney asked us not to proceed until he had an oppor-
tunity to talk with his client. It was not long before he assured us
Berchtold had been given an ultimatum: "*Get that girl back to
Pocatello or you'll be charged with child endangerment.*"

Saturday afternoon, the phone rang and Bob answered it.

"Dad, I'm at the mini-dome and need you to come and get me,"
Jan said. "You need to bring the car." She offered no explanation
and hung up.

As Bob drove into the parking lot, he spied Berchtold's car. He
could see Jan standing nearby, surrounded by shopping bags.

Seeing Bob approach, Robert hurriedly climbed into his car. He
had no intention of speaking to him.

Shouting out an open window, "Thanks for everything," Robert
blew Jan a kiss and sped off.

Bob was livid.

13 double jeopardy!

August 1976

Jan threw open the door and stormed into the house, her arms filled with bags. She ran down the stairs to her room, unloaded the merchandise, and was out to the car again. Bob removed several items from the back seat and deposited them on the garage floor. Neither spoke a word. I was silent also, allowing the situation to play itself out. It was obvious that Berchtold was trying to buy her affection.

Finally, Bob finished the unwelcome chore and slammed the car door. He walked in the back door carrying a portable sewing machine, his eyes inflamed.

"This is only one of the gifts Jan received for her birthday. He bought her a camera, hordes of new clothes, all kinds of trinkets, and who knows what else. I told her it is all going back. She is very upset, and so am I."

He was not calm as he stormed out of the house toward the patio.

I called at him through the screen. "Did you ask Jan why she flew up there and where the money came from?"

133

"No! I'm too angry right now to be reasonable. Berchtold is . . ."

He paused, never finishing his thought, but clenched his fists and shook them furiously.

Jan kept silent as she flitted up and down the stairs, carrying her new possessions. I called after her, "I'm so thankful you are back. Could we talk?"

Avoiding eye contact, her answer was curt. "Not right now."

Later that evening, I overheard Karen quizzing her. Enthusiastically, Jan talked about her excursion. "Working at the Fun Center was okay, but I don't like to play those pinball machines. I helped take money, make change, and stuff like that. The most fun was going to the Pink Garter Theater. When I'm old enough, I'm going to be in plays there. The people were really nice to me. Jerry and me did some shopping, but I didn't stay long enough to earn much money. I want to go back."

To our bewilderment, teenage rebellion had raised its ugly head. Perhaps a professional could identify her defiance and why she was determined to follow Robert's demands. Our immediate concern was finding a counselor.

Bob and I gave orders that no one was to speak with Berchtold when he called, and to leave the phone off the hook.

"But, he'll really be mad if you don't take me back to the doctor," Jan said.

"What doctor?" I asked aggravated. "He took you to a doctor?"

"Yeah, to an allergy clinic. Brother B said he had to see what was wrong with me."

Annoyed, I snapped at her. "Oh good grief! You had allergy tests when you were five years old. Robert knows that."

"But he said I need some good medicine that will help me."

I was furious and spouted off, waving my hands. "What's he trying to prove? He's not your father. As if you needed those aggravating tests again."

Jan shrugged her shoulders as I fumed over his interference.

"Well, I told him I didn't want to, but he said he couldn't get medicine for me unless I did." She pulled a face, drawing her shoulders forward as if she was still feeling the irritating itch from scratch tests.

"I guess you know that we're pretty upset over what you did. You are not allowed to talk with him, Jerry, or any of the Berchtolds."

Jan turned her colorless face upward and looked at me, her eyes wide and questioning. "But why?" she whispered.

"You belong to us, not him. Even though you might think our decisions are not the best, it's our job. He's trying to take our stewardship away and we're not going to let it happen. He told me he would take you far away and we would never see you again. I couldn't stand that."

Teary-eyed, Jan said no more. She sat on the kitchen chair with teardrops falling down her cheeks. Her arms slid across the table and she dropped her head on them. Gentle sobs emerged as she wept. I chose not to console her. It was more important that she knew we were not giving in. If we were going to keep Robert away, we had to be tough.

After Bob arrived home from work, we sat on the patio while I ranted over Robert's motives. "Why would he make her go through allergy tests again? He's up to something."

"That's the pattern of his life, but there might be something else Jan's not telling us."

Looking anxiously at Bob, I knew the probability of Jan being violated in some way by Berchtold was high. "What do you think he's done?"

Bob put his face in his hands and heaved a heavy sigh. "I can't even think about it. I get too sick. Do you think Jan would ever tell you?"

I threw my head back, grabbed my neck and moaned. Thinking about the challenge, I paused before responding. "I don't know, but I'll try."

That night, I attempted to have a mother-daughter talk with Jan. I felt awkward and stumbled around trying to find the right way to bring up the sensitive issue. After a few feeble efforts, I decided she needed to know that the FBI thought Robert to be a man who preyed on children. She listened intently, but never commented. Her eyes were sympathetic as she watched me struggling. I hoped she could feel safe and tell me if there had been any inappropriate behavior from Robert. She said nothing. Exasperated, I finally blurted out, "Has Robert done anything bad to you? If he has, you need to tell me."

Jan emphatically shook her head to assure me. "No! That's sick!"

Seeking legal advice, Bob went to an attorney. "What rights do we have to protect ourselves from Berchtold? He continues to harass us with phone calls and he threatened to take Jan again."

Scowling, the attorney's bushy eyebrows formed a straight dark line across his brow. "Basically, none. He isn't breaking the law unless he attempts to hurt one of you. Legally speaking, your personal rights aren't in jeopardy unless he commits a criminal act."

"What if he's molested our daughter?" Bob asked.

"Without her admission, or any evidence, he's off free, but I'd get her to a counselor, pronto." The attorney paused, scratched his head and leaned back in his chair. "Why don't you file a civil suit against him? Whether it would do any good, I don't know, but he might leave you alone and it would certainly bring some attention to the authorities."

"Once he hears that, he'll be even more volatile."

"He'd be a fool," the attorney said.

The following afternoon, I picked up the phone only to be confronted with a tongue lashing from Robert. He heard from Jan that the FBI said he was a child molester. The hair on the back of my neck bristled as I blurted out, "You rotten snake. I know you've molested Jan and we'll get the truth. I hope they throw the key away when you're sent to prison."

Robert screamed back, "You told Jan I had little girl problems and didn't have the capacity to enjoy adult women. How could you be so low to say that to her? I will have Jan, so help me God. I have made promises to her I intend to keep!"

When I scolded Jan for talking to Berchtold I was given the silent treatment. Later in the day, Jan ignored her father's warning and rode her bike to Caroline's. Determined to make his point, Bob drove over and brought her home. Reasoning with her why we were being so protective didn't seem to make an impact. "Just let me go back up to Jackson," she demanded.

"No, Jan! I can't let you. Your mother and I don't want Berchtold near you. You don't understand how dangerous he is. He might take you again."

"Dad, I want to marry B!"

The words were thunderous for Bob to hear. Flabbergasted, he didn't know what to say. He blurted out, "Jan? What are you saying? You're too young to even think about marriage."

Refusing to look at her father, Jan stared ahead as her father drove down the street.

"Because something has happened that is bad, and I don't want to live in sin the rest of my life. If I married him, I wouldn't have to."

Bob flinched at the news, swallowed the thick lump that stuck in his throat, and for a time could not breathe as he tried to digest her words. His face turned white and he fought back tears. "Can you tell me what has happened?"

Jan shook her head.

Bob felt his throat tighten as he pled with her.

"Whatever has happened, you don't have to marry Berchtold. It would be the worst mistake of your life."

Jan hung her head, silent and unresponsive. Tears dropped from her chin.

"Don't give Berchtold another second of your life. He is telling you lies and making you feel guilty. He's a wicked man. Please listen to me. I will not let him do anything to hurt you. Let me help."

When he arrived back home, Bob was an emotional wreck. Jan was subdued and remained silent. The following day was Sunday; Jan ignored Bob and I. Our only consolation was seeing our three girls relate with each other normally.

On Monday morning, August 9, 1976, I went to pick up a few items at the grocery store. Upon my return, Jan was gone. I panicked and called Bob. Shortly she returned, but sat outside in the garage looking extremely distraught. I was relieved to see Bob drive up.

Jan watched him get out of the van and walk into the house, then began screaming. "Now you've done it! You finally got to him. B said he never wants to see or talk to me again. I hope you're happy!" She ran downstairs to her room, slammed the door and stayed there most of the day. We looked at each other and wondered what brought that on. Bob invited her to join us for family night, but she refused.

We all noted her nervousness as she paced in and out of her bedroom, then into the family room. She would not stay while anyone was there. Later, I asked if she would watch TV with me while I ironed, but she refused and returned to her room. It was after midnight when I concluded she wasn't going to talk to me and went to bed.

Jan's diary, August 10, 1976: I'm really scared but I have to do this. If I don't, something terrible is going to happen. I've done everything they told me. I wish Mom and Dad knew. B said they will soon. I hope so. My family is the best. Nothing bad better happen to them. They need to understand that I have to do this and can't fail.

■ ■ ■

Jan stood trembling in the cool night nervously watching for a blue sedan to appear. Her shivering could not be attributed solely to the night air; it was 1:30 A.M., an odd time for a girl barely fourteen to be standing in the shadows of her house waiting for a ride.

Her conscience was causing her doubts about the entire situation. She thought wildly, I can't believe this is happening. I don't want to go, but I have to. *Emotions tugged at Jan's heart and tears welled up as she anticipated her family's shock when they discovered she was missing again.*

Twice tonight, Robert had tapped on her window to let her know he was there. The first time, Jan silently mouthed the words, "Mom is still up" and motioned toward the family room. Finally, Mary Ann went to bed and turned off all the lights. Jan sat nervously in her dark bedroom anticipating Robert's next signal. She nearly jumped out of her skin when she heard three soft taps on the windowpane.

Remembering distinctly Zada's intrusion in her life, right in her own bedroom, Jan was not sorry to leave this house. She was constantly afraid of hearing that awful voice again. Now it was time to do what she had been dreading. Jan quietly slipped down the hall to the storage room and crawled through a small basement window which was partially open. There were cobwebs around it which made her shudder.

My parents can't understand, *Jan thought.* I've tried to find an explanation, but . . . if they would just let me be with him . . . things would be different. Dad doesn't want me to see him again. I wish they knew. Someday I won't have to hide all these secrets.

Shivering as she contemplated her assignment. Jan felt a knot inside her chest, pushing hard against her ribs. It's going to be okay, *she tried to reassure herself, although the horrendous anxiety made her breathless.*

Jan surveyed the neighbor's unlit homes before slinking behind a pine tree at the corner of the street. She glimpsed a car slowly creeping down the darkened street with its headlights off; her heart thumped wildly. Robert told her he was going to park around the corner by the mini-dome and would be in a blue Ford sedan. That's it! *she thought, stepping out momentarily so Robert could catch a glimpse of her before she darted behind the tree again.*

A flicker of the car's headlights gave Jan assurance that Robert had seen her.

Jan remembered the sharp words exchanged with her father earlier. *If they only knew this is for all of us. Zada told me that once B and me get married, everything will be okay. B keeps reminding me that my parents have to believe in me.*

Jan quickly glanced at the neighbor's bedroom window, knowing she was in view of the widow lady. Hurry, B, *Jan anxiously thought as the car moved cautiously along the quiet street. Again, trying to justify her actions, she reminded herself,* Dad and Mom both think B is bad, but he's been so good to me. What would happen to me if B wasn't around to protect me? He's scared, too.

The car stopped; Robert reached over and opened the door. Jan dashed from her hiding place into the front seat of this unfamiliar car and pulled the door shut. Even the clicking of the door sounded unusually loud.

"Hi, angel," *Robert said, smiling affectionately.* "I see you got the backpack."

Distressed, Jan responded breathlessly, "Yeah, I kept it hidden in my closet, but I didn't bring any clothes."

"Good girl!" *he squealed in a shrill, approving voice.* "That's what I told you. This is the beginning of a whole new life. I'll take over from here and buy you everything you need."

With that remark, he put his arm around Jan and pulled her close. She looked from the corner of her eye toward her home, thinking about her unsuspecting family. Robert left the lights off until he reached the end of the block. He turned onto Center Street, then guided the car toward the Interstate. A hard, sickening lump lodged in Jan's throat as she read the word overhead indicating the direction they were headed . . . Salt Lake City.

Robert watched Jan struggling with her emotions as she dabbed at her eyes. "Quit your worrying. Everything is going to be okay. Bob and Mary Ann will understand soon enough. Did you do everything I told you?"

"Yes, I . . . I think so." *Jan's voice quivered.*

"Did you have any trouble getting out the basement window?"

"No," she answered. It was open."

"Yeah, I know." Robert snickered slyly. "And did you leave the note for them?"

"Yes," she replied in a shaky voice. Jan knew she was going to cry and she was trying not to. After all, this was the time she wanted to prove that she was strong enough to go through with the plan. Crying might make her look like a boob.

"Did you write it like I said?" he inquired.

Annoyed, she responded, "Uh huh!" She swallowed hard, feeling pressure from Robert's interrogation.

Robert giggled. "That's great, honey! Once they realize you're not their little girl anymore, we'll be able to settle down into a good relationship with them."

"I don't want to talk about it anymore," Jan said.

"Okay," he replied. "I'd rather talk about our future anyway." With a smirk on his face, he stated, "Can't wait 'till we go to Hawaii, snorkeling and cruising from one island to the next, you in a grass skirt doing the hula. Woo, Woo!

Jan didn't say anything as she desperately tried to keep her emotions in check.

"How about a jungle safari? Africa would be a fabulous place to go. Most people think of it as a big adventure, but it's a very romantic place." Looking longingly at Jan, he pulled her closer. "We'll need a couple of rifles. I can teach you to shoot. I'm a pretty good marksman." Squealing with delight and giving her a squeeze, he proclaimed, "Our lives are just beginning."

Determined to change Jan's sullen attitude, Robert asked enthusiastically, "Where would you like to go?"

Jan stared straight ahead into the dark night, shrugged her shoulders and remained silent.

"Hey, cheer up. It's not the end of the world, you know." When Jan did not respond, Robert asked, "Is Dolly tired?"

Jan pursed her lips together and nodded.

"It has been a hard day . . . for me too." Robert continued to probe. "What happened after you called me today? What did Bob and Mary Ann say when you told them I never wanted to see you again, which is a big fat lie," he declared with gusto.

"Nothing. I didn't want to talk to them so I just went to my bedroom and stayed there all day." Jan swallowed hard. "Zada tried to tell me Mom and Dad aren't my real parents. I don't believe them."

"Oh Dolly, be careful what you say. You know they hear everything. This is hard for you to understand because Bob and Mary Ann are wonderful people and have had an important purpose in your life. But honey, you're a special angel, a chosen spirit. I knew that the moment I laid eyes on you. Try to be patient. Everything will fit in time. Remember when Zada . . ."

Jan's anxiety level began to rise at the mention of her name and she cut Robert off. "I don't want to talk about it! I get scared every time I think about them." Agitated, she began to squirm, put her hand over her mouth and shouted, "I feel sick!"

Robert patted her leg gently, hoping to comfort her. He couldn't see her face well enough in the dark of the night to tell if she was really sick, but supposed it was nerves. He said with a firm voice, "You'll be okay."

A few moments later, Jan announced, "I'm going to throw up!"

Robert slowed the car. "Hold on till I stop." He pulled quickly onto the side of the road, reached across Jan, and opened the passenger door. Jan immediately bent over and hung her head out the door. Holding her stomach, she swallowed hard and waited. Nothing happened.

Robert asked, "Are you okay, Dolly? What can I do?"

Jan moaned and waved her hand; she just wanted Robert to stop talking to her. The cool night air brought her some relief and she soon announced that she felt a little better.

Robert looked closely at Jan's pale, perspiring face, then hit the steering wheel with a vengeful blow and snapped, "Hell, this is hard. Why can't Bob let go? You don't deserve this." Robert rummaged around in his pocket and pulled out a pill. "Here, this will help. It's a relaxer; I think you've got a case of the jitters."

Jan swallowed the pill, then slid down on the seat, curling into a ball.
"I think I'm okay now," she responded weakly.

Robert tenderly patted her small form as he pulled back onto the high-
way. "Just remember everything you've been told. The Black family is very
nice. I wish you could have met them when they came to Jackson Hole this
summer. You'll love being in California. They have a cute little room wait-
ing for you and there is nothing for you to worry about. Everything has
been planned out perfectly."

■ ■ ■

The following morning, Bob went down to Jan's bedroom
before work, hoping to redeem himself. Instead of finding Jan, he
found a note laying on her pillow.

Dear Bob and Maryanne
    You won't let me do whats right so I will do whats wrong. I am
leaving without B, and do not plan on coming back until you accept
me as me. I cannot except your religeon or your screwed up morals,
I just want to be me and have B. Please before all of us are
destroyed let me go.
                    Jan

Referring to us as Bob and Maryanne was distressing besides
the fact that she had misspelled my name. I found every word of
the note extremely alarming. What had Robert done to her?

Bob called Pete Welsh, giving him a brief explanation. Pete
was at our home almost instantly.

I lamented, "She seemed to be doing so well until this summer.
Robert had me as his open door to Jan. I wised up, but now it's too
late. He got her anyway."

Pete shook his head. "Berchtold is a master at deceit and has a
convincing tongue. Her note indicates she left on her own which

most likely will preclude the FBI from involvement. Do you want me to report this to the police?"

Not wanting media coverage, we were hesitant. Pete explained his reasoning. "If she is reported as a runaway, it will protect you from the press because runaways aren't released to the public. Unfortunately, the downside is the fact that runaways are not actively sought by law enforcement like a missing person is."

We preferred keeping her disappearance quiet. Our emotions were so fragile that dealing with anyone but family might push us over the edge.

"I still have the tape recorder," Pete announced. "It hasn't been used since you last had it. I'll bring it by."

His advice and support were appreciated. "Record every call that comes in. Be calm and talk to people as you normally do. Things worked out the last time—maybe not perfect—but we did get your daughter back."

Pete paused as he looked at our shocked faces. "Are you guys going to be all right?"

As soon as we assured him we were okay, he left for the police station.

Later in the day, George Shail, a big, burly detective, stood at our door with a friendly smile and a warm handshake. Ready to assist us, he needed details so he could begin an investigation.

I hadn't expected to hear from Robert. There was no doubt in any of our minds that he was behind Jan's disappearance. Consequently I was more than surprised when I picked up the phone that evening and he was the caller. He sounded frantic. I recorded his call for the police.

"What in the hell has happened there? I just had a phone call from Jan saying she ran away from home. Do you know how she left . . . what she took . . ."

"Stay out of this, Robert," I warned. "We'll take care of getting Jan home."

"Oh!" he whimpered. "It's all my fault. I shouldn't have told her I never wanted to see her again."

His false emotions were unbearable and I snapped back, "That's the smartest thing you've ever done. Be sure you mean it."

"It's obvious you're not concerned about Jan," he snarled. "That little girl could be anywhere, and you couldn't care less."

For once, *he* hung up on *me*.

Robert called again the next day. I was not home, but Bob answered. As soon as he heard Robert's voice, Bob hung up. He called back, begging Bob to hear him out. He declared he was drunk and had been for three days. He cried, saying Bob could have everything he owned; his car, money, kids, anything Bob wanted was his, if he would give him permission to marry Jan.

"Over my dead body!" Bob declared emphatically and slammed the receiver down.

Two days later, Robert called again. "Have you heard from Jan?" Robert asked.

"No," I replied.

"Neither have I. I tried drinking myself to death and just spent twenty-four hours in the Jackson Hospital. I'm so worried about Jan." His voice was whiny. "Jimmy's here with me, but I'm taking him back to Ogden today. I'll come back here in case Jan calls me." Again he asked, "Have you heard from her?"

"No!" was my short and curt reply.

"What in the hell got into her?" Robert asked. "I tried so hard to convince her things could be worked out, but she wouldn't listen. I did tell you she was going to run, Mary Ann."

There was a brief pause as I waited for him to say more and I wasn't disappointed. "There's something else I need to tell you, Mary Ann. I don't want to add any more worries, but I think Jan is a lesbian."

"You damn liar! Does everyone you know have to be perverted?" I banged down the receiver.

An hour later, I had another call from Robert. Breathlessly, he said, "Mary Ann, I just hung up from talking to Jan. She called me collect, but wouldn't tell me where she is. You'll never believe what she did the night she left."

Every word he uttered, I monitored with skepticism, hoping there would be a glimpse of Jan's whereabouts. "Okay, I'd like to hear."

Berchtold's singsong voice was full of drama. "I can't believe she did this, but she walked up to the Interstate and flagged down a truck driver. She told him she was a runaway and wanted to go home. Can you believe that?"

His explanation did not ring true. Firmly, I said, "I don't believe that. Jan's afraid of the dark and would never have the nerve to do such a thing."

Miffed by my response, he fired back. "Well, that's what she told me. Obviously, you don't care. I'm just relieved to hear from her."

I was silently seething from his lies, but bit my tongue and let him continue his uncouth dialogue.

"She told me not to worry because she has money and is getting a nice suntan." He laughed. "Isn't that good news? She sounded really good. Now I can take Jimmy home. If I hear anything else, I'll call you."

I was repulsed.

As the police began their investigation, they found Berchtold had opened a checking account under the name of Jan Broberg at the Jackson State Bank. At the allergy clinic, she was listed as Jan Berchtold. She had been given a prescription for medicating allergies.

But all that seemed irrelevant to the question that pounded in my head every second: *where was Jan now?*

■ ■ ■

When Jan arrived at the Black's she was full of confusion and anxiety. What did her family do when they found out she was gone? And where was B? He gave her that pill to help her relax, but what happened after that?

Robert hadn't told her much about the Blacks except they were nice and would take good care of her. She didn't need to be afraid and he was certain they wouldn't pry into her life. She wondered, "Are the Blacks some of them?" They didn't ask her any questions about why she was there, and within a few days, Jan's fears about them decreased. The family made no demands, treated her well, and allowed her to be a recluse.

Robert kept telling her she had to be brave because everything would be over soon so she could go back home. How would that happen? Jan wondered. The unknown caused her sleepless nights and soon black circles appeared under her eyes.

Robert's daily phone calls were the only thing that kept Jan sane. She begged him to come and get her—soon. He worried about the FBI throwing him into jail again, but more than that, he feared the demands Zada was making.

"We have to do what they say or they will take Susan. It doesn't matter what they do to me, but it's you. Be brave, Dolly, for just a little longer. Your folks have to give in. Crap, I wish they knew what we're going through."

The indecision about her future kept Jan feeling edgy. She was experiencing nightmares—reliving the vivid experience she encountered two years ago. "Why me?" she often asked. Nightly, when she tried to sleep, the memory of the fateful day she was held captive by the aliens invaded Jan's mind. With all her might, she exerted great effort to erase the thoughts, but they would not turn away.

■ ■ ■

It had been two weeks since Jan disappeared. There was no clue from local police as to her whereabouts.

On Wednesday afternoon, Bob was at work and answered the phone to hear a shaky voice say, "Dad, it's Jan." There was a tremor in her voice and she was trying hard to not cry.

Stunned, Bob slumped onto a stool and cried out, "Oh, honey, where are you? What's going on? We miss you and want you to come home. Tell me where you are and I'll come and get you."

Sounding frightened, the strain in her voice alarmed Bob. "I can't tell you where I am, but I want to come home and go to school. Have you signed the papers?"

"What papers? What for? I haven't seen any papers."

"Giving me permission to get married," she blurted out. "You should have gotten some."

"From who?"

"I don't know." The trembling in her voice was still apparent.

Remaining definite, Bob stood firm with his former decision. "Jan, I have told you before and I still mean it. I will never give you permission to marry that devil. I love you too much to do that."

Bob waited for a response. All he heard was a soft guttural sound. He pleaded, "Please, come home."

Jan sniffled quietly. "I can't, Dad. Not until you sign the papers."

"Honey, I can't do that, but I love you and we miss you. Please know that. I would do anything in this world for you, except let you marry Berchtold."

Jan's voice was weepy. "If you love me, you will sign the papers."

Realizing she was not going to abandon the issue, Bob encouraged, "Jan, call your mother. She's missing you terribly. Please, will you do that?"

She cleared her throat in an attempt to control her emotions. "I don't know. I might."

An operator came on the line asking for a deposit of more coins to extend the call.

Anxiously, she exclaimed, "Dad, I've got to go! Just sign the papers and everything will be all right. I want to come home!"

Most people don't have a kidnapping scrapbook.
The following pages contain items I collected during
our ordeal in the mid 70's.

Jan in 6th grade, 1973

Jan in 8th grade, 1975

Karen, Jan, & Susan, Easter 1974

Broberg Family, 1977
Mary Ann, Jan, Susan, Karen, Bob

Robert Berchtold and Jan, 1973

Jan in the role of Oliver, 1975

Sisters, Christmas 1977

*Jan and "friends," in old bedroom
on her birthday, July 31, 1973*

Karen and Jan horseback riding, 1975

Karen, Jan, & Susan with their cousin, 1973

Christmas 1974

David Broberg, Brad Barnard (Jan's cousins), Jan, and best friend Caroline Hansen.

Daddy-Daughter Date
Jan and her father Bob, 1973

Jan in 7th grade, 1974

Robert Berchtold, 1975

Girl Missing

FBI Files Kidnap Charges Against Pocatello Man

Federal kidnapping charges have been filed against a Pocatello man missing with a Pocatello girl since last Thursday.

FBI Idaho-Montana division special agent Robert W. Evans said today charges have been filed against Robert Ersol Berchtold, 38, 107 S. 18th. Berchtold is former president of the Freight Outlet furniture store in Pocatello.

Berchtold is charged in the alleged abduction of 12-year-old Jan Broberg, a daughter of Mr. and Mrs. Robert Dean Broberg, 171 S. 16th. The girl reportedly was picked up by Berchtold from her music lesson Thursday. The two have not been seen since.

Power County sheriff's deputies Friday found a 1974 Maverick registered to Berchtold abandoned in American Falls. FBI agents today said they now believe Berchtold and the girl may be traveling in a 1973 orange GMC motorhome.

The Broberg girl is four feet six inches tall and weighs 68 pounds, according to FBI sources. She has light brown hair, blue-green eyes, and has a lump on the ring finger of her left hand. A description of the girl's clothing the last time she was seen was not available today.

Bond for Berchtold on the kidnapping charge, which carries a maximum life imprisonment sentence, was set Monday at $100,000 by U.S. Magistrate R. Don Bistline. Berchtold also faces a warrant issued by Pocatello police charging him with second degree kidnapping.

A friend of the Broberg family, Berchtold reportedly had permission from Jan's parents to pick up the girl from her music lesson. The two never arrived at an intended horseback riding activity later that day.

JAN BROBERG
Allegedly Kidnapped

ROBERT E. BERCHTOLD
Former Merchant

Oct 24. 74

FOR MISSING PAIR . . .

FBI Search Spreads Out

FBI agents continued an inter-state search today for the whereabouts of a 12-year-old Pocatello girl allegedly kidnapped by a Pocatello man one week ago.

Federal kidnapping charges carrying a maximum life imprisonment sentence were filed this week against Robert E. Berchtold, 38, 107 S. 18th. The former Pocatello merchant is charged in the alleged abduction of 12-year-old Jan Broberg, a daughter of Mr. and Mrs. Robert D. Broberg, 171 S. 16th.

Information gathered during investigation of the incident indicates the Berchtold and Broberg families have been close friends for a number of years and have often engaged in social and recreational activities together. Berchtold reportedly had permission from Jan's parents to pick the girl up from her music lesson last Thursday afternoon and take her horseback riding in American Falls. The two have not been seen since.

Power County sheriff's deputies late Thursday found a 1974 Maverick registered to Berchtold abandoned in American Falls. Inside the vehicle, deputies reportedly found blood near a smashed window. FBI agents now believe Berchtold and the girl may be traveling in a 1973 orange GMC motorhome.

According to informed sources, Berchtold told the Brobergs several weeks he had sold his motorhome. However, Mrs. Berchtold and Mrs. Broberg, while driving around Pocatello early last week, reportedly spotted Berchtold working on the motorhome at a storage lot.

After Berchtold and the Broberg girl disappeared, authorities checked the storage lot. The motorhome was gone.

Search Still On

Pocatello FBI agents said this morning the Federal Bureau is continuing its search in the western U.S. for 12-year-old Jan Broberg, daughter of Mr. and Mrs. Robert D. Broberg, Pocatello, believed kidnapped eight days ago by Robert E. Berchtold, 38, a former Pocatello merchant. Spokesmen reported earlier the pair is believed to be traveling in an orange 1973 GMC motorhome.

Search Continues For Missing Pair

FBI agents continued an interstate search today for 12-year-old Jan Broberg, Pocatello girl believed kidnaped 11 days ago. No new leads were reported.

Federal kidnap charges were filed last week against Robert E. Berchtold, 38, a former Pocatello merchant who reportedly picked up the Broberg girl from her music lesson the afternoon of Oct. 17. The two had intended to go horseback riding in American Falls later that day. They have not been seen since.

Berchtold, a friend of the Broberg family, reportedly had permission from Jan's parents to pick up the girl the day of the alleged abduction.

Informed sources today verified that Berchtold has been a patient at the Clinic for Behavioral Therapy in Beverly Hills, Calif. It also was learned Berchtold has been in contact the past several months with a Salt Lake City psychiatrist and LDS social workers concerning an emotional problem.

Berchtold's wife, Gail, reportedly told authorities she had noticed some of her husband's personal items disappearing from the family's Pocatello home prior to Oct. 17 and suspected he was preparing to leave. Among the missing possessions presumed to be with Berchtold is a small handgun, she said.

Mrs. Berchtold told authorities she does not feel her husband will harm the Broberg girl. She said she expects he will return her to Pocatello. Contacted at her home today, Mrs. Berchtold had no comment on the matter.

Power County sheriff's deputies Oct. 18 found a car registered to Berchtold abandoned west of American Falls near Register Rock. Inside the car, deputies said they found blood near a broken window.

Berchtold and the Broberg girl are believed to be traveling in a 1973 orange GMC motor home received by Berchtold as partial payment for sale of the Freight Outlet furniture store in Pocatello. Berchtold also reportedly has with him some $27,000 he also received from sale of the store.

JAN BROBERG
Allegedly Kidnapped

ROBERT E. BERCHTOLD
Former Merchant

Broberg Girl Found Unharmed in Mexico

An intensive month-long search for a missing Pocatello girl that spanned 50 states and two foreign countries ended Saturday night in Mexico when authorities arrested Robert E. Berchtold and found 12-year-old Jan Broberg unharmed.

An FBI spokesman in Pocatello said Berchtold was arrested early Saturday evening by agents of Mexico's Federal Police in Mazatlan, a coastal city of about 75,000 people some 875 miles southwest of the U.S.-Mexican border at Ciudad Juarez and El Paso.

"The girl is in "fine condition,"" said the FBI spokesman," and will be taken care of now by her family," Jan is the daughter of Mr. and Mrs. Robert D. Broberg, 171 S. 16th.

The spokesman said the matter is now in the hands of the U.S. State Department, which will arrange for Berchtold's extradition from Mexico.

"The arrest was the culmination of an extensive search in every state as well as Canada and Mexico," he said. No other details on the arrest were available Saturday night.

Berchtold and the Broberg girl disappeared Oct. 17. A friend of the Broberg family, Berchtold had been given permission by the family to pick Jan up after her music lesson Oct. 17 and take her horseback riding in American Falls. But the two never arrived at their destination.

Federal kidnapping charges carrying a maximum life sentence were subsequently filed against Berchtold, 38, 107 S. 18th. He also faces a warrant issued by Pocatello police charging him with second degree kidnaping.

Jan and Her Parents Reunited in Mazatlan

The parents of a young Pocatello girl missing more than a month were reunited with their daughter in Mexico late Sunday evening.

Mr. and Mrs. Robert D. Broberg traveled by air Sunday to Mazatlan, a city on Mexico's west coast where their 12-year-old daughter, Jan, was found unharmed by agents of Mexico's federal police Saturday. The girl reportedly stayed with her parents in a Mazatlan hotel Sunday night.

Meanwhile, federal authorities have started extradition proceedings against Robert E. Berchtold, 38, a former Pocatello merchant taken into custody Saturday in Mazatlan on federal kidnap charges in the Broberg girl's disappearance. Berchtold's extradition will be handled through the U.S. Department of State.

Jan's uncle, Richard P. Broberg of Pocatello, said today his niece was "in beautiful shape" when reunited with her parents in Mexico Sunday night. "She had not been harmed by the abductor," he said.

Broberg said his niece and her parents could return to Pocatello as early as Tuesday, depending on when they complete "legalities" in Mexico.

An FBI spokesman in Pocatello today would not disclose particulars about how

ROBERT E. BERCHTOLD
In Mexican Custody

Berchtold and the Broberg girl were traced to Mexico. The FBI's month-long search for the missing pair had crovered all 50 states, Canada, and Mexico.

Berchtold, a close friend of the Broberg family, reportedly had permission from Jan's parents to pick up the girl from her music lesson the afternoon of Oct. 17. The two never arrived at a horseback riding activity they were to attend later that day in American Falls.

The next day, a car registered to Berchtold was found abandoned near American Falls. Power County deputies said they found blood spots inside the car near a broken window.

Berchtold and the Broberg girl have been believed traveling the past month in a GMC motorhome Berchtold received as partial payment for sale of the Freight Outlet furniture store in Pocatello. FBI agents in Pocatello said today they were not certain as to the whereabouts of the motorhome, although Richard P. Broberg said today the motorhome "is believed to have been sold."

PARENTS WANT TO DROP CHARGES . . .
Berchtold Pleads Innocent to Kidnap Count

By PAUL SMITH
Journal Staff Writer

Robert Ersol Berchtold, 107 S. 18th, pleaded innocent today to a federal kidnaping charge involving a 12-year-old Pocatello girl, after his attorney filed affidavits from the girl's parents that she was not taken "by force" and was not sexually molested — and that they do not wish Berchtold to be prosecuted.

Federal District Court Judge Ray McNichols continued the case for arguments by counsel at an indefinite date, on defense lawyer Patricia McDermott's motion for dismissal.

The 38-year-old former merchant was apprehended in Mazatlan, Mexico Nov. 23, after allegedly disappearing with the girl on Oct. 17. Jan Broberg was found unharmed in Mazatlan.

Appearing in court nattily dressed and groomed, the small, slender Berchtold waived a reading of the federal grant jury indictment.

The indictment charged that on Oct. 17, 1974, he "wilfully and knowingly took and caused to be transported in interstate and foreign commerce from Pocatello, Jan Broberg "who had thereto been unlawfully seized, confined, inveigled, decoyed, kidnapped, abducted, and carried away and held . . . by the defendant . . . for ransom and for other purposes, including sexual gratification."

Ms. McDermott's dismissal motion challenges the indictment on grounds, such as the contention neither Berchtold nor his counsel were informed of the grant jury sitting, so Berchtold could exercise his constitutional rights; and that the indictment otherwise violates the defendant's constitutional rights.

In support of the motion, Ms. McDermott filed duplicate affidavits sworn to by Robert Dean Broberg and Mary Ann Broberg, both of 171 S. 16th.

Both father and mother state: "My daughter was not taken by force or against her will . . . The defendant and my daughter and our families have been close personal friends for the past two years.

"After my daughter left with the defendant, I contacted the Pocatello Police Department to assist me in ascertaining my daughter's whereabouts. At the time, I requested that the . . . authoritiers hold the matter in complete confidence. I further informed them of the fact I did not desire to have criminal charges initiated. I still do not."

Each of the parents stated Berchtold requested no ransom. They state she was "unharmed in every way and was not subjected to sexual intercourse or molestation of any kind or sort." The latter contention, the Brobergs say, was substantiated by an examination of the girl by two physicians (a pediatrician and a gynecologist) after her return from Mexico.

Assistant U.S. attorney Dan Dennis, Boise, told the judge today he needed time to refute Ms. McDermott's motion. Judge McNichols said the government prosecutors may wish to submit "counteraffidavits."

The judge did not set a date for arguments because they will have to be fitted in with the Idaho Legislature schedule of Ms. McDermott, Pocatello Dist. 34 representative, who is Democratic minority leader.

Meanwhile, Ms. McDermott said Berchtold must leave immediately for Salt Lake City where his 12-year-old son has been flown for medical treatment of a severe illness. She also reported Berchtold has an employment offer in Salt Lake City.

Berchtold again was released on $50,000 bond, with indications the status of his case will be determined by the court during the next two or three weeks.

Berchtold still faces different kidnap charges filed by state authorities. A preliminary hearing on the state charges was scheduled this afternoon in Pocatello.

Souvenirs from a sudden trip to Mexico

Berchtold Bound Over for Trial

Robert E. Berchtold, 38, was bound over Wednesday afternoon to Sixth District Court for trial, following Magistrate Dell W. Smith's denial of a defense motion for dismissal of the case on grounds of insufficient grounds for prosecution.

Berchtold has been charged by the state with kidnaping in connection with the Oct. 17 disappearance of 12-year-old Jan Broberg, Pocatello, reportedly later found unharmed with Berchtold in Mexico. His attorney is Patricia D. McDermott.

In an attempt to provide an explanation for affidavits filed in the Federal and Sixth District courts, the Broberg family released the following statement late Wednesday afternoon through Deputy Bannock County Prosecutor Howard L. Armstrong, Jr.:

Statement from Robert and Mary Ann Broberg:

"Due to the statements that have been made and due to the possible misinterpretations and misunderstandings that might have been placed upon our affidavits, we wish to make the following comment:

"Because of our anxiety and the traumatic experience that we and our daughter, Jan, have gone through during the past few months, we feel that this is a period in our lives that we would like to forget and certainly wish had never happened.

"With this in mind, and being grateful for all of the help that we have received, and for the fact that our daughter has been restored to us unharmed and just as pure as when she left, we felt that the easiest way for us to pick up the threads of our lives was to have all connections with the last few months severed as soon as possible.

"That is the reason we gave our affidavits, being under the belief that everything would then be terminated and that Jan and we could commence living our lives once again. We now realize that this was foolish and that there is nothing that we can do or say that will alter the things that have happened since October 17, 1974. We are now prepared to go forward with whatever testimony we have and tell the truth and will sincerely trust in the law enforcement officials, the courts, and all concerned to see that justice is done."

Pocatello, Idaho U.S.A.
November 29, 1974

LIC. OCTAVIO RIVERA FARBER.
APARTADO POSTAL NO. 47.
MAZATLAN, SINALOA
MEXICO

Dear Sir:

We hereby give you full permission to follow through on the Marriage/annulment of our 12 yr. old daughter JAN BROBERG, who was according to Mexican law; married Nov. 15, 1974. to ROBERT ERSOL BERCHTOLD.

On Monday, November 24, we conferred with the Chief of Immigration (MR. Baietz). He reccommended your services and at that time gave you a few details over the telephone, concerning the kidnapping of this same girl, from our home on October 17, 1974. We are enclosing a copy of the newspaper clipping concerning the kidnapping and also a copy of the marriage certificate we received from Mr. Bietz.

Our daughter had no legal papers with her, neither to enter into Mexico, nor for any such marriage. We did not give her permission to marry.

If more information is needed, please advise at once. Let us know what the fee will be so we can send you the money covering your services.

Please annul the above said marriage as soon as possible.

Sincerely yours,

Robert Dean Broberg
Father

Mary Ann(Buck)Broberg
Mother

ADDRESS: MR. ROBERT D. BROBERG
171 So. 16 Place
Pocatello, Idaho 83201
U.S.A.

Letter to Mexican officials

FBI Finds Missing Broberg Girl in L.A.

Today's Chuckle

Years ago we hid our family skeletons in closets. Now we let them parade around in bikinis.

IDAHO STATE JOURNAL

VOL. LXIV NO. 204   POCATELLO, IDAHO   WEDNESDAY, NOVEMBER 17, 1976   15 CENTS

Fair

Sunny and warmer today, patchy fog and low clouds tonight. Variable cloudiness Thursday and cooler. High today 16, low tonight 31, high Thursday 10.

COPYRIGHT, 1976—Idaho State Journal, Inc.

Prosecutor Charges Berchtold
With Kidnaping, Ransom Demand

★ ★ ★

Former Pocatello Merchant to Fight Extradition

By DAN FLYNN
Journal Staff Writer

Missing for three months, 14-year-old Jan Broberg of Pocatello was found alive Tuesday in Los Angeles by Federal Bureau of Investigation agents, Garth Pincock, Bannock County prosecuting attorney, announced late Tuesday. Robert E. Berchtold, 42, formerly of Pocatello, is charged with kidnaping the girl and making a "consent to marriage" ransom demand, the prosecuting attorney said.

The 14-year-old girl was last seen in Pocatello Aug. 16, Pincock said.

Until FBI agents located her in Los Angeles Tuesday, Jan Broberg was last seen Oct. 3 between Salt Lake City and Ogden, Utah.

Berchtold's sentence in that earlier federal kidnaping conviction was five years in prison with all but 45 days suspended. The former Pocatello merchant served part of that federal jail time in the Bannock County Jail, from Sept. 1 to Sept. 14, 1976. A federal court clerk said Berchtold was

---

Jan's note, written Aug. 9, 1976

Dear Bob & Maryann
You won't let me do whats right so I will do whats wrong. I am leaving with out B, and do not plan on coming back until you ~~let~~ ~~accept~~ me as me.
I cannot except your religeon or your screwed up morals, I just want to be me and have B. Please before all of us are destroyed let me go.
Jan

Flintridge
Sacred Heart
Academy

Brochure from Flintridge Academy where Jan was hidden for four months

Copy of one of Robert's intercepted letters, written while in prison

Fire Loss Undetermined

By DAN FLYNN
Journal Staff Writer

Pocatello's downtown Dietrich Building is dead today, but might be brought back to life if somebody wants to put up the dollar, local fire and building authorities told the Journal today.

"It definitely has a future," city building inspector Wayne Ellis said. "The basic structure is good." Ellis reported after making a preliminary inspection at the building involved in an all-night blaze that began Monday evening.

Ellis credited a firewall between Atkin's Florist Shop and Maag's Prescription Center with preventing the Pocatello landmark at Center and Arthur from total destruction.

If the building is restored, Ellis said, builders will be required to bring the structure up to date and comply with all city building codes.

The man who would have to put the money together if the Dietrich Building is restored told the Journal today the price

...tag might run between $300,000 and $500,000.

"That's not even a ballpark figure," David J. Anderson of American Land Title Co. added.

Davey Anderson, who was at Grand Targhee when the fire began Monday night, said that until negotiations are finished with insurance adjusters, it's hard to say what the fire's cost will be in dollars and cents.

"The whole story was people," according to Anderson. American Land Title Co. records were removed from the burning building Monday night by dozens of citizen volunteers.

"Friends came out of the woodwork," Anderson said, in appreciation of their efforts. "Our spirits are not dampened."

American Land Title Co. plans to resume services this week in a former retail store at 200-624 W. Center. The company's telephone service has been restored at that address with the same number.

Many Tenants of Dietrich Building Doing Business in Other Locations

In human terms and dollars and cents, the fire was made tough for Bob and Mary Ann Broberg, owners of Atkin's Florist.

"I wish we knew what we were going to do," Mary Ann Broberg commented. "It's all up in the air."

The fire began after someone broke into the rear door of Atkin's, according to local police. The flower shop and its contents were totally destroyed in the blaze.

"We love the business," Mrs. Broberg told the Journal. The florist's fire insurance is minimal. Mrs. Broberg offered a "wild guess" of $100,000 when asked to estimate their fire loss, but she added that insurance will cover only $15,000.

"It's a terrific loss," Mrs. Broberg continued. "It's difficult to think of going anywhere else," noting her husband has spent 10 years at the site.

The Brobergs were planning to meet with Dietrich Building owners today.

Another businessman forced out of the building by the blaze—Gregory Maag of Maag's Prescription Center—said he could not determine his loss. Until meeting with insurance adjusters, Maag said he could not even offer a guess.

Maag's Prescription Center began service today at 331 W. Center, just across the street from the old location. Maag said prescription records were saved, and the telephone number remains the same.

Reportedly, Homefield Finance Corporation of Pocatello will be moving in next to Pocatello Realty on North Arthur Gem State Mutual, which was on the Dietrich Building's second story, will also be moving to another spot.

The place at several other businesses in the damaged building were unclear at presstime today.

For the Pocatello fire and police departments, the Dietrich Building fire continues today as an arson investigation.

That investigation remains hampered because detectives still can't get into the basement where the fire started, Fire Chief Hal Call said.

Arson investigators were canvasing this morning at the fire station, presumably to decide how to proceed. Walt Jensen, chief of detectives, said authorities did not expect to make an arrest today. Other sources in the police department indicate detectives are following up "good leads" in the investigation.

Firemen maintained a firewatch at the Dietrich building last night. Call said several spots are still smoldering within the structure.

Authorities today expect to be heard up the Dietrich Building and open the portion of Center Street that has been closed since Monday night.

John Nurse, a fire department lieutenant who sustained a fractured back while fighting the blaze Monday night, is listed in good condition today at Bannock Memorial Hospital.

Call said another fireman, Glen Adams, was sustained smoke inhalation, was released from St. Anthony Community Hospital.

Asked about his own sprained hand, Call replied, "It's fine."

Authorities Thwart Berchtold Letters

An attempt by Robert Berchtold, 40, a former Pocatello businessman, to smuggle letters out of the Bannock County Jail to 14-year-old Jan Broberg has been thwarted by authorities.

Berchtold is charged with first degree kidnaping in the 1976 disappearance of the Pocatello girl. He pleaded innocent to the kidnaping charge and is being held at the jail on a reduced bond of $50,000.

According to a police report today, Berchtold was writing letters to another Pocatello girl who was supposed to hand deliver them to Miss Broberg. The girl's sister told their mother who reported the incident and gave local police the letters intended for Miss Broberg.

Berchtold's Mental Defect Results in Acquittal

By JUANITA RODRIGUEZ
And DAN FLYNN
Journal Staff Writers

Robert Ersol Berchtold, a former Pocatello businessman, Tuesday afternoon was acquitted of first-degree kidnaping by reason of "mental defect," according to an order signed by Judge Arnold T. Beebe, a Seventh District Court judge from Blackfoot.

Berchtold, 40, was charged in the 1976 disappearance of Jan Broberg, 14, of 171 S. 16th. Miss Broberg, a daughter of Robert and Mary Ann Broberg, owners of Atkin Florist on West Center, was located by the federal Bureau of Investigation at a Catholic school in Salt Lake City last November.

According to the judgment of acquittal signed by Beebe at 3:28 p.m. Tuesday, Berchtold is committed to custody of the Idaho Department of Health and Welfare. In a temporary order, Beebe ordered Berchtold's admittance to the Idaho Security Medical Facility at Boise.

Berchtold still stands accused of arson and burglary in the Jan. 24-25 fire that destroyed Pocatello's landmark Dietrich Building. Arson investigators determined that blaze started in the Broberg family's florist shop.

After the court received reports from doctors Dean R. Ackley and W.A. Dietzge, the defense moved for acquittal based on mental defect in the kidnaping case.

_____, Bannock County prosecuting attorney, did not contest the defense motion. Earlier, on Nov. 16, 1976,

_____ told reporters, "We will fully prosecute our charges."

Beebe's Tuesday order states: "The defendant at the time of the criminal conduct charged, suffered from mental disease or defect, which substantially impaired his capacity to conform to the law."

Still speaking of Berchtold, the order continues: "He is hereby acquitted of the charges set forth in the information upon the ground of mental disease or defect, excluding responsibility."

Beebe further orders that Berchtold be placed "in an appropriate institution for custody, care, and treatment, provided, however, this commitment is subject to the existing jurisdiction of this court."

According to the order of admittance to the Idaho Security Medical Facility, Berchtold will be held for "psycho-social diagnosis and recommendations as part of the pre-trial or pre-sentence procedure before this court." The matter before the court is an evidentiary hearing concerning Berchtold's alleged "dangerousness."

On Tuesday, Lloyd R. Lockhart, who earlier pleaded guilty to second-degree arson in the Dietrich Building fire and was sentenced to a prison term not to exceed 10 years, pleaded the Fifth Amendment and refused to testify in the evidentiary hearing.

Berchtold pleaded guilty to federal kidnaping charges after an earlier disappearance involving himself and Miss Broberg in 1974. More than a year and a half after being apprehended in Mexico, Berchtold was sentenced to five years in prison by a federal judge, with all but 45 days suspended. Judge

J. Blaine Anderson also placed Berchtold on five years' probation. Before pleading guilty, Berchtold was found mentally competent to stand trial. After the federal court action, the State's second-degree kidnaping case against Berchtold was dropped.

After Berchtold was again taken into custody by the FBI on a fugitive warrant based on first-degree kidnaping charges filed in Bannock County resulting from Miss Brogerg's second disappearance, she was found at a Catholic school in California.

_____, in announcing the recovery of the missing girl after three months, said Berchtold had made a "consent to marriage" ransom demand involving Miss Broberg. "We do believe there was a ransom involved or we would not have charged first-degree kidnap," _____ said.

Miss Broberg was returned safely to her Pocatello home from California under a tight security escort by authorities.

Berchtold was bound over for trial in district court after a four-day preliminary hearing. He pleaded innocent to the kidnaping charge.

After earlier asking for dismissal of the charges, the defense entered a motion indicating they would use the "mental defect" defense. The court ordered the mental examinations based on that order.

The disappearance of Jan Broberg, which was investigated as a kidnaping, was probably the most expensive investigation in the history of the Pocatello Police Department, according to John Perkins, chief of police.

Robert Ersol Berchtold

Mary Ann & Jan
Sept. 2003

Bob sat stunned, the receiver in his hand; he choked up and began to weep.

By chance, I stopped at the shop just minutes after her call. I found my husband extremely distraught.

Faulting himself for not getting through to Jan, he was experiencing bitter despair. "She wouldn't listen. She kept saying over and over that I had to sign some papers. I don't even know what she's talking about. I felt so helpless. What else could I do?"

Having no answer, I leaned against his shoulder and cried with him.

Two days after Jan's call to her father, I heard from Robert. He asked if I had tried calling him, afraid he had missed my call.

"What reason would I have to call you?" I asked.

"I thought Jan might have called you or Bob."

Thinking about Jan's phone call to her dad, I said nothing. Had he been with her when she made the call? I hoped he would explain about "the papers" to the recording machine.

Berchtold continued, "I've been in Phoenix for the last four days."

"In Phoenix? Why there?"

"I have people who are helping me search and one of them thought he had found her, but it turned out to be a false lead."

"That's too bad," I replied blandly.

"She told me she was getting lots of sun, so I figured Phoenix was a good lead."

My response was a grunt.

He stammered, "Uh, by the way, it's the end of summer, so I'm closing up the Fun Center."

I said nothing.

After a brief few moments, he said, "Did you know Gail and I were divorced? It was finalized a couple of weeks ago here in Jackson."

Surprised, I replied, "Oh, I didn't know."

His nonchalant attitude was expected. "Oh, we haven't been compatible for years. Gail knows this is best for both of us. I'll still take care of her and the kids, but I've got to get on with my life and find happiness."

I could have puked. Everything was now convenient for him to marry Jan. *Where was he hiding her?*

deception upon deception

Sometime in August

It was a hot, sticky day in southern California. Perspiration beaded Sister Maria's forehead as she hurried down the stairs to answer the telephone. The temperature was soaring again for the fourth consecutive day. Combined with the unlimited stacks of paperwork, the scurrying only added to her discomfort.

"What a day for the air conditioning to be out," she remarked. The ringing phone persisted as she scolded, "I'm on my way! Patience, you little talk box. I don't know why God didn't give me wings . . . Heaven knows I could use them today."

The sister paused to push back a few damp strands of hair under her habit as she picked up the receiver.

"Flintridge!" she answered breathlessly.

The voice at the other end of the phone responded anxiously, "Yes, hello, is this the Sacred Heart Academy?"

"Yes, that's correct," the Sister replied, sounding a bit annoyed. "May I help you with something, sir?"

"To whom am I speaking?" he asked.

"I am Sister Maria Terese."

"Please, I'm needing to talk with Sister Charlotte."

"I'm sorry sir, but Sister Charlotte is not available until this afternoon. Would you like to leave a message for her?"

"What is your position?" the caller asked.

"I'm a teacher at the Academy."

"Are you in charge?"

"In charge of what, sir?"

"Enrollment!" he fired back.

"Well, yes. All the sisters have responsibilities here for enrollment, but Sister Charlotte is the decision maker on many school matters. But I think I can help you if you're making inquiries about criteria for placement."

"Fine, I guess you'll have to do. I'm desperate and need help in the worst way."

His voice was quivering and full of emotion. Sister Maria's posture shifted as she heard the stranger's desperate plea.

"Please, Mr.—uh," Sister Maria groped for a name. *"Sir, what can I do for you?"*

"This is an extremely difficult situation and extremely confidential," the caller said.

"All information that comes to us, stays with us. We never discuss anything you choose to tell us," Sister Maria explained.

"I trust you. I'm an agent for the CIA and am on assignment for President Ford. I've been stationed in Laos for some time. I'm sure you've heard what's happening there at the present time."

Sister Maria thought for a moment, not wanting the caller to think she was ignorant of world affairs.

Excitedly, the man went on. *"The communists are overtaking the country and all Americans are being evacuated before they are killed. I'm one of those who barely escaped with my daughter. It has been a horrible ordeal."*

The caller's voice choked up and he was obviously attempting to gain his composure before he could continue his tale. Sister Maria pictured the dramatic scene of a family escaping destruction and running for their lives.

She carefully steered her body toward a straight-backed chair and plopped down. As she listened to the heart-wrenching story, tender feelings of concern went out to this pitiful mystery man. Searching for the right words to say, the sister expressed compassion. "Oh my dear man. I'm so sorry to hear of your tragedy. I hope everything is going well for you at this point and time. I will pray for you and your daughter and . . ." Sister Maria hesitated, then added, "uh, what about your wife?"

Again emotion was heard as the voice exclaimed, "My wife is dead."

"Oh no," shrieked Sister Maria. "May God bless you." She crossed herself.

After a few moments, the voice continued. "My wife died not in the conflict, but of terminal cancer just a few weeks ago. My young daughter is still grieving her loss. This is a terrible shock for her and she is one sad little girl. She needs lots of love and support. My job doesn't permit me to spend as much time with her as I would like. I'm going to talk with Jerry—oh, pardon me—I mean President Ford and see if he can give me a new assignment. This invasion has been doubly hard for her, first to lose her mother, and second to be uprooted from her home in Laos leaving her mother buried there, not knowing if she can ever return."

By this time, tears were blurring Sister Maria's vision as she thought about the emotional pain and turmoil this family was experiencing.

"Sir, how old is your daughter and what is her name?"

"I do apologize. I forgot my manners. My life is in a very precarious situation at this very moment because of the secrecy of my assignment and I can't reveal my name. I worry like hell that my daughter's life is in jeopardy too."

"Sir, you should know that anything you reveal to me will be kept in confidence and will not be divulged to anyone outside these sacred walls. However, Sister Charlotte needs to know. How we can help you?"

"I need a private school for my daughter to attend. She is a bright, intelligent girl who needs the security and safety of your school. Her mother would be very happy to know she is attending a Catholic school. She was so devoted to Catholicism and we both tried to raise our daughter with a knowledge and love of God in an extremely Buddhist country. Janis is a very religious little girl."

"Oh, Janis!" Sister Maria replied, grateful for somebody's name.

"Yes," the caller acknowledged. "Her name is Janis Tobler. But please, you must promise to keep her identity hidden from anyone who comes to inquire. I couldn't stand it . . ." the voice quivered with emotion as the caller continued his plea, ". . . if something should happen to her. She is my only reason for living. She's my life."

"Of course, I understand. I promise you, we will look after her. But, uh, Mr. Tobler?"

"Frank Tobler," came his response.

"Well Mr. Tobler, I don't know if your daughter will fit into this school . . . her age and all. Our students are of varying ages and come here from all over the world—"

"I know she will fit in. Your school has been investigated by the secret police, and there is nothing I don't know about the Flintridge Sacred Heart Academy."

"Oh!" was the stunned reply.

"Let me tell you about Janis. She is barely fourteen, rather small for her age, but she's had to learn a lot about life in the last little while. You'll find her quite mature. Janis has been very brave these last few weeks, but I know she will be very sad because I can't be with her. I'm all she has left of a family. My assignment is so demanding right now."

"Yes, Mr. Tobler. I'm sure it is very hard for you, too."

"I need to tell you the details of Janis's arrival. She is in hiding at the present time. I have an important meeting with President Ford and members of the Chief of Staff in Washington, D.C., these next few days, but I will be coming to Los Angeles this weekend. I can bring her then."

"Mr. Tobler, our school doesn't open for two weeks. You'll need to speak to Sister Charlotte."

The caller ignored her comments. "She is very homesick right now and is longing for her home, besides being very frightened and apprehensive. Please don't ask her a lot of questions. I will answer anything you need to know. She only has a few things because we escaped Laos with only the clothes on our backs and nothing else. I'm surprised we're alive. Some of our friends didn't make it." Choking sounds were heard while he continued the frightful event. "Janis is quite traumatized. She is worrying about her Laotian friends that were left behind and are now part of the bombing and ravaging."

There was a long pause as Mr. Tobler was heard sniffling and clearing his throat.

"Sir . . . Mr. Tobler? You needn't worry about Janis. We will take excellent care of her," Sister Maria said. "We will look forward to meeting her."

"When can you take her?" he asked.

"I'll discuss that with Sister Charlotte. She will have to make the decision."

"If only you could find a place for her at your school. My biggest concern has been making certain she is protected from outsiders. I could care less about what happens to me, except she would be left all alone. I can't let that happen. She's been through so much."

"I will speak with Sister Charlotte and see what we can do. Where can I reach you?"

"I will call you in the morning. Time is critical. Please tell that to Sister Charlotte."

"Well, we do have another early arrival. Perhaps we can make this exception as well."

"Oh, it will mean so much to know she is with you wonderful sisters."

"Certainly. Please call tomorrow . . . and God bless."

■ ■ ■

Jan's diary, August 20, 1976: B called yesterday and said he was coming today. I can't wait to see him. Hope he has some good news about me going home. The Blacks are really nice. They have two daughters older than me. They think B is my dad. I think B met them in Jackson when they visited Lydia. Mrs. Black said she and Lydia went to school together. They are very Catholic. Every time they bless the food, they cross themselves. Maybe they want me to. Makes me feel funny. I wonder how Susan and Karen are doing? Fine, I hope. I sure love them!

■ ■ ■

It had been three weeks since Jan disappeared. Registration was two days away and school would be starting. Jan would not be there. It had been difficult telling her friends she was out of town over the past three weeks, but what would I tell them when she didn't start school? I had to give an explanation to the drill team advisor. I was desperate and called Gail.

"Robert is back from Jackson and tells me Jan wants to marry him," Gail commented. "She sounds very persistent. I know this sounds awful, but if it were my child, I would give my permission. How can you stand it? I'd rather have her married and know where she is, rather than go through this uncertainty. Think of all the horrible things that could be happening to her."

"Oh Gail, have you lost your senses? Think if it were Jill, fourteen years old, asking for permission to marry a forty-year-old man. You would be dying, like we are. We are desperate to have Jan home, but not under those circumstances. Have you heard from her?"

"No, but Robert is here. Do you want to talk to him?"

I didn't, but hoped he would give me some help.

Robert came to the phone, taking advantage of my near hysterical state. "I talked to Jan a couple of days ago and she told me about calling Bob last week wanting permission to marry me. She thought you would have called me. Jan's pretty desperate, but said she won't come home until you let her marry me. Just to get her home, can't you say yes? I have a Salt Lake attorney who would put some papers together. Would you like me to talk to him about it?"

"What happened to your Pocatello attorney?"

"I fired him! I wouldn't be serving any jail time if he'd done things right."

Arrogantly, he gave me his next set of instructions. "I want you and Bob to come down and meet with my new attorney—to discuss this with him."

I wanted to scream at him, but didn't dare. His phone calls were important for the investigators and I had to keep my cool. However, I couldn't contain my emotions on this matter and raised my voice. "Do you think we're crazy? Whatever is going on, we won't be a part of it."

"You want her back, don't you? You wouldn't listen when I tried telling you about Jan. I told you she was needing some help because she was so mixed up. Now look what's happened."

Getting myself under control, I spoke in a civil tone." Robert, just get Jan back home. That's all we want."

"She's pretty determined about this marriage thing." He drew a deep breath before continuing, "I have a solution, but it will freak you and Bob out."

He hesitated and I waited for him to tell me his anomalous plan.

"We could go to a Justice of the Peace in a small Utah community and it could be done very quietly. No one even needs to know. It sounds like the only way to get her home. This is pure hell not knowing where she is."

Sickened by his proposal, I terminated the phone call. His determination to marry Jan was beyond belief. I hoped what he said could be used as another blackmail plot and the law could charge him. Detective Shail was informed.

Pete stopped by to listen to the recording. "Until Berchtold comes up with a document, there's no legal proof he's intending to marry Jan. He's smart enough to know that, so he's putting all the blame on Jan to free himself of any legal entanglements."

Detective Shail agreed. "It would be hard to prove in court at this point that he is leading her into marriage. He's getting close to doing something, but we still don't know where your daughter is, and we don't want to jeopardize her safety."

Bob agreed. "He expects we are desperate enough to give our permission. I could never live with myself if I did that, no matter what the outcome might be."

Robert Berchtold was clever and moving very cautiously while he tried to manipulate us to give in to his deviant desires. Obviously, Berchtold was the only link to Jan's whereabouts and it was an advantage to the law for him to stay on the loose, at least for now.

We all agreed that keeping news of the investigation from Berchtold was imperative for Jan's safety and recovery. If he felt less threatened from law enforcement, he might take some liberties or talk more freely. Given enough rope, he might hang himself. Could we stay focused and not become rattled?

Detective Shail offered a small shred of hope. "Berchtold closed Jan's checking account at the Jackson State Bank on August 27 and presented the teller a card which bore her signature. Not only that, but a few days earlier, he picked up a prescription under the name of Jan Berchtold at that allergy clinic. And he doesn't know where she is? That's hard to believe."

Pete, still anxious to be involved again, couldn't officially enter the case. Sympathetic to our dilemma, he said, "Waiting is tough. Keep yourselves busy. It will help.

We did our best to follow Pete's advice, but found it incredibly difficult. This ordeal required much more patience than any parents could be expected to have. We wanted Jan back—NOW!

15 school days

Anxiously, Jan peered from the attic window watching cars pass down the street. B said he would be in a rental car because he had flown in. She scrutinized each passing vehicle with anticipation.

We're going to some fancy hotel when he gets here, she thought. At last a car stopped in front of the house. As she strained to see who it was, she recognized B climbing out of the drivers' seat. Her eyes brimming with tears, she grabbed her small bag and bounded down two flights of stairs to the main floor. He had hardly walked through the door when she breathlessly appeared.

In the midst of greeting the Black family, he paused and exclaimed, "Hi Dolly." Jan flew into his arms, grateful to see a familiar face. He bent down and hugged her. "How's my girl doing?"

"I think she's happy you're here. She's been rather quiet—and lonely." Mrs. Black said.

After Robert's expression of thanks for their help in protecting his daughter and taking care of her needs, Jan's voice trembled as she gave her appreciation for their kindness. Once in the car, Jan expressed over and over her feelings of relief. She was so thankful to be safe with B.

"It's so good to see you too," Robert said. "You don't know what a hard week this has been. It's been a worry having you stay with people you didn't even know. What a trooper you are."

"When am I going home, B?" Jan asked anxiously.

Robert shook his head and confessed, "Not for a while. Things haven't worked out yet with your parents. We need to talk. I've been working on some things and you're going to have to stay in California for now."

Jan's response was full of emotion. "I don't want to stay here any longer. I want to go home."

"Let's go get a bite to eat and we'll talk about it. It's only for a little longer. I want you home too. I hate you being here when I'm so far away," Robert said. "I'm not going back until I know you're safe."

Robert awoke in the dark hotel room startled to find that Jan was not in bed. Hastily he scanned the darkened room and spied her curled up in a chair near the window.

"What's the matter?" he asked with alarm.

"I couldn't sleep. I've just been thinking."

He hurriedly went to her. "About what?"

"About school. Me . . . pretending to be Catholic . . . going there today."

"Oh, I see."

"I can't be Catholic. All that stuff—the rosary, catechism, confirmation, confession. I don't know what they're talking about. I don't want to go!"

Since Robert's arrival, he had deliberately avoided discussing how Jan was to approach her new environment. She felt unsure of how she was to talk with people who viewed her as Catholic.

"Oh, Jan. It wasn't supposed to happen this way. I would take it all away if I could, but Zada insists this is what you must do until Bob gives in. You have to do what they say. Please, honey, you've got to go through with this."

"I want to go home," she cried out. "I don't want to go to a Catholic school. This is stupid. I'd rather be dead than have to do this."

"Don't talk like that!" Robert tried to gather her into his arms but she struggled to free herself from his hold.

"I'm not a little kid," she protested.

"It's going to be okay, Jan, believe me. It'll just take time but I know it won't be that long. If Bob and Mary Ann knew why you wanted to marry me, they wouldn't hesitate for a minute."

"Then tell them!" Jan blurted out.

"You know what would happen. Nobody can know, at least not yet. Could you really stand to see those terrible things happen to your sisters? I know how much you love them both. Can you think of Karen being blind or them taking Susan and her going through this?"

Jan closed her eyes while her body trembled. "No," she whispered.

"Please be patient! It will all work out for the best. Believe in Christ and do everything we have been told." Robert drummed his fingers nervously on the arm of the chair while he watched Jan's disappointed reaction. "I've something else to tell you."

Jan looked at him fearfully. "You're not supposed to know, but . . . one of the Catholic sisters is part of the plan. That's the reason you are going there."

Startled, Jan questioned, "What? One of the sisters? Who?"

"I knew this would freak you out. I shouldn't have told you. I don't know which one. I haven't been told yet. Dolly, don't be frightened. Whoever it is, she will be on our side. She's going to protect you from any evil. She knows what this is all about. I was told she will always be near to help you with anything. These nuns are women who have devoted their lives to God."

"Is she like Zada?"

"Oh, I really don't know. This sister has a different job. She's going to protect you and keep you safe so you'll be ready for . . . well, to complete your mission when it's time. Just remember the plan—your mother died and I am your father. But no one will ask. Look to the future and think *about how it will be, you and me, and all your family happy for us. You will be safe here till it's over, I promise. I've never lied to you, have I?"*

Sniffling, Jan looked away, unable to answer his question.

Robert handed her a tissue. "Somehow your parents have to let go. It's all up to them. Maybe your mom will listen."

Jan turned away from him. With no response, Robert jumped up from the chair, clapped his hands and said cheerfully, "Hey, we should go to the beach today and get some more of that golden sunshine. You've got the beginning of a beautiful tan, and it looks ravishing on you. Come on. Get your bag. We'll have a beautiful day. We won't have to think about anything else except having a good time."

He crossed the room to where she was standing, pulled her face up, and kissed her.

The beach was crowded and hot. Buried to her neck in white sparkling sand, with sunglasses covering her eyes, Jan was trying to block out thoughts of her new assignment. Robert picked up a handful of sand and slowly dribbled it over her small frame.

"I hate to see the fun end, honey, but I have to drive all the way back to Utah today then go back up to Jackson," Robert said. "It's time to close up the Fun Center."

Jan remained motionless. He studied her exposed face, examining every feature. "Crap, you're beautiful. I love all those cute little freckles across your tiny nose." He rubbed his finger softly across her nose and cheeks. "And those high cheek bones are just like your mother's. Why did God make you so perfect?"

With eyes closed, Jan remained still. He carefully pulled the sunglasses away from her eyes blowing gently on her face. "Look at those eyelashes—so long, dark, and simply wonderful. If our children look like you, they will be awesome."

Why did he have to say that? *she thought angrily. Bounding out from the cool mound of sand, she stood up. "I'm ready to go . . . now!" Picking up her beach bag, she marched hastily over the hot sand toward the dressing room.*

Knowing his impulsive words were ill-stated, Robert tried to rectify his position. "Jan! I shouldn't have placed that burden on you. I wasn't thinking. You've got enough to worry about. I'm sorry. Wait, I'm coming!"

Jan entered the dressing room ignoring his apology and changed from her swimsuit to a pair of pink shorts and a striped top Robert had bought her on their shopping spree. At the car, he again begged forgiveness.

"It's okay, B. I'm just very nervous," she stated coolly, trying to forget his remarks.

Both were quiet as they began the ride to Flintridge. Jan peered out the window while the car climbed up the mountainous road toward the school. Pine, palm, and oak trees lined the roadside preventing a peek at the view beyond. The quiet roadway was an extreme change from the busy, chaotic freeways only miles away.

Flintridge campus crowned a peak of the San Rafael Hills, sprawling across fifty-two acres of canyons and semi-developed terrain. The Spanish-style buildings where the sisters and students lived had once been the Flintridge Biltmore Hotel. On top of the hill was a library building and an auditorium. Included on the beautifully landscaped grounds were a swimming pool, tennis courts and the music department—surrounded by small cottages. The entire grounds were enclosed and protected by security guards.

Robert had insisted Jan visit the school two days ago. When they had pulled up to the front of the Academy, Jan had remarked, "This looks like a fancy hotel. Are you sure it's a school?"

A large green canopy sheltered the marble steps in front of the building. Curiously, Jan ascended the steps, wondering what experiences waited beyond the doors. As they walked into the foyer, a sister came scurrying to greet them. She identified herself as Sister Ignacious. She and the other resident sisters greeted them with a great deal of warmth. Jan hadn't been around Catholic sisters except when she played Gretel in The Sound of Music*—and those nuns weren't for real. With some apprehension she watched and listened to each sister. It was a relief not to feel threatened. Instead, their friendly attitude was appealing. Robert seemed to know them.*

He joked about a wolf that someone said was on the hillside. "I almost changed my mind about bringing my daughter to this untamed territory."

"Oh yes, this is undisturbed nature," Sister Maria said. "They were here long before we were and God would want them to stay in their natural habitat. The wall around the campus keeps them off our grounds. We've never had a casualty yet from an aggressive wolf."

"We respect them and they respect us," Sister Ignacious concluded.

Following the introductions, Sister Charlotte took them on a tour of the grounds pointing out the surrounding vistas. "Students come from around the world—fifteen foreign countries to be exact—and from the immediate neighborhoods of Pasadena and Glendale. Some are day students, but you will be a permanent resident," she said to Jan. The word "permanent" made an impression on Jan's mind.

"Learning, and living together, the girls build strong and enduring personal friendships with both faculty and students. Some of our students are motherless, so the sisters are accustomed to being mother, friend, and tutor, as well as teacher." Sister Charlotte paused as she realized her words might sound a bit harsh to Janis since the recent loss of her mother must be difficult. Receiving no indication of distress from the young girl, she continued her lecture.

"At Flintridge, there is special emphasis on fine arts. The drama teacher is an actress who has toured, understudied and 'starred.' She knows theater arts and can teach drama and the appreciation of it. The music department is outstanding, and attracts especially gifted students . . . "

Excitement welled up within Jan as the speech continued. Someday, I'm going to be an actress, she thought. B said being here would require the finest performance of my life. He's going to help me get in a movie. Wow! I might like it here a lot.

Sister Charlotte pointed out Jan's new temporary residence. "Janis, you will be staying in one of the cottages with myself and a darling girl from China, Jacinta Lobo, just until school starts. Then you will move to the dormitory which the Sisters and students share. Jacinta is a fine musician, and I hear you are too. I think you will like her very much."

Robert graciously thanked Sister Charlotte as they returned to the office building, telling her Jan would be moved in on Tuesday afternoon before he left for Washington.

Having the chance to look over the campus and realizing the favorable opportunities brought excited chatter from Jan for the remainder of the day.

Robert had taken advantage of Jan's upbeat mood and enthusiastically said, "Isn't Flintridge everything I told you? You're going to love it. Now, we're going to celebrate. I'm taking you into Hollywood to the wax museum, then the Chinese Theater. And tonight, we're going to a very romantic place for dinner."

"But B, I don't know anything about Catholics. You've got to help me."

"I will, but not today. We're going to have the time of our lives and talk about that later."

■ ■ ■

August 16, 1976

Since school was soon to begin, I called the principal and told him Jan would not be coming because some difficulties had arisen. I couldn't discuss the situation with him, but would he pass the news to the drill team advisor? Mr. Soderquist wished her well and said, "She will be missed. Jan is a good student and well-liked by both teachers and students." Later, I wondered if he thought it odd we never requested her transcripts or school records.

Keeping the matter of Jan's disappearance secret would be challenging since it had been imperative to let family and close friends know. With her case highly profiled, word of her absence could spread through the community like wildfire, botching confidentiality.

Karen faced questioning daily from Jan's peers. Where was she? Why wasn't she in school? Drill team had started rehearsals without her.

Karen remained loyal to our decision and said, "Jan is staying with my grandma. She'll be home soon." Among her friends, only Caroline and her parents knew the truth.

■ ■ ■

As Robert pulled the car up to the entrance of the school, Jan was suddenly filled with anxiety. If only I could feel the way I did two days ago, *she thought. But the apprehension of facing a totally new and foreign environment was so frightening, she could hardly think straight.*

"Are you ready?" Robert asked. "Do you know how incredible you are? I know you can do this . . . for us . . . and for them. The only thing you need to remember is, you are Janis Tobler, and nothing else. I've asked the Sisters not to question you about anything because you are having a hard time coping with the death of your mother. Okay? I can't tell you enough how much I love you. This is going to kill me—leaving you like this."

Quietly, Jan said, "I know. Don't worry. Do what you have to do."

"What a girl." Robert took her hand and kissed it. "I love you," he whispered passionately. After a few searching looks, wanting her approval, he opened the door and jumped out, motioning for Jan to slide across the seat to exit his door. He removed two small bags of new clothes out of the trunk. Because the students wore uniforms to class, Jan didn't need an extensive wardrobe. Other than necessary underwear, socks, shoes, and nightwear, her only other needed items were dance leotards and tights, and a few articles to wear during off-hour activities.

With Jan standing beside Sister Charlotte, Robert repeated again how sorry he was to leave and parted with instructions to "take good care of my daughter." He said he would call the following day. Planting a friendly parental kiss on Jan, he confidently got into the car, put on his dark glasses and drove slowly out the driveway. With the security gates closing behind him, Jan felt she was beginning her prison sentence.

Jacinta Lobo was an energetic, bright, happy, and friendly roommate. Her petite form, almond shaped eyes, and dark, short hair fit the image Jan expected. What she didn't expect was the immediate response of caring from this much-needed friend. Because the two girls' circumstances brought them both to Flintridge early, they had two weeks to develop their friendship, which seemed to save Jan from worrying too much over her precarious situation.

While Jan studied Catholicism, Jacinta practiced the piano. Although Jan was adept at the keyboard and took her turn practicing and playing, listening to Jacinta was intimidating. She either practices for hours every day or she's a prodigy, *Jan thought.*

Each morning, the girls attended worship services, and soon Jan was proficient with reciting the rosary and other set prayers. The ritual of crossing herself became a habit although it never felt natural. When they finished studies and small chores assigned to them, they enjoyed playing tennis, swimming, and relaxing in various sections of the outdoor gardens talking about girl stuff. Jan avoided talking about herself, and Jacinta never probed. Sister Ramona had told Jacinta about Janis's mother dying and the terrible flight she experienced escaping from Laos. Jacinta's impeccable manners would never allow her to press for information.

<u>Jan's diary, August 26, 1976:</u> I miss my wonderful parents. I wish I could tell them how very thankful I am for them. My mom for doing so much for me. For having patience with me. For loving me. For teaching me how to be a good person. For our wonderful talks. I really love her. I'm thankful for my dad because of all he did for me. For providing for me. For loving me. For teaching me the gospel and helping me make decisions. And for the time he spends with me. If I didn't have my parents I couldn't live. They've got to understand and let me come back.

■ ■ ■

On the first day of September, I had a surprise visitor. Gail had just delivered her ex-husband to the county jail for his two-week stay. *Hardly justice for the kidnapping of Jan nearly two years ago*, I thought.

"Have you heard from Jan?" I asked hopefully.

Gail's demeanor was cool and distant. She emphatically replied, "No, but I've come to pick up the sewing machine Robert gave Jan for her birthday. It was very expensive and I could use it."

"Gail, I'm sorry, but I'm not returning anything Robert has given Jan until she is back in her own home. Tell him that," I said. Her stay was brief and I felt friction between us. I was determined not to give an inch to Robert and was sorry he continued to manipulate his ex-wife.

■ ■ ■

Night was the difficult time for Jan. She wrote:

September 20, 1976: B brought me this tiny TV but I'm not allowed to watch it in my room. I sneak it under the covers and stick my head under so I can watch "Charley's Angels" and "Love Boat." That makes me think about home. I wonder what Sister Ramona would think if she saw the antenna sticking out from the covers? Jacinta thinks it's cool and laughs at me. Hah! Hah!

But usually Jan couldn't watch TV, and with lights out, Jan had a hard time turning off her thoughts about home and her future. Then her tears became unstoppable. The first time Jan broke into sobs, it took Jacinta by surprise.

She arose from her bed and knelt by Jan's side, gently patting her back. After the crying subsided, Jan asked Jacinta, "Do you ever get so lonely for your family you can't stand it?"

"When I feel so bad like you, I just blow my troubles to the wind. That makes me feel better," Jacinta said.

"Sometimes, I feel like I want to die. I don't think I can stand feeling like this," Jan said, choking back a sob as her dear friend placed her hand on Jan's face and comforted her.

"Tomorrow we will go to the top of the hill and throw all our troubles away. You will feel better. Okay, little Janis?"

"Okay, Jacinta." Jan responded between sobs. "Thank you for being such a good friend. I need you." Jan threw her arms around Jacinta and hugged her. "I'm feeling better already."

"I don't like to see you sad," Jacinta said.

Jacinta returned to her bed while Jan tried to forget about the turmoil engulfing her life. Guilt was overwhelming her. She didn't feel good about the way Robert touched and caressed her. It was wrong. She knew it. Yet Robert kept telling her this was the plan.

"Oh, I hate it," she whispered.

16 spy stories

After Robert was released from Bannock County Jail on September 15th, I desperately wanted to follow him since I felt certain he would visit Jan. I realized it was an irrational thought. But on the weekend, I persuaded Bob to go with me to Salt Lake. I became convinced in my mind that spying on Robert might be the only way we would find our daughter.

Robert was employed as a salesman for an arcade and pinball machine investor, and I had the address of his employer. Parking on the street near the building, I hoped to find activity at the business, but it was Saturday. The business was closed.

Our next stop was the Salt Lake Airport. As Bob drove around the parking lot, I spied Gail's green station wagon. Pulling into a vacant space, Bob cautioned me to be careful. He didn't want me accused of pilfering. I went over to the car, tried the door, and found it unlocked. Waving to Bob, I got in. Laying on the seat was the entry ticket into the parking lot marked September 19, 1976. My heart raced with anticipation. *He's gone to see Jan,* I thought. After looking through other papers in the jockey box and on the seat of the car, I walked back to report.

"According to the parking ticket, he came in here yesterday at 11:18 A.M. I also found a receipt from Mountain West Distribution showing the purchase of a JVC TV-Radio yesterday."

"Undoubtedly another gift," Bob said. "Let's go in and check airline schedules."

Salt Lake Airport was large enough to make the job unrealistic. It was mind boggling to check all the flights which left around noon. After a few hours of gathering up airline pamphlets with flight schedules, we returned to the city.

"If he left yesterday, I doubt he'll come back today," Bob stated.

At the motel, I stayed up late studying each schedule, anxious to figure out a destination. Certainly the Lord was on our side and would let one of us see him when he got off a flight. It was a sleepless night while I worked through a dozen different scenarios. What would I say if we saw him? Should we avoid him or make him nervous by letting him see us? Will there be a scene? Would Jan be okay if Robert felt threatened?

We spent Sunday at the airport watching passengers get off various flights. Bob was at one end of the airport while I positioned myself at the other. Becoming weary of watching arrivals, we decided to talk with ticket agents. "We're trying to find out if a relative is on this next flight? Would you mind checking your passenger list for Robert Berchtold?" We also checked for aliases we knew he had used: Frank Farr, Hank Hutchinson, and Bobby Tobler. And of course we checked for Jan Broberg. Several of the congenial agents let us scan their lists. To our disappointment, neither Robert nor Jan were listed on any of the incoming flights.

Bob was growing perplexed. "We can't watch every flight, my dear. And what can we do if he does get off, unless Jan is with him? There is little chance of that."

Troubled about the seemingly hopeless situation, he urged me to give up the search.

I knew we needed to pick up our girls at my mother's and go

home. Reluctantly, I left, knowing tonight, tomorrow, or in a few days, Robert would be getting off a flight, but that it was futile to catch him.

Returning to our car, we noted that the green station wagon was still in the parking lot. With heavy hearts, we drove out of the airport and headed home.

Our decision to hire a private investigator was not hasty. On the day Jan was reported as a runaway, a private eye had seen her name on the police log and called us. With the police department just beginning their investigation, we didn't feel his services were necessary. Weekly, he called to solicit us and we said "no." As time passed with no clues, desperation changed our minds.

After ten days on the job, I asked for an accounting of his work. Although his information coincided with everything from the police department, he believed Jan was in Ogden, Utah, disguised with heavy makeup, and hiding out. It was just a matter of finding her. Realizing he was inexperienced, we terminated our contract and asked for his bill. It arrived immediately, amounting to thousands of dollars. I took his bill, walked into his office, and asked that he itemize his charges.

He was unable to do so. I told him to "stick it in your ear!" and furiously marched home. Eventually, we sent him a check when we agreed upon a fair amount.

From that moment on, every day became a search mission. Knowing Jan's life demanded challenges, I concentrated on important details of her personality. She had to be busy either in school, the arts, or craft projects.

During the first kidnapping, Robert was chagrined because Jan's boredom centered around her desire to return to school. *Okay,* I thought, *What kind of school and where? She had to be reasonably close, but invisible to law enforcement scrutiny.*

For the next several days, I poured over volumes of telephone directories at the local library searching for private schools in surrounding states, drafting and mailing letters:

To whom it may concern:

I am writing to you with an unusual request by asking for your help in locating our missing daughter. We have reason to believe she has been placed in a private school by an individual who claims to be her father. A description of our daughter is below:

Name: Jan Broberg
   (could be under the alias of Berchtold)
Birth date: July 31, 1962, Age: 14
Weight: 85 lbs., Height: 4'10"
Hair: light brown, School year: 9th

She has a sprinkling of freckles across her nose, a dimple in her chin, and a distinctive bump on the first knuckle of her left hand ring finger. She is very petite and very active, has a charming personality, loves drama and acting, plays the piano, sings, is bright, intelligent, loves outdoor activities such as swimming, horseback riding, and gymnastics. A picture is enclosed.

As concerned parents, we are most anxious to locate her and would appreciate a collect call from your school should she be enrolled or has inquired about enrollment.

The individual responsible for her disappearance has several aliases. His given name is Robert Ersol Berchtold; alias Frank Farr, Bobby Tobler, and Hank Hutchinson. He has blonde, wavy hair, 5'8" tall, 145 lbs., and is 40 years old.

If you have any questions regarding the validity of this

request you may contact the Pocatello Police Department and ask for Detective George Shail.

Thank you for your time and we hope you have good news.

Out of the several letters mailed, I received one reply from the Judson School in Scottsdale, Arizona.

Dear Mr. and Mrs. Broberg:

We received your letter and are in deepest sympathy with your dilemma. I am sorry to inform you that we have had no contact with your daughter, however. If she does come here, we are keeping your address and letter in our files and we will contact you immediately.

We wish you good luck. Enclosed is a picture of your daughter being returned.

Sincerely,

Henry G. Wick, Director

Robert's phone calls became sporadic, but he always said, "Jan won't come back until you give her permission to marry me." Our response was consistent. "Sorry, but tell Jan that will never happen."

"How can I tell her? I don't know where she is," Robert said.

"You seem to have more contact with her than we do," I said. "When or if she calls, tell her we miss her desperately and to please call home."

"I guess it's up to me to find her since you don't seem to give a damn," he declared angrily.

Bob's excited voice rang through the telephone wires on the morning of October 4, 1976. "Mary Ann, guess who Tom saw yesterday on his way home from Salt Lake? Berchtold."

"Okay," I said, waiting for him to explain his excitement.

"Yeah, there was a girl sitting on his lap," Bob said. My heart leaped with anticipation. *Maybe I owed the private eye an apology,* I thought. "He was out near Lagoon when Robert passed his car. A bunch of the kids in Tom's car laughed when they saw a young girl driving and made snide remarks about old Berchtold cuddling some chick."

"Do they think it was Jan?" I asked, hoping for a positive response.

"No," Bob replied. "Tom said she was small, blonde and a cutie, but it wasn't Jan. She looked younger than Jan. But the boys had a better look and talked about it for a few minutes, then dropped the matter."

My rush of adrenaline drained out with this disappointing news. I groaned and began to cry. "Oh, that sick, perverted idiot. I want to tear his heart out like he's doing to mine. Where is she? What has that creep done with her?" I shrieked.

"I'm calling George Shail," Bob said. "Mary Ann, things are going to be okay, I know they will. Just hang on."

My imagination went wild. *Now another young girl is being victimized, and where is my daughter?* Thinking the worst, I continued to bawl going from room to room wringing my hands, pounding on door casings, verbally beating myself into a frenzy. Furious, I shouted loudly, *How stupid, blind, and ignorant can one person be. Look at what you've done. You are disgusting. How can you stand yourself? It's your fault. And who's paying for your stupidity? Your innocent daughter. How do you feel?*

The anguish of letting Robert con me weighed so heavily on my mind that I felt I was being crushed. Again, I was driven to my knees in the most mournful and sorrowful plea I had ever uttered. Full of hostility and resentment, I asked, *Why should Jan be the one suffering? This isn't her fault. How could this happen to her? Why is Jan paying for this awful crap. I deserve the punishment, not her! Where is thy justice and mercy, Lord?*

Losing complete control of my emotions, I bellowed, *I hate this depraved, deceptive, corrupted liar! He has twisted and distorted everything that was good in my life. He's a devil . . . a sick monster!* Sobbing uncontrollably, I felt as if my entire lower extremities were being severed. I experienced indescribable physical, emotional, and spiritual agony. If this was *justice* for a battered soul, would *mercy* follow when the price was paid?

Eventually, my petition changed to submission and humility. *Oh Dear Father, what more can I do?* Choking with emotion, I pleaded, *Let Jan be safe . . . let her come home . . . give me another chance to be her mom . . . let me continue to teach her, give her the help she needs and the love she deserves . . . let her heal and be whole.* In return, I promised a soul which would be more righteous, repentant, devoted, and indebted to Him. At that moment, I received the most overwhelming witness of Christ's death on the cross and my contribution to His great suffering.

Overcome with grief, I sprawled limply on the floor. Lying there, my body heaved sporadically as the sobbing began to subside. My head was pounding so hard I thought it would explode. It felt huge, out of proportion. Slowly, my emotionally bruised and battered soul began reviving. Gradually, my quivering muscles relaxed and I pulled myself to a sitting position where I cradled my head for a very long time.

Bob came for lunch to observe a puffy, red-eyed, weak, and subdued wife. His loving arms were a welcome embrace for one who recognized this forgiving, understanding giant as my greatest strength.

"George talked to Tom. He wants an eyewitness account from the boys, too. George wants to be *sure* it wasn't Jan," he said.

After school, the three boys were interrogated at the police station. George explained the reason for them being questioned and told them Jan was missing again and that Berchtold was a suspect. "Do any of you think it was Jan Broberg? Just speak up. It's okay. I want to know if you are absolutely sure it wasn't her."

The youths didn't think it was Jan. They knew her well. But after brief discussion, one of the boys thoughtfully contemplated Detective Shail's words. "Well, I only saw her from a side view and I'm not absolutely sure. It could have been her."

Detective Shail jumped to his feet and said. "Would you be willing to appear in court with that testimony, if we need it?"

The boy nodded.

Detective Shail was excited. His search could now proceed outside the boundaries of Idaho. Police records stated: *Jan Broberg was sighted in the Salt Lake area on October 3, 1976, in the company of Robert Berchtold.*

Within a few days, George enticed a close friend, Ken Corbridge, to fly him to Salt Lake. Ken became acquainted with Detective Shail when he trained at the local police academy before lucrative business opportunities lured him away. Putting his dream aside never purged his desire for police work. I discovered Ken had combed secluded hills around Idaho and surrounding states in his twin engine Piper two years ago, searching for Berchtold's orange motor home. He was excited for a second chance to look for our daughter.

George, insisting on my presence in Utah, asked me to meet them at the local airport before dawn. The breeze was chilly, reminding us that cold and snow was not far behind. In Salt Lake, we were met by a police officer who transported us to the downtown station. Pictures, present information, and past history of Berchtold and of Jan's kidnapping were discussed.

When we had finished there, the accompanying officer took George and me to Ogden where, once again, we repeated our story. I furnished them with information about Robert's relationship over the past year with a divorcee who worked for Robert's attorney. Her daughter, Crista, was a few years younger than Jan. The Ogden police force were eager to "nail this guy" since children in their community were at risk.

We were driven to the elementary school Crista attended. I waited in the car as George and the police officer went into the school to speak with the principal and show him a photograph of Jan. Not to alarm the targeted student, they asked that Crista be shown the picture of Jan to see if she knew her, but not to mention the fact that Jan was a missing child.

After lengthy discussion of how to do so without divulging any information, a plan was formulated. A school event was in the planning stages which would require a group of students to be representatives for an inner-school project. Student input was necessary and ideas for the project had already been discussed in small groups. One representative was to be selected from each class to present their project to the District Administration. By inviting the students to comment about their classmates, a better informed decision could be made on the selection of representatives. Crista was escorted into the principal's office along with other students where pictures of students were displayed. Jan's photo was among them. The students were asked to point out photos of students they knew and indicate who they thought would be a good representative. Crista was specifically asked if any of the students were friends of hers or if she knew them. Crista studied the pictures for a few moments. She pointed to a couple of students stating she knew them, but passed by Jan's picture. Her blank expression didn't reflect any sign of recognition. She returned to class unaware of the intense search.

The children were out for recess when George came out. He pointed Crista out to me and said, "Do you think she could pass for Jan?" I nodded in the affirmative, thinking it unfortunate that Crista was another of Robert 's targets.

The lawmen felt pleased that contact had been made with the young girl. They would attempt to talk with Crista's mother and find out what type of association the family had with Berchtold. George concluded Jan was not, nor had been, in the area. I hid my disappointment and said nothing, but my stomach was churning. I thought, *If she isn't here, then where is she? What has he done with her?*

I didn't pay much attention to the conversation between the men as we traveled back to Salt Lake. It was police talk and I wasn't in the mood to hear anymore success and failure stories.

Instead of returning to the police station we pulled into the parking lot of an apartment complex. George said, "While we've been gone, our pilot has been doing some detective work. He obtained a search warrant to Berchtold's apartment. I wonder if he found any evidence?"

Immediately my spirits revived. A combination of nerves and excitement made the hairs on my arms stand on end. As I watched the housing unit anxiously, a man dressed in overalls and carrying a toolbox exited. Smiling broadly and giving a thumbs up, I recognized it to be Ken as he walked towards us.

George asked, "Any luck?"

"No one was home, but the manager let me in," Ken said. His next comment caused a shiver down my spine. "There were some little girls clothes in the closet, but too small for a 14-year-old." I wilted. Jill's clothes, no doubt. Ken continued, "I did find a manuscript under the mattress which I think Berchtold is writing. He calls it *Seasons in the Sun*. Since I didn't have much time, I only read the first and last chapter. His 'love' is a 12-year-old girl he teaches in Sunday School. At the end, when he gets out of prison, she runs across the street to see him, but is hit by a truck and dies. What a scary guy. I took a few snapshots of his place and his writings. There isn't much stuff around. I don't think he spends much time there."

"Oh criminy. I was sure you would find something that would give us a reason to put him behind bars. That big jerk." Turning around, George said, "Sorry, Mary Ann. I'd liked to have gotten more, but we're going to get this guy, believe me."

As the plane headed for home, I crowded into my little spot in the back and laid my head on a crossbar. The noisy engine drowned out the conversation going on between the pilot and the detective. I was left to my own thoughts, and went over the disappointing activities of the day. What a waste. Jan's photograph was left with several officers, but it all seemed so hopeless. I tried not to be discouraged, but giant tears rolled down my cheeks.

It was late afternoon and the sun bounced off the mountaintops making the world look hazy and glittery. As I strained to look out the small window nearby, I spied a small cemetery nestled peacefully on a hillside.

I thought, *There's the Garland cemetery and somewhere down there is my dad's grave. Do you know how much I need your reassurance, Dad? What are you doing right now? Please, if you can, be with Jan. Give her your sweet, comforting spirit. I'm going to make it through this, Dad. That's what you'd expect me to do, and I'm not going to disappoint you.*

me, the spy?

October, 1976

Immediately after my return with George Shail, I had a new surge of optimism and began pressing Bob for another trip to Salt Lake. Just maybe, I dreamed, Robert is bringing Jan into Salt Lake, or hiding her in his apartment. I felt doubtful he would be that brazen, but I had to make sure.

I had no idea what we could accomplish, but doing nothing brought exhausting anxiety. Even without a sensible reason, I couldn't stay at home with my thoughts and fears running rampant. Sometimes I felt I was smothering as desperation and hopelessness invaded my thoughts. Each morning I would awake with new hope that we would hear positive news or that Jan would be found, but by nightfall, the grim reality of nothing brought a tightness to my breast.

Often I stood alone at the dining room window when the rest of the family was in bed, staring into the dark unfriendly world, wondering about my little girl: *What are her feelings and thoughts? Is she being tormented?* I was trying to console my own bleeding heart and finding little comfort. Silently, I would pray that she knew

181

how much we loved her—unconditionally—and that we missed her desperately. If I could receive a portion of peace, I would be able to face another day. How benevolent the Comforter was to my soul as I was lulled into sleep.

Bob was scheduled to attend a wholesalers holiday open house in Salt Lake the next week and I was determined to go with him. My jogging partner, Karlene, helped me work out a disguise for our trip. I borrowed her blonde wig, a loose fitting blouse, a long skirt, round-rimmed reading glasses, and funky shoes. I would look like a hippie, and I laughed at this "out of character" costume. I remarked, "Oh Karlene, am I nuts? I'll look like an idiot." At her urging, I laid the items in the car trunk, determined to accomplish something to further my cause of finding my daughter.

We drove to Utah, and while Bob went to his open house, Susan, Karen, and I headed for the apartment complex where Robert lived. Seeing his Lincoln Continental parked near the entry made my heart leap.

Information gleaned from Detective Shail indicated Robert lived with an artist named Lydia, whom he had met in Jackson Hole. According to police reports, her main residence was in Park City, but she rented a small shop in Jackson Hole each summer where she could peddle her paintings. Jan had briefly mentioned Lydia after her brief stay in Jackson, stating she was a "large lady and really nice." It was assumed she had never married. Since residents of the apartment didn't know her, it was thought Berchtold might have simply used her name to secure the apartment in order to remain anonymous.

My heart practically jumped out of my skin when I saw Robert come out of the building, look around, and then open the trunk of his car. Fortunately, we had parked among several other cars a distance away. The girls ducked down, frightened, but I wanted to observe what he was doing. He was moving something from the back seat of his car into the trunk. I had a spy glass, but my view was hampered by trees and cars, and I didn't dare move into a better position.

Shortly, he got into his car and drove away. I was tempted to follow him, but knew it would be foolish. Susan volunteered to go into the complex and find the apartment. I approved her proposal and told her "if she weren't out in three minutes, I would be in after her."

Susan charged from the car, ran up the walk, and disappeared into the building. Karen looked at me with alarm. "Where's my brain!" I blurted out. Karen stared at me with anxiety. "Hurry, Susie," I said anxiously, "hurry up and get out of there."

Within two minutes, Susan was racing back down the sidewalk. "I found it!" she said breathlessly. "I listened at the door and I could hear *Gilligan's Island* on TV."

Excitement mounted. "Are you sure it was the right apartment?" I asked.

"I think so."

"Well, somebody's in there. Maybe it's Jan and he's gone to get them a treat. I'm going in," I said.

"Mom, we don't want anything to happen to you," Karen said fearfully.

"Nothing's going to happen."

"What are you going to do?" Karen asked.

"Just listen at the door. Maybe I'll knock and see who answers," I replied.

Confidently, I placed the blonde wig over my dark hair and positioned the glasses on my nose. "How do I look, girls?"

"Weird," Susan said, laughing.

Karen joined in, "Very silly. I don't even know you."

"Good. That's what I want."

I opened the car door, then carefully closed it. Butterflies began dancing in the pit of my stomach as I firmly forged ahead to Robert's apartment building. I opened the door and tackled the stairs. As I walked down the hallway, a door opened and I panicked. A fellow leaving his apartment looked strangely at me out of the corner of his eye. I nodded and kept walking ahead like I knew where I was going. He turned around to glare at me when I reached the end of the hall and exclaimed, "Whoops! Wrong floor," and started walking back towards him. He went down the stairs and out the door. I assumed he left the building.

I turned around and put my ear to Robert's apartment door. At first, I thought I heard someone moving about, and my skin began to crawl. I quickly retreated down the hall. A few minutes later, I crept back and listened, but heard only silence. Not wanting to run into Robert should his errand be short, I exited the building.

As I hurried down the walkway toward the car, I ducked to avoid a low branch. I didn't stoop low enough and felt the wig lift off my head. I looked up and saw it dangling on the tree. I quickly retrieved it and dashed to the car to find my daughters laughing hysterically. I began to chuckle too, as I thought of my ridiculous charade.

"Well, do you think the FBI will hire me as a undercover agent?" I asked.

"Only for comedy routines," Karen answered.

"What did you do in there, Mom?" Susan questioned.

"Not much. I don't think Jan is living here. Let's go find your father."

Back home in Idaho, we tried to make the best of life. George Shail called occasionally with no information. He was waiting for Berchtold to make a move and give them a lead. He encouraged me to keep taking Berchtold's phone calls and have him talk as much as possible.

Pete checked in nearly every day to keep our spirits up, reminding us how much time it takes for a criminal to feel comfortable enough with his crime to begin taking chances. Pete suggested we might consider hiring a local retired FBI agent who could spend quality time checking on Berchtold and perhaps observe him on a daily basis. He gave us the person's name and address; the retired agent lived only blocks away!

Vern Jensen was a handsome man in his mid-sixties, with silver hair, a kindly manner and an unassuming demeanor. He made no loud acclamations about his life, service, or accomplishments, but his firm handshake and warm smile reassured us that he had the capability needed to do the job.

Taking this assignment would interrupt his long-desired solitude and cramp his fishing, hunting, and secluded cabin living, but he still wanted the job. As a family man with grown children and now a grandfather, this crime was intolerable to him.

Bob and I were honest about our limited finances, but Mr. Jensen preferred a "gentleman's agreement" which would require no contract and the "pay back" could be worked out in the future. He assured us that his time and expenses would be kept to a bare minimum. We were free to call him anytime with information and he would call us when he had anything of importance. He emphasized patience.

"Berchtold is a man with a criminal mind and has taken a great deal of time plotting out this devious scheme. He's no fool."

Mr. Jensen had done his homework, and the information Pete gave him was all he needed to get started. His personal and professional refinement brought us a quiet peace and new hope.

Vern Jensen's approach to investigating was methodical. He warned us not to expect quick results, but assured us he would be thorough. His surveillance of Robert proved effective when he reported Robert's absence from Salt Lake City for a number of days. Upon Robert's return, his Mark IV had a dented fender. Mr.

Jensen found that an accident report had not been filed in Utah. Perhaps it occurred out of state, but where?

Late in the month, I received a phone call with Robert's excited voice stating, "I have some important information on Jan. One of my connections has told me he sighted her."

Considering his past barrage of false information, I expected he had nothing new to report. "What did he say?" I asked skeptically.

"I can't talk over the phone. I know you have this phone bugged and I'm not telling you anything except in person. Meet me at the Crossroads and I'll tell you."

"I don't think so," I said, unsure.

"Too bad. It's something you should know," Robert declared.

"I'll call Bob. Maybe he will come with me."

"Mary Ann, you either come alone or not at all. I don't want Bob there."

Without hesitation, I replied. "Okay, where shall I meet you?"

"At the Crossroads Cafe. Two o'clock this afternoon, alone."

"I'll be there!" I replied with conviction.

I called Bob and relayed Berchtold's message. Determined to hear what he had to say, I insisted I needed to go. Bob tried to talk me out of it. "Call Pete. Have him listen to the tape. Let him advise you."

Pete Welsh listened and then asked, "Are you afraid for your life?"

"No, he has no reason to harm me. He has something on his mind and I want to know what it is."

"I really don't think you should go alone. You can't trust this guy. He's such a liar. No one knows his state of mind."

"Pete, I have to go. Even if it's all a lie, I have to hear what he has to say. It's been ten weeks with no word about Jan except his lies. I'm sure it's another one, but what if he really does know where she is and is willing to share it with me? I guess I'm hanging on to any little hope that comes my way."

Pete understood my desperation. "Mary Ann, you're not going unarmed. Come down to the office and take some protection with you. Do you think you could use a gun to preserve your own life, if necessary?"

I floundered. "I don't know." Then, realizing what was at stake, I confidently replied, "Yes, I would."

Immediately, I called Bob and told him what I was doing. He wasn't pleased with my decision.

I argued, "Robert might drop some hint. I'll stop by before I leave, but first I'm calling Mom. Maybe Randy could be in the parking lot and serve as my hidden protector."

My youngest brother, Randy, was a postal employee who lived in Tremonton with his young family. The Crossroads Cafe was right off the Tremonton exit. Berchtold had never met him and I felt confident Randy would be just another face in the crowd.

"Mom, will you call Randy and ask him to drive over to the Crossroads parking lot? I would feel a lot safer if I knew someone was watching. If he can't get off work, I'll understand."

Expressing fear for my safety, my mom didn't agree with my decision to meet Berchtold. I tried to reassure her it would be okay, realizing those were empty words after asking for protection.

When I went to the FBI office, Pete placed a small handgun in my palm. "Let me show you how to use it. Have you ever used a gun before?"

I nodded. I shot a rifle at a target range many years ago, but I had never used a handgun.

After a quick course on using it, Pete told me to keep it in my purse. "Don't zip your bag, and keep your hand near the opening so the gun could be accessed in a second. If Berchtold should make any move toward you that's threatening, use it."

I gulped.

"I never tell people it's okay to shoot another person, but I know this guy could wipe you out if he is pushed against a wall," Pete said. "I'll be responsible for legalities afterwards."

Feeling determined, I placed the gun in my purse. "This gives me an eerie feeling. I hope I don't have to use it."

"Call when you get back home. I'll come by and retrieve the gun."

Bob's look of dismay almost caused me to change my mind. After a lengthy embrace, I told him to pick up the girls from school. I would call him from my mother's after I saw Robert. I needed to hurry. It was just past noon.

Robert was waiting in the parking lot when I arrived. I had been praying that I would not react to him in any way and use my best judgment in what I said. I waited in my car briefly, scanning the lot to find my brother. There were several pickup trucks parked around the cafe, but I didn't see my brother's car.

This was a farming community, and the Crossroads Cafe was the most popular coffee shop in the area. It not only attracted local farmers, but long-haul truckers as well as many road travelers. The cafe was situated on a dangerous two-lane stretch of highway which provided the main thoroughfare to the Idaho-Utah border and eventually connected with the Interstate.

The day was overcast and gloomy, and Malad Pass was treacherous when surprise winter snows blanketed the area. I didn't expect my visit with Robert to be lengthy and hoped to be home before dark.

I nervously picked up my purse, clutched it tightly, and got out of my car. Robert approached me and cordially asked, "How are you, Mary Ann?"

"Oh, not so great," I replied.

"I'm half crazy worrying over Jan," he said. "Let's go in and sit down. I'd like a piece of pie." He motioned toward the cafe.

I was relieved because I didn't feel anything would happen around a group of people. I should be safe. I noticed Robert nervously looking over the customers. I didn't recognize anyone in the cafe. We found a booth near the door and sat down. I ordered a soda; he had apple pie.

Our exchange of words was guarded. He wasn't ready to reveal anything until he scrutinized the situation. He questioned what we had done about finding Jan and if the police or FBI were involved. I knew our local authorities hadn't been in touch with him, so he was clueless. I wanted it to stay that way.

"I've told you before, we reported Jan as a runaway and were told it was put over the police wire service. That's all we know. The police said runaways are not actively sought by local law officers. They are generally found when they get in trouble or turn up dead. That's really a positive outlook to finding Jan. We have no other leads. I'm hoping you have some news."

"I do, but I won't talk in here," Robert said in a low tone. "It's Bob's fault that she left. If he'd given his permission for Jan to marry me, we wouldn't be going through this. Bob said it was because he loved Jan that he wouldn't allow her to marry me. I know it's because he hates me, and now neither one of us has her."

"Bob had to do what he felt was best for Jan," I said. The contemptuous look he gave me was unnerving. I moved beyond his angry presence and said, "I came here to talk about Jan and find out what you know."

Stubbornly, he persisted, "This *is* about Jan! She will never come home until Bob gives in. What a stubborn, hardheaded fool! He's always been like that on things he wants."

I studied the hateful look in his eyes, but sat quiet, not responding to his remarks. Realizing I was not giving him any ammunition to take shots at my husband, he sat and glared at me.

"I should have finished the bastard off when I had the chance," Robert remarked through clenched teeth.

My heart skipped a beat as I heard his admission. Too frightened to ask, I stared at him without moving a muscle.

He continued, "I was in that parking garage the morning he went down to do flowers. My gun was pointed straight at him."

Moving his eyes down, he abruptly shoved away the last few bites of pie. "I don't know why I didn't do it."

Too shaken to respond, I finished my drink and squirmed nervously.

Robert said, "Let's go out to my car. I won't talk in here about Jan. What I heard won't be easy for you." He threw some change on the table and went out the door.

I felt panic. *What does he intend to do when I get in his car? What if he drives off?* No matter what, this is the reason I came. I picked up my purse, thinking about Pete's instructions. If I had to, did I have the guts to use the gun? His confession left me shaking.

Unlocking his flashy red and white Mark IV, I apprehensively got in. Sitting with my purse on my lap, I nervously fidgeted with the zipper until I realized that might be drawing Robert's attention. The thought occurred that he could grab my purse and use the gun on me. Turning my attention to him, I listened intently.

"I don't know where she is, but I've been told she is living in a commune with a lot of other people."

"Where?"

"I said I didn't know," he answered, irritated. "He wouldn't tell me."

"Who wouldn't tell you?" I pursued.

"Some guy Jan knows. He lives in this place where she's at. She asked him to contact me. He said the information he was offering had to be secret because he doesn't want the law investigating their place. It sounds like they have some illegal activities going on."

"Like what?"

Robert bit his lip, a worried look on his face, then slowly began to relate what he knew. "He told me Jan is . . . shooting herself up." He paused, carefully taking his time.

"What are you saying, Robert? Jan's a druggie? Jan, who can't stand the thoughts of a shot?"

Trying to be emotional, he whimpered, "I know it sounds crazy, Mary Ann. It's the last thing I ever expected to happen. But, this guy told me there is a lot of illegal stuff going on. Somehow, I've got to find her and get her out of there."

"So, what's your plan? How do you expect to find her if you don't even know where she is?" I asked. "And how can you believe this guy?"

Robert began to fidget. My hand moved to the purse opening, carefully placing my hand near the open zipper. My heart was beating at an accelerated pace. Frantically, I thought, *Don't do anything stupid, Robert. I don't think I can do this.*

Robert played with his keys, turning them over and over in his hand. "I haven't worked this out yet, but I have an idea she is in Montana."

"Oh!" I said, startled.

He went on. "I've spent a lot of money trying to find her. Hell, I'm about broke. I found out that there is a community somewhere in Montana that is run by a group of hippies. I'm going to spend some time looking into it. It scares me to death because I don't want to endanger Jan's life."

I tried to appear gullible to his stratagem, but inwardly I was enraged, thinking of how rotten he was to continue such deceit.

"It didn't have to end this way," Robert said. "It could have been so different. Jan is so stubborn. When she makes a decision, even hell can't persuade her to change it. My biggest fear is some creep taking advantage of her."

I studied him carefully, thinking he was putting on a very poor performance of a man whom I believed had already robbed my little girl of her innocence. His ploy to deceive me was over, but this wasn't the time to confront him.

"Anything else?" I inquired.

"No. I hope to hell this guy was lying."

"Do you think he was?"

"I don't know. But I'm going to do everything in my power to find out."

Robert started to put his keys in the ignition. I relaxed and opened the door.

"Will you call me if you have any news?" I asked.

Robert smiled at me slyly. "You can count on it."

As I got out of his car, I turned and said, "I wish you had better news for me."

He nodded. "I don't think Jan can keep this up much longer. I know if I find her, she will be begging to go home. I'll be calling you."

"I can't wait," was my sarcastic reply.

I went over to my car and watched as Robert pulled out of the lot onto the highway. He headed towards Brigham City, but I couldn't predict his intentions. I was anxious to leave. I pulled out and watched as a pickup exited the lot. I drove to my mother's home, two miles away, watching carefully for any sign of Robert. Only the pickup continued to follow at a reasonable distance.

After circling the block once, I pulled into my mother's carport and went into the house. Within a few minutes after my arrival, Randy came in the back door. His friend, who had furnished the truck, dropped him off. I related the incident to Mom and Randy before calling Bob to tell him I was safe and would be home soon.

"We about had a heart attack when you got into Berchtold's car," Randy said. With a twinkle in his eye, he continued, "Craig had a rifle in his truck and wondered if we should shoot out his tires. But we decided if he took off, we'd follow you. I'm glad you didn't go any place."

"Me too! I'm relieved this is over," I said.

After thanking Randy for being there as my protector and assuring Mom I would be okay driving home alone, I departed. I knew it would only be a matter of time before Robert presented a new scheme. Over the past months, his calls had become a painful aggravation. If he thought his dishonest information would freak us out, he sorely misjudged our resistance. Still though, waiting had become our enemy, and every day was a raging battle, with only fragments of hope.

It was disappointing that the only news he delivered was a cunning lie by a person whose whole existence was a sham. Why had it taken such gigantic, horrific consequences before my eyes finally opened in regard to Robert's true character?

Before Mr. Jensen entered the case, Detective Shail had presented a piece of evidence which he emphasized was highly confidential. "I can't tell you how I got this, but look at Berchtold's phone bill for the months of June, July, and August—an enormous amount."

Looking over the list, George pointed out the numerous calls made to our personal number from Jackson. I acknowledged that he did call often, but there were calls made to other numbers, many of them pay phones.

"Now, look at all the collect calls he received from Pocatello. Most of them were made from pay phones, too," George declared. "How would you like to pay his phone bill every month?"

Nearly every day there was one call placed, and some days, two or three. George identified the locations of the calls from phone booths on Center street, the mini-dome, a gas station, and a trailer court. It was staggering.

"I wonder how many of these calls Jan was involved in?" I asked curiously.

"Who knows, but I suspect most of them. None of the calls were long, just often. You can tell when you guys went on vacation, but the day you got back, they increased again. What kind of an influence does this guy have on your daughter?"

I shook my head wondering the same. "What are these other calls?" I asked, pointing to numbers with area codes.

"I don't know. Call them and find out," George said. Handing me the list, he issued a stern warning, "If anyone finds out you have this, it could mean trouble. I'm not about to lose my job or retirement over this little piece of paper. Swear you will not let anyone else know you have it."

I nodded. "I promise."

Putting the list in a safe place, I didn't forget it. I thought about the unknown numbers constantly. Who would I find at the end of the line? What would I say if I did call? Would it give me a clue about Jan or would I mess everything up?

Finally, mental anguish overcame indecisiveness. While studying the numbers one evening, I decided to place one phone call. I thumbed through the phone book and found the area code was Oregon. It turned out to be a game machine company with a message giving business hours. I was disappointed.

A few days later, I brought the list out again and called another number. *Wonder what this business sells? It's in Arizona.* Results were the same, another game business. I thought they probably were all businesses, so why not try each one to satisfy my curiosity. My third call was a number in California. A lady with a mature, strong eastern accent answered. "Mary Mount," she said.

Blood rushed wildly to my brain and I felt faint. "Pardon me, what did you say?" I asked excitedly.

"This is Mary Mount. May I help you?" the voice stated.

"Yes! Are you a school?" I was flustered and felt a warm flush on my face.

"We are a Junior College."

"May I ask where you are located?" I asked excitedly.

"Los Angeles," the person said.

"Oh!" was my startled reply.

Again the person asked, "Is there something I can do for you?"

"Well, I'm not sure. I'm looking for someone, but I don't know if this is the right place. Can I call you back?" I didn't know what else to say.

"Certainly. Call back anytime."

"I need your name, please."

"Sister Patricia Ilene." With that reassurance, the conversation ended.

The news was exhilarating. Filled with anticipation, I could hardly speak as I dialed Bob to give him this overwhelming piece of luck.

"Call Vern," he shouted excitedly.

When I called, Mrs. Jensen reported her husband was in Salt Lake. "Let me call his motel and leave word for him to call you."

My stomach was in my throat all day. Finally, Vern called. As I related my discovery, he cautioned me, "Don't you make one more phone call. I'm coming home and we'll talk tomorrow."

I was elated. It was the renewal I needed to keep my sanity.

I broke my promise to George when the phone numbers were revealed to Vern, but I told him I couldn't tell the source. Vern smiled and assured me it wasn't necessary.

"Be patient. This will take some time to investigate." He gave us no clues of what or how he would do it, just assurances. "Don't get your hopes too high," he cautioned.

Vern kept us informed by simply stating the investigation was proceeding and his contacts in California were handling the situation very cautiously. Days later, Vern reported personally. His kind eyes expressed disappointment. "Jan wasn't there, but don't be discouraged. Law enforcement in California are working with us and they are continuing to search. We'll find her."

18 found again!

Approximately a week later, I was doing my Saturday cleaning when the phone rang. I hurried to turn on the recorder, then picked up the receiver. A strained, quiet voice on the other end of the phone said, "Hi, Mom." I knew it was Jan.

"Jan!" I shrieked. "Honey, where are you? Oh, it's so good to hear from you." I was crying and laughing at the same time.

"Is Karen there?" Jan asked. "I want to talk to Karen."

"No, she's over at Caroline's," I reported anxiously.

"Caroline's?" There was a touch of excitement in her voice.

"Yeah. You know, just doing whatever, not much," I said, trying to be casual. With a lump in my throat, I gushed, "Oh Jan, we all miss you. How are you? The girls will be sick they missed your call. Are you okay?"

"I can't talk to you. I have to talk to Karen or Susan." She sounded strained and anxious.

"Susan is over at Cindy's, but she'll be home soon. Honey, I can't stand not knowing where you are . . . or how you are. All your friends keep asking about you. When are you coming home?"

I was trying to keep levelheaded and be wise in my choice of words.

"I don't know," she said. "I have to talk to Karen or Susan! When do you think they will be home?" She sounded very disappointed.

"Really soon. They'll be so sad to know you called and they weren't here." My heart was pounding so hard, I thought it would explode.

"Well, I've gotta go now," she said. There was a little tremor to her voice.

Panic set in. What else could I say to keep her on the line? Everything seemed so trivial.

"Jan, are you well? Are you doing okay?" I asked.

"Well, I've got to go. I really wanted to talk to them. Maybe I can call back, but I don't know," she said hesitatingly.

"Yes, honey, call back. I will have Karen and Susan come right home. They've missed you so much. You've got to call them, okay?" I begged.

"If I can . . . but I don't know. I'll see. Gotta go. See ya."

The phone clicked and the dial tone came on. Surprisingly, I didn't cry. A myriad of emotions overwhelmed me as I sat clutching the receiver stunned, grateful, confused, exasperated, and very concerned. I stared into space, thinking of every little thing that was said. *Why wouldn't she talk to me? She sounded okay, but not great. Not scared, but sad. Homesick? Maybe, but, what if she weren't?*

I dialed Bob with the news. He was ecstatic. "I'll be right home," he said.

Caroline's father said he would bring Karen home.

"Please, let Caroline come," I said eagerly.

Soon, the house was buzzing as the girls quizzed me about Jan's call. I rewound the tape and urged them to listen for themselves. Shrieks of emotion pierced the room as they listened to Jan's recorded voice.

Bob said, "Okay, that's enough. We can't tie up the recorder in case she calls back right away. So, calm down and don't get overly excited. Let's talk about what you're going to say to her."

After sufficient drilling, we huddled around the kitchen table for snacks, and waited. Karen was appointed the official phone answerer. When three fitful hours had ticked away, my faith began to waiver. But the girls felt positive Jan would call back.

The anticipated call finally came. "Hello, Karen? This is Jan! How are ya'?"

"Real good. How are you doing?" Karen asked with enthusiasm.

"I'm fine." Then, with a quivering voice, she stated, "I wanted to call and tell you I love you so much and I miss you so much." Her voice broke down and she began to cry.

Jan's emotions sparked Karen's as she began bawling too. "We miss you too and love you!"

"I just wanted to call and hear your voice," Jan blurted out.

"Susan's on the other line," Karen said. "She wants to talk to you."

"Huh?" Jan questioned, not sure she heard.

"Yeah, it's me! Hi, Jan. How are you doing?" Susan asked.

Jan squealed, "Susie! Hi. Just wanted to hear your voice. How's piano going for you?"

"Good. I've started on my festival pieces and they are hard."

Karen broke in. "Jan, you've got to come home."

"Oh, I want to, I want to come back and visit you so much. It's all up to Mom and Dad right now. Did they get my letter?"

"I don't know! I can ask Mom—she's right here," Karen stated.

"Tell her I sent her a letter and it has everything in it. It has all my reasons and explains everything. Oh, I sure love you guys. How are you, Susie Q?"

"I'm doing great, but Karen's having trouble in drill team. She needs help. If you were here, you could help her," Susan said. Her comment evoked a spark of interest.

"She needs help in drill team, huh?"

I stood in the background coaching their conversation, whispering to ask certain questions.

"Jan, you've been gone a long time. When are you coming home?" Susan said.

"It seems like forever, doesn't it? Well, I'm not going to say right now. I just had to call and tell you . . ."

Karen interrupted her by telling her the family poodle wanted to say hello. "Here she is, she has her ear to the phone. Talk to her."

Excitedly, Jan said, "Hi, Tiffy, how are you! Oh, I love you."

Karen stated, "Tiff acts like she knows it's you. She's still so cute."

"I just want to talk to you guys for a minute . . ." Jan paused.

Karen anxiously said, "Don't hang up, Jan. Caroline is here."

"Caroline's there?" Jan shrieked.

At that moment, the operator broke into the conversation and said Jan had only thirty seconds left. Jan was too emotional to let that detail interrupt her. Caroline's exclamation of "Hi Jan" brought a response from both girls.

Their weeping and wailing was deafening. The hysteria between girlfriends and sisters was a gratifying sound. I knew at that moment Jan wanted to be home. Whatever phony, wicked, and unscrupulous plan Robert had devised, he hadn't destroyed the love and devotion she felt. Jan had plenty of genuine feelings as her true emotions became ammunition for the crossfire enabling the continued conversation. The exchange of chatter was unimportant, but it verified the fact that they were all united spirit to spirit.

Jan fired off questions to them as rapidly as they did to her. She continued to express her love for each one of them as she repeated over and over, "I love you guys so much. Oh, I'm just so happy," in a quivering voice.

Again, the operator interrupted the gabfest and asked Jan if she desired to extend the call. Jan enthusiastically exclaimed, "Yes!"

I picked up an extension and was trying to listen, but there was so much crying, I couldn't hear what was being said. It was useless to try and calm any of them as they were so electrified with their reunion. Their conversation resumed after Jan deposited the needed coins.

Jan asked, "Are you guys all on the phone?"

"Yes!" they blubbered in chorus.

"So am I, Janny!" I joined in.

"How are you, Mom?" she asked.

"Great, honey. I love you."

"I love you, too. Did you get my letter?"

"No! What letter?" I asked.

"I sent you a letter. It explains a lot of things." Her voice became shaky.

"Um, when did you mail it?" I said.

"Oh, I don't know." She paused, trying to determine a date. "It should be there pretty soon."

Jan changed the subject. "I had to call and tell you all . . ." she hesitated, "and hear your voices." She was choosing her words carefully.

Karen proudly announced, "Jan, I'm going to drill team every morning. I marched in the Homecoming parade."

"I'm so proud of you," she exclaimed.

"It was really hard. I had about ten blisters on my feet," Karen complained. They all laughed.

"Do you like it?" Jan asked.

"No!" Karen stated emphatically.

"No?" Jan responded. They all chuckled again.

"Everybody misses you. They want you to be the leader. You're the best!" Karen said.

"Well, that's the breaks," Jan replied.

I jumped back into the conversation. "Janny . . . are you okay? Have you been well? I've been worrying my head off."

"Yes, I'm well. I just miss you all."

"Are you homesick?" Susan asked. "Do you want to come home?"

"Oh yes." she responded enthusiastically. "Sometimes. I'm getting by okay. I just wanted you all to know I love you." Again it appeared she was weighing her words. "Well, I've got everything in my letter."

"I wish it would come," I said.

"Relax. You'll be getting it pretty soon."

"What's in the letter?" I asked.

"Well, I'm not going to discuss much of anything. It's all in the letter."

Annoyed with my persistence, Jan asked other questions. "How's Tiffy? Has her hair grown back yet? Put Caroline back on."

Determined not to let go, I persisted. "Have you seen Robert lately?"

"I haven't talked to him for a couple of weeks. He wanted me to contact you before I called him."

"Why?" I boldly asked.

"So . . ." she paused. I thought she was being prompted. "I want you to tell him I called. Call him so he knows."

"Why does he need to know?"

"I don't know. You call him or something, and tell him I've called."

"I don't have his phone number. He's never given it to me. He always does the calling. Do you have it?" I asked.

"Well, I don't either."

Abruptly, she directed her next questions to the girls and asked about school. I allowed them to converse as I tried to plan what I should say next. She had just stated she was going to call him after her contact with us, then claimed she didn't have his number.

Karen and Susan were both getting straight A's and Jan was excited.

Jan inquired, "Is Dad there?"

"No, he had to go back to work," Susan said.

"He'll be sad he missed you!" Karen added.

"Oh, that's okay."

"He misses you and loves you desperately," I blurted out.

Jan wistfully said, "I'm glad to know I'm still loved."

The connection went fuzzy and we thought the call was over. When it cleared, Jan was trying to figure out where we had gone. She said again, "I just wanted to hear you guys. You sound so good. Just do whatever my letter says. I want to come home and see you so I can be around you. Put Caroline back on. I'm short for time."

Caroline answered her request. "I'm here, Jan."

"Oh good!" They spent a few moments chatting when the operator came back on the line. Jan began saying her good-byes and said, "I'm out of money."

"Can I send you some?" I screeched.

"I'm fine. The letter tells every way I feel. Susan, I love you, and keep up your grades."

Susan expressed her love for Jan and began weeping again. Caroline had never stopped her bawling. Karen, crying, said, "I love you, Jan."

"Karen, I love you too. Hug Tiff for me. Caroline, I love you. I love you all." Jan was sniffling.

"Please come home!" I begged.

"I want to! I'm out of money and gotta go."

The last words she said to me echoed in my ears. "I want to marry B."

A disturbing note on which to end our conversation.

The girls shouted into the phone, "Jan, come home! We love you. Hurry home!"

"Know my love, and I'll see you later," Jan shouted back as the call terminated.

The mood following the call was solemn and a time of reflection on how Jan sounded, what she said, and the uncertainty of her overall attitude. The girls expressed valuable opinions.

When Bob arrived home, we continued our discussion of how Jan seemed at times to be very excited or homesick, but when talking about the letter, her attitude was quite bold and unfriendly. Bob and I theorized that perhaps she had to be that way for the sake of whoever might have been with her.

Pete was notified. He contacted Vern Jensen and Detective Shail. The group arrived at our home a short time later. Pete brought with him the area manager of Mountain Bell, John McDonough.

Listening to the recording, George complained about the girls and their emotional outbursts. "Couldn't you make them stop? Girls, listen to how awful you sound. We can't hear what Jan is saying."

"They were so emotional and happy to hear from their sister," I said, defending their right to be noisy.

"It's okay," Pete stated. "We're glad you all got to talk to her."

All of us listened intently to the recording. My heart pounded as I again heard Jan's voice. Mr. McDonough scribbled on a piece of paper. At the conclusion, the men conversed and parts of the recording were replayed. Mr. McDonough took a black book out of his pocket while he listened closely to the sound of coins being dropped into the toll box. He had it played again.

His announcement about the number of nickels, dimes, and quarters deposited was profound. Taking a large map from his coat, he unfolded it, and placed it on the coffee table. With a pen, he drew a large circle on the map. "From the amount of money she put in, she has to be somewhere in this area."

The encircled area included parts of six states surrounding Idaho. The most significant spot that stood out was Los Angeles. The men continued to speculate over the entire circled area, discussing all possibilities that existed in any of the cities in the circle.

Leaning towards the Los Angeles area, the men decided it would be most advantageous to concentrate efforts there. Law

enforcement officers had already been contacted and if that did-
n't pan out, then other cities would be considered.

■ ■ ■

<u>Jan's Diary, October 31, 1976:</u> Wow! B just left today. He was here
this weekend and there was a lot going on at school for the big
Halloween bash. I think he felt a little left out. But he was a good
sport and just hung out so I could do some things with my friends.
I got to call home yesterday and talked to everybody except Bob.
Caroline was there. That was a big surprise! Everybody sounded
so good. It made me homesick. B told me what to say in the letter. I hope Mom understands. They have to let me go and do what
I have to do. I wonder what will happen when they read it?

■ ■ ■

Anxiety mounted as we waited for news. My thoughts ran rampant as I considered Jan being moved from one place to another.
*Who has her when Robert is in Utah? Do her captors treat her with dig-
nity?*

A week after Jan's call, her letter arrived. At Pete's request, I did-
n't open it, but called to inform him. The contents would be
inspected for fingerprints and analyzed by their agency.

Interestingly, the envelope was covered with a blitz of postal
stamps from locations around the United States and the stamps
hadn't been canceled with a date.

Shaking his head, Pete said, "He must have a string of criminal friends from every state in the Union. This was not sent through
the post office." He concluded that someone had dropped the letter in our mail box.

Later, when we were allowed to read the letter, I tossed it aside
in disgust. "When did Jan grow into an adult? Does he think we

are that naïve? Robert dictated every word of this to Jan. It's her handwriting, but not her thoughts. What an evil man."

Dear Mom:

B said he won't talk to me again until I make contact with you so I am contacting. He said you told him that you couldn't understand why I left home so I'll tell you a few of the reasons.

I was sick to death of putting on the little girl act just because its what everyone expected of me. I had all I could take of the battle between you and me over B. He had been mine from the beginning and you have no right to him. I never again want to be around a man who's either happy and loving or running around hating everyone including himself screaming and throwing fits.

I'll never come back to the fighting between you and dad. We never knew if we were going to have a home or not, or if the sheriff was going to come and take everything away for the whole neighborhood to see. I felt like an outcast in my own ward. And I was sick and tired of the bishop and Dad's relatives bugging me about someone I loved so much. Through the whole mess there was only one thing I could hang onto that was B and his love for me. To this very day I know he would die for me but more important than that he's willing to live and endure everything you and the whole world can throw upon him! He'd go through it all for me. I feel that you just want to own and control me. For what reason I can't imagine, so help me God I can't.

I begged Dad on the phone to let me just have B and be me. But he acted like I was stupid and the whole thing was a big joke. B said you told him I've never stated what I felt. I've begged and pleaded for a year to let you know how I felt and then you'd say I was acting or that I really didn't know what I wanted. I'm telling you that I do know what I want a lot more than you or dad do. I want B and I'm going to have him.

I've begged him to come and live with me. I could care less

about marriage for marriage sake. But he won't leave his business and family to risk being with me. I want you to know I blame it all on you and your jealousy and hatred. If you could learn only a little bit of the love you always claim to have, you wouldn't do this to me or B.

I would like nothing more than to start a new relationship with you on a women to women basis. Maybe then we would learn to know and enjoy each other. I would love nothing more than to be around my sisters and enjoy them during all the good times. I know we will have together in the future. However I know we will have these good times with or without you and dad.

Most of all on this earth I want to be B's wife. I will make him a good wife and our love which I know has existed forever will go on into eternity no matter what you or dad or anyone else on this earth does to us. I know this more certainly than any other thing in my life.

Please, Mom, please give me the chance I have fought so hard for and given up so much for. I have found a new life here and can find happiness of a sort, but not like I know belongs to me and B and all of you living as sensible people loving and understanding each other.

I hope you understand what I am saying. I haven't meant to hurt anyone now or in the past. But you have left me no choice if I am going to be able to live with myself.

Please do what ever needs to be done so I can return and marry B. I know life can be good for all of us and nothing has to be lost if we will give the true measure of love Christ gave to us. I pray to God you finally understand how I feel.

Love, Jan

Anxiety grew as the days passed. Finally, a bombshell exploded when we were informed that Robert had been arrested and was in a Salt Lake jail. Vern Jensen's fine detective work was passed on to federal authorities in the Salt Lake office after Vern discovered Robert was not living at his reported residence, the apartment complex. He only used the address as a front. He actually lived in his motor home at a hidden location.

The arresting officers were not certain what to expect when they approached. They had used their vehicle to gently ram his motor home. Robert had opened the door with a puzzled look on his face, surprised by the officers' intrusion. He was placed under arrest on a federal warrant for flight to avoid prosecution and for violating parole by not notifying federal authorities of his change of address. A detainer was filed in the District of Utah for probation violations.

A search of his motor home revealed a number of wigs and disguises. Among the items collected were tapes that an officer described as "strange." Unfortunately Jan's whereabouts were still unknown.

Placed in the Salt Lake Jail, Robert fought extradition to Pocatello. He denied any knowledge about Jan and proclaimed his innocence.

I couldn't believe he was in jail. In anguish I moaned, "Bob, why did they do that? Robert will never tell anyone where Jan is. What next?"

"Let's think positive. Pete and George have never stopped in their pursuit of Berchtold and they won't stop until Jan is found," Bob answered. "And I'm certain Vern has done things we will never know, he's so modest. This is progress."

Bob's confidence in the positive nature of Robert's arrest helped me cope.

Over two weeks had passed since Jan's phone call, and three days since Robert's arrest. I was suffering from great anxiety when Pete called and said with excitement in his voice, "Mary Ann, I have some news. Would you have Bob come home and I'll drop by?"

An immediate rush of adrenaline charged through me. Pete didn't use the word *good* news, so the next half-hour seemed a lifetime.

We opened the door the second he drove up. Hearing him say, "Jan's been found" brought a shriek from me and a raised fist of triumph from Bob, followed by tears and exclamations of gratitude.

"Can we sit down?" Pete asked. "I don't have a lot of details yet, but Jan was located in a private girls school in Pasadena, California. She is safe and appears to have been well cared for by a group of Catholic nuns."

Bob and I looked at each other in shocked silence.

Pete continued, "She was identified by the FBI and was going by the name of Janis Tobler. I guess they discovered her last week, but until Berchtold was behind bars, it's been a confidential matter. Sorry I couldn't tell you anything when they arrested Berchtold, but the situation was still being investigated."

"We've spent a panicked weekend. I'm without words." Bob wiped silent tears for a moment, unable to say more.

The excitement in Pete's voice kept my pulse beating fast. "Hearing that the agents who found her thought she looked healthy is good news. I guess she was scared and tried to deny her real identity, but she cried when one of the agents told her they knew who she was and that Mr. Berchtold had been arrested. She didn't react, just remained quiet. The agent I talked to said she appeared to be rather humiliated, but she wouldn't give details about how she got to the school.

"A Catholic school. Who else but Robert would have thought of it," I said, shaking my head in disbelief.

Claiming to have no further information, Pete said, "I'm not sure when she'll be home, but Detective Shail is making arrangements to fly there and get her. The sister in charge asked that Jan be allowed to stay at the school until authorities from Pocatello arrive to pick her up.

With energy drained from our limp, weak bodies, we needed strength and comfort from a greater source. Once more, we were privileged to rejoice that Jan was coming home. Certainly, complications would line our path, but we would endure. Tears of gratitude flowed freely.

Inexpressible joy had visited us again.

jan in jail

November, 1976

My thoughts raced with apprehension as Jan's circumstances were made known. It had been over
three and a half months since her disappearance. I couldn't begin
to imagine her state of mind. I was so relieved that the nuns would
take care of her until she could come back to us. I didn't want her
to have any more bad experiences in jails. I couldn't get my mind
off her; what was she thinking? What was she feeling?

■ ■ ■

*November 16, 1976 was a terrible day for Jan. Sister Charlotte called
her into her office in the morning and there were two men from the FBI waiting to talk to her. She was scared stiff. They asked what her name was and
she said "Janis Tobler." One of the men said he thought her name was Jan
Broberg and she couldn't believe it. She told him it wasn't, but they had a
report and knew exactly who she was. When the one man asked her again,
she admitted it. They said Berchtold was in jail and Jan should just tell
them what happened. She wouldn't tell them anything. Sister Charlotte*

210

talked to Jan and was very kind. She asked the agents to let Jan stay with her since she didn't want Jan going to a juvenile correction center. They agreed and left her in the care of Sister Charlotte. Later in the day, two deputies from the county sheriff's office arrived and told Sister Charlotte that they had to keep her locked up because she might run again. Her night in the detention center was horrendous. Jan didn't dare go to sleep. The other girls looked older and talked terrible, hollering at each other. They were very rough and keep asking the guards for a smoke or to bring them drugs. Some of them asked Jan why she was there. She shrugged her shoulders, avoiding conversation. A couple of girls with tattoos repeatedly threatened to beat the "s—t" out of others. The night seemed endless, a waking, living nightmare. Jan had never been so glad for daylight. When Detective Shail showed up the next afternoon, Jan was worn out, confused, full of mixed feelings. She wanted to go home, but hated to leave Flintridge. It seemed like years since she had seen her family. How would everyone treat her?

■ ■ ■

Pete came by the house on Tuesday to remove the recorder. "Are you prepared to face the press again?" he asked. "I'm preparing a news release and I expect they won't be too happy that we kept Jan's disappearance from them."

He was right. The newspaper people were miffed. Nevertheless, reporter complaints didn't change the circumstances that this had been the best way to handle an irrational, obsessed man.

The evening news was filled with Jan's second kidnapping and being found in a Catholic school. The evening journal carried the new story:

FBI FINDS MISSING BROBERG GIRL IN L.A.
BERCHTOLD ACCUSED:
CIA IMPERSONATION OCCURRED AT SCHOOL

Since we ourselves had been given scant information, we chose to ignore the blitz of phone calls. Needing all the strength we could muster, we decided to focus our energy strictly on our family.

Pete explained the legal procedure Jan would face when she returned. Because she was reported as a runaway, she would have to spend the night in jail, then appear in juvenile court before a magistrate judge who would decide her fate. Pete felt certain she would be released to us because she was a victim, not a juvenile delinquent.

Anxious for news of Jan, we sat up late awaiting word. Attempting to be calm and patient, each of us had our diversion. Karen and Susan watched TV and worked on a challenging puzzle while Bob nervously read the newspaper. I tried to read, but had no power to concentrate; my thoughts were far removed from the printed pages I absentmindedly turned. Everyone was more quiet than usual. Occasionally, a brief conversation broke the silence of the tense atmosphere.

When the minutes began ticking past midnight, we abandoned our vigil and went to bed. It hadn't been more than half an hour when the sounds of a chiming doorbell brought us to an upright position. Bob and I clamored out of bed, threw on our robes, and let Pete in.

He apologized for getting us out of bed, but knew we would want the latest news of Jan. For the first time in our two-year ordeal, Pete's vibrancy and positive attitude appeared deflated. Pete sunk into the couch, his voice weary as he related his experiences of the last few hours.

"I was at the airport shortly before eleven o'clock and drove right up to the steps of the plane after it landed in order to save Jan from the news media. Reporters were buzzing around the airport like flies. All other passengers exited before Jan and George appeared at the door of the plane. I got out of my car and waved. I think she was glad to see me from the way she descended those stairs—practically running. She flashed a forced smile and said, 'Hi Pete.' I asked her how she was and she just shrugged her shoulders. I whisked her into my car and she said, 'this isn't the same car you had the last time I was with you.' I said, 'You're right! I got a new one. How is it?' and she said, 'Okay!'"

We all chuckled at Jan's notice of something as insignificant as a different vehicle. "Sounds like she hasn't changed," Bob mused.

"Then we drove to the police station where they did a preliminary check-in. She placed a few personal possessions into a basket—she didn't have much—I think a ring and watch, maybe a little change in a coin purse, but that's about it. The officer checked it into a locker. She wasn't talkative at all. I explained what was going to happen to her and why she had to stay overnight in jail."

Pete's voice cracked as he tried to gain control. After a lengthy pause, he cleared his throat. "She didn't say anything, but just stared at me with a hauntingly wistful look. It was awful."

Pete paused for a moment. "Maybe I shouldn't say anymore. I'm sure it's not easy for you."

"No, no!" I urged. "We want to hear."

"How does she look?" Bob asked.

"Oh good, I guess. Tired, like she hasn't had much sleep. She looks the same, but her quiet demeanor bothered me. That isn't your daughter." Pete continued to review the events by constructing the last moments before knocking on our door.

"I stayed in the cell with Jan for quite awhile. I asked her if I could get her anything, if she wanted something to eat, and she shook her head no. I told her I was going by her house and tell her folks that she was back and okay. She nodded her head, but didn't say anything. I tried to think of things to say that would make her feel okay, like 'Were you treated well? How was the plane ride? Your folks are fine and really happy you're home.' But nothing seemed to affect her.

214 Mary Ann Broberg

"When I got up to leave, I asked her again if she had thought of anything I could do for her and she said she was cold and wanted a blanket. After I brought one back, she wrapped herself in it and cowered into a corner of the bed with the blanket pulled up to her neck. She was shivering a little." Pete paused. "I don't know if she was cold . . . or it was just nerves. She just sat on the bed looking forlorn and scared to death. I told her I would be back early in the morning to see her."

Pete's voice wavered as he put his hand up to stroke his chin. "I hated leaving her alone. It was like leaving my own daughter in that jail. I felt like a heel."

"It's okay; you couldn't do anything else. We're glad you were there and she could feel some encouragement," I said.

Bob added, "It's hard, but she's home. Who knows what she's gone through? And Berchtold is behind bars. What more could we ask?"

Pete pulled himself up from the couch. "I need to go and let you get some sleep. I'll be at the police station early. Don't worry about Jan. You'll hear from me as soon as I know what's happening."

As Pete went out the door, he tried to be reassuring about Jan, but feeling the pangs of this unusual night left us feeling apprehensive.

The next morning, shortly after eight o'clock, Pete called. "Jan's having breakfast—well, that is, the food is sitting in her cell. I don't think she has much of an appetite, but she's okay. I still don't know about the hearing, but I'm going to take her with me so she doesn't have to stay here. I'll bring her home when we get through."

Five hours later, Pete pulled into the driveway. I watched through the kitchen window as Jan climbed out of the car. Pangs of anxiety swelled inside my chest. She looked the same, except she was wearing a ball cap covering hair that was longer, and her clothes were unfamiliar. Most concerning was the look of complete desperation imprinted on her face; her eyes were filled with fear. I swallowed hard and told myself not to become emotional.

As Jan came through the front door, I opened my arms and scooped her into them. "Oh Jan," I cried. "I'm so glad you're back."

"Hi, Mom," Jan said quietly. She allowed me to hug her, but her posture was rigid, and she was unresponsive.

I wanted to burst into tears as I continued to hold Jan close, but I held back and just enjoyed coddling her as I had desperately yearned to do every moment for months. After releasing Jan from the bear hug, I waited for her to reciprocate. She did nothing but stare blankly. I felt awkward and wondered what to do next.

"Well," I said clumsily, "you have some new clothes."

"Yeah, I guess so."

"How are you, honey?" I asked, cautiously.

"Fine." Her voice was flat.

A small cut on the bridge of her nose was just healing over. I asked, "What happened to your nose? Looks like you ran into something."

"Oh, I was in a car accident with B. He was letting me drive when a car ran a stop sign and hit us."

I raised my eyebrows at her unexpected answer. "You were driving?"

Realizing she had just admitted to an illegal act, she looked away and pressed her lips tightly together. Turning to Pete she asked, "Is it all right if I go downstairs?"

Pete looked wryly at me and I nodded. "You're home now and your parents are in charge," he said.

Jan walked downstairs while I rolled my eyes and frowned. "Vern told us that Berchtold's car had been in an accident. What an idiot. I'm just glad she didn't get hurt."

"Thanks to Jan, we now know what kind of accident," Pete said, shifting from one foot to another. I motioned to a chair and he sat down. "How's Bob doing today?" Pete questioned.

"He's okay. We had a hard time going to sleep last night thinking about Jan being in that deplorable jail."

"I had a miserable night myself. I woke my wife up when I got home and told her I needed to talk. I was still wide awake at three this morning worrying about your daughter. Jan was pleased to see me, but complained that she didn't sleep last night either."

I heaved a heavy sigh. "She looks it. She has very dark circles under her eyes."

"Considering where she was, I didn't expect she'd get much rest. It's terrible—listening to jailbirds hollering most of the night," Pete said shaking his head. "Oh, by the way, I told Jan she will be seeing Doctor Rush for an exam tomorrow."

"What did she say to that?"

"She wanted to know why. She claims nothing has happened—that she's fine—and she doesn't want to go." Pete shrugged, pursed his lips, and shook his head.

"I wish it were true, but this time, she will get counseling immediately."

"Any ideas what counselor she will see?" Pete asked.

"No. We're going to make inquiries through my doctor. We're open to any good suggestions. I only know one child psychiatrist in Pocatello, and I'm not impressed."

"A hearing will be coming up real soon, but if she could be seen before the trial begins, it would help."

"How did Jan's court appearance go with the Judge this morning?"

"Okay. There were no surprises. He released Jan to your care with a warning for her to listen to you and he gave a lecture about why she was cited as a runaway. He was stern, but also sympathetic to her predicament."

"Anything else?" I asked.

Pete sat back on the dining room chair and took a deep breath. "Oh yes. When George picked her up in California, she was at a juvenile jail."

"She was in jail? I thought she was left at the school with the nuns."

"That was the plan. The head sister begged the FBI to leave Jan with her, and they did. But Wednesday, when the Pocatello police contacted the California sheriff's office and told them she was a runaway, a deputy went to the school and incarcerated her because they were afraid she might run. They didn't know Jan's situation. A good share of their juveniles are drug users, prostitutes, and streetwise teens who have no sympathy for anyone but themselves—lots of hardcore delinquents. George said the language from those females was worse than obscene, and he found Jan hiding in a corner of the center looking like a frightened rabbit. By then, she was quite traumatized."

Stunned, I groaned. "No wonder she looks so pathetic. Pete, I wonder why she stayed at that school so long without telling somebody who she was?"

"Brainwashing. When you find out, let me know," Pete said as he stood up and turned toward the door. "I'm going to run. Call if you have any concerns. I'll check later to see how things are going. Tell Bob I'll be by the shop and see him."

I nodded, and thanked Pete for everything.

"It's just part of my job. You guys have your hands full, but I'm glad she's back. By the way, happy Thanksgiving—again."

"This is getting to be a habit, but I promise you, this is the last time."

"I'll hold you to that promise. I hope we can keep this guy behind bars for a very long time."

missing flintridge

Jan was not easily persuaded into talking. She appeared apprehensive about anything I said, examining every word I spoke as if I were planning some type of retribution because of her absence. I hadn't planned to pressure her for details regarding the past four months. I concluded she was in shock from everything that had happened. I couldn't imagine how horrendous it had been for her.

Jan's reaction to her father was startling. She stood back several feet and would not get close to him. As he approached her, she recoiled and a look of panic crossed her face. He glanced at me with a questioning look. Bob used his good humor to lighten up the situation, and expressed his happiness at having her home. Later, he commented how frightened she was of him. "I need to give her time, but I wonder what's happened?"

Bob was extremely patient with Jan. Although she would talk to him, she did so at a safe distance. I remembered a friend of mine, who as a young adult used me as a shield whenever a male invaded her space. After Mona established my trust, she confided her experience of being sexually assaulted. We were certain that some type of sexual abuse had occurred with Jan. Hopefully, she would find the courage to reveal the extent to a confidante.

The most encouraging aspect of her homecoming was the excitement, laughter, and chatter when her sisters arrived home from school. There were no barriers.

Jan's Diary, November 18, 1976: I got home today. It feels weird. Everybody acts different and I don't want to talk to anybody except my sisters. I think Dad was going to hug me. I don't want him to touch me. I heard Pete tell Dad that B will probably be transferred from Salt Lake to our jail on Monday. I'm glad he's coming. I miss him a lot and maybe I can see him. I wish we could get married and people would stop blaming him for everything. Nobody cares how I feel. They treat me like a criminal and think I don't have feelings. I hate being here and want to go back to Flintridge. I wonder what the Sisters told my friends about me leaving?

The following day, I suggested Jan call Flintridge and let them know she was home. Her personal belongings were there and the staff needed to know what to do with them. Jan shrugged her shoulders, lowered her eyes and didn't answer.

I said, "If you don't, I will. I'm not going to ask them any questions, but they need your address. Do you want to talk?" Jan shook her head and retreated to the living room.

Sister Charlotte answered the phone. The moment I opened my mouth, I found myself emotional. "This is Jan Broberg's mother—uh, you know—Janis Tobler?"

The sister greeted me warmly and asked how Janis was doing. My voice trembled and I began to cry. "I don't know how to adequately express our overwhelming joy, but we are so indebted to all of you. The Lord heard our pleadings and allowed her to find refuge with you. You are the miracle we prayed for. Please let the others know of our deepest gratitude."

After Sister Charlotte expressed concern for Jan and sympathy to us, she conveyed her feelings and that of her coworkers. "Janis is a fine girl. She has been exceptional while with us. Not only is she a good student, but she has a great rapport with her peers. She has always been thoughtful and kind to everyone. We will miss her."

"I'm pleased to hear that. Jan is a wonderful daughter and we are so grateful to have her home. Mr. Berchtold has been a major problem to our family for quite some time, but hopefully, he is out of our lives and things will be better for all of us."

"I understand this wasn't the first time. May God bless all of you, and please, give Janis our love."

Little by little we were informed of Robert's situation. After he learned that Jan had been discovered, he admitted to parole violation by leaving Utah without permission. He had tried to convince a federal judge that he traveled to Phoenix on business and had made two trips to Los Angeles in a desperate effort to convince Jan she should return home. They didn't buy his story. Idaho would be given first chance on new charges and then he would have to deal with charges on the federal detainer.

Robert didn't fight extradition and was moved to Pocatello on a first degree kidnapping charge with bond set at $500,000. If bail were raised on the kidnapping charge, the federal detainer would not allow the county sheriff to release him from jail. He would stay put.

Later, Robert was charged by a United States Marshal for impersonation of a CIA agent. A federal warrant was filed against him out of California. The bond charge for that offense was $5,000.

Over the next few weeks, Jan began to reveal events which occurred at Flintridge. Exposed to a new life outside her guarded small town culture proved to be an education in itself. Theater and drama were an important part of the curriculum and Jan enjoyed these classes the very most. Following Christmas holidays, the theater students were traveling to New York for a workshop and Jan had been planning to go. She expressed disappointment over the change of plans. Among her drama classmates was Melissa Sue Anderson of *Little House on the Prairie* fame.

I thought, *Berchtold certainly knew what he was doing when he found this hideaway. Jan is enthralled.* We recognized that after months of exposure to an unaccustomed lifestyle, Jan wasn't emotionally ready to face school or peers. Talking about returning to junior high frightened her. Recovery was necessary, but it would take time. I discussed the need for counseling with her. She begged us to send her back to Flintridge. She insisted that the sisters at the school didn't want her to leave and most of them were already counselors. The diversity of classes at Flintridge was far different than classes at Franklin and she was doing excellent school work. Why should she have to change?

We hadn't entertained the thought of her returning, and a private Catholic school was out of the question. However, Bob diplomatically stated, "Let us think about it, Jan. I want to do what is best for you and our family."

Jan's Diary, December 15, 1976: I've been thinking about Flintridge today. I want to go back. I remember when all the freshman got assigned a senior for a big sister, and I got Sharlene. She had blonde hair and was really tall. Our big sisters took us places and were supposed to look out for us. But all Sharlene wanted to do was party and make out. That college party she took me to was crazy. Some creepy guy kept following me around. He was drunk and was acting weird. I thought he was going to attack me so I crawled behind a garbage can on the patio and put the lid in front of me so he couldn't see me. I stayed there for hours so he couldn't find me. Sharlene finally came out of the house, but was drunk. I thought we were going to wreck before she got me back to the school. When I told B, he wanted to tell Sister Charlotte, but I didn't want him to. I'd get in trouble with Sharlene if she found out I squealed on her. I miss my friends at Flintridge. I know my parents are going to make me go back to school here, but I feel like a dodo.

We sought advice from our physician, and presented him with Jan's plea. The good doctor stated, "What would it hurt for her to go back there—now that Berchtold is out of the picture?"

"But," I replied, "it's a Catholic school. Would you send one of your Mormon daughters there?"

"I might, if I thought it was best for them. I worry about Jan's reputation among her peers. There's a lot of information that will be brought out in the trial which could damage her. People are cruel, especially kids."

"We know that," Bob replied, "but Jan is too vital to our family circle. We want her to feel secure and loved no matter what comes out. I can't let her go back there."

I nodded my head in agreement. "I think Jan has to face what has happened and as much as we don't like it, pay the consequences. What we need is a good psychiatrist. Do you have any recommendations?"

We were given the name of Dr. Smith, a child psychiatrist in Salt Lake City. I called immediately and scheduled the first appointment for mid-December.

Jan didn't lack for things to do; she kept busy with projects. She also went to the floral shop with Bob and began helping make small Christmas arrangements under her father's tutorship. She seemed proud of her accomplishment.

Occasionally, she asked about Berchtold. I didn't have any news. A hearing was scheduled for the first week of January. Jan asked if she would see him. I nodded.

A box arrived via Greyhound bus containing Jan's possessions from Flintridge. She unpacked a school uniform consisting of a plaid skirt, white blouse, and blue blazer, then a small TV/radio.

Seeing the TV, I pointed to it. "Oh, I found a ticket for this in Robert's car at the Salt Lake airport, most likely the weekend he brought it to you."

Jan glared at me and said nothing. Among the few items in the box were some beads. I picked them up and said, "These are a bit strange. Did you wear them?"

"No," Jan said. "They are rosary beads." She took them from my hands and placed them on her dresser. "They have a special meaning to me. I don't think you would understand."

Wow, I thought, I better learn more about the Catholic religion so I know what's tucked away in my little girl's brain.

Jan wanted to do something nice for all the sisters at Flintridge. The next few weeks found her sewing kitchen aprons and pot holders for each sister. She carefully cut characters and flowers from old greeting cards, placed them on bars of soap, then dipped them in wax to preserve the emblems. For each of her close friends she hand-strung and tied a necklace of colorful wooden beads. After attaching special notes of love, gratitude, and good cheer, Jan carefully wrapped each gift in festive Christmas paper and packaged them for mailing. Now this seemed more like our old Jan. Our hopes soared.

struggles

Jan's complaints about not sleeping were verified by the dark circles under her eyes. Realizing she had good reason for insomnia, I longed for the chance to bear some of her heavy burdens. One night I made a goodnight visit and found her crying. She said she had bumped her shoulder sharply on the corner of her hanging bench. "That hurt," she complained, rubbing her bony shoulder. Seeking pity, she continued, "I'm hungry, but nothing sounds good, and I think I'm getting sick. My throat is sore."

I listened to her pitiful lamentations, wondering what she was really crying about. I expressed sympathy for her supposed illness, offering to get her an aspirin, then inquired tenderly, "and what else hurts, honey?"

She turned away and began to sob mournfully. "Oh, I miss B so much I can hardly stand it."

I gathered her frail body into my arms and cradled her close. The sobs increased.

"What am I going to do?" she asked. "I can't eat. I can't get excited about Christmas. I can't sleep. I just worry about him. If I could just talk to him. I was so close to him the other day, yet I couldn't tell him how I felt or ask how he was. I can't stand it."

It was hard to comprehend her agonizing plea, but remembering being manipulated myself helped me understand. I had to temper my anger and listen to her pathetic cry for help.

"Could I write to him or just do something?"

"No, that isn't allowed," I replied.

She cried for several minutes as I held her in my arms and stroked her hair. I felt helpless. It would be two more weeks before her appointment with the psychiatrist. *What is the key to unlocking her mind and removing Berchtold from her life?* I wondered. His control over Jan was frightening.

"Jan, I'm going to get you a tranquilizer. It should help you calm down."

As she gulped the pill down with some water, I studied her swollen red eyes. This was the first time she had shown any real feelings over the past three weeks. Bob and I wondered if she had an emotional system left.

Sitting on the bed next to her, I begged, "Honey, whatever is inside you, please get it out. I want to help you, but you have to talk. Cry . . . scream . . . holler . . . anything—but get it out."

Again, she broke into heartrending sobs as I tenderly embraced her. My own emotions began working their way to the surface. This was the first time she had allowed any affection between us.

"He's such a part of me . . . I don't think I can stand . . ." she paused for a few moments. "I just want to prove to you that I can."

"Can what, honey?"

"Be a good wife and mother," she blurted out.

"Oh!" I said in surprise. It felt like a knife had pierced my heart. "I know you can and will be one of the best. No one in this whole world has more to give than you."

Her voice raised in exasperation. "How come you wouldn't . . ." She broke into sobs again. "When will B get out of jail?"

I shook my head. Groping, I asked, "Jan, do you believe the Lord loves you?"

She didn't answer.

"I know He does. You need to pray for strength to endure whatever is coming."

Jan didn't acknowledge my advice. "But Mom, I don't want to have a trial here. Not for B or me or any of us. All those people in court want to have it here. Will they?"

"I don't know. There has been some talk about moving it to another county, but I don't know." I knew the prosecution was fighting to keep it in Bannock County while the defense felt Robert wouldn't have a fair chance here.

Her lamentations continued. "Oh, I miss him. I just want to know that he's all right."

Little sobs were catching in her throat from the upheaval of her long outburst. Her sporadic sobs were the only sound in the quiet night as she sat on my lap holding a handful of tissues. Occasionally, she blew her nose. The medication was beginning to calm her down.

In a forlorn, whisper, she said, "This room is sometimes the happiest place in the whole world and sometimes the most sad. I wonder how it can be so lonely?" Answering her own question, she replied, "I guess because it's so far away from the rest of the house."

She slid from my lap onto her bed, lying face down on the pillow. I looked around the room at her mementos and personal possessions. I thought, *B helped build this room. Does it remind her of him? Probably. We need to redecorate it real soon.*

I began rubbing Jan's bony back, massaging her neck and shoulders. She began to relax. I patted her gently and said, "I'll be right back."

I raced upstairs, pulled a heavy quilt out of the linen closet, picked up Tiffy and hurried back down to her room. Jan snuggled the dog as I covered them. Bending down to kiss her, she said, "Thanks Mom, I love you."

"I love you too, sweetie. Are you going to be okay?"

She nodded drowsily.

"Sleep tight," I whispered.

I wearily climbed the stairs, heartsick and concerned for Jan's mental well-being. I choked back feelings of sadness and despair. Kneeling at the side of my bed, I prayed for courage and wisdom.

Our first trip to see Dr. Smith was a two-day session. Jan refused to talk to him, but he wasn't bothered. He remarked he was used to the "cold shoulder" of young people. We faithfully attended weekly appointments. Dr. Smith met with each of us separately.

Early into the therapy sessions, Dr. Smith asked for our approval to contact a child psychologist who worked for the Salt Lake school system. He knew Donna Carr was competent with her testing of children who suffered with emotional problems. Jan protested, but I agreed to having her evaluated. Jan met with the pleasant, attractive woman in a regal home on South Temple. The four-hour testing brought encouraging news.

"Mr. and Mrs. Broberg, are you familiar with art therapy?" Ms. Carr asked. Our response was negative. "I had Jan do some art work for me. Let me show you some of the pictures I asked her to draw. Disturbed children, or those whom have been severely abused, draw images in their pictures which show a lot of violence, anger, hurt and distrust."

She showed us a few frightening examples.

"In contrast," she said, "Here is one of Jan's pictures."

She handed us a simple drawing. As we looked at the picture Ms. Carr proceeded, "I asked her to draw a picture of her family and how she sees them. She could draw anything she wanted. It was all up to her. Now, look how she drew her family. Do you see anything abnormal?"

Bob and I studied the picture Jan had drawn. We both said, "No."

Ms. Carr explained her perception from the sketch. "First of all, Jan has put an apron on you, Mrs. Broberg, cooking in the kitchen, and you, Mr. Broberg, have a newspaper in your hand. Her sisters are holding some items too—a book, a doll—and Jan drew herself carrying pom-poms and dressed in—oh, probably her drill team outfit. Everyone has a smile on their face. Take note of the roof she has drawn to put all of you together in the house, even your dog. I find that very significant as to the way your daughter feels about her family. She feels you belong together."

The session rejuvenated us. Keeping her home with us was the right decision. Bob never doubted. Although that news was positive, there were still lots of hurdles to jump with Jan's emotions. Church attendance was one. Jan attended church with us for the first few weeks, then began resisting. We decided not to push and gave her a reprieve.

After a two-week vacation, Bob and I decided it was time for her to return. I awakened the girls to prepare themselves for church, but Jan didn't appear. Ten minutes later, I called to her again.

"I'm not going to church. I'm Catholic now," she called back.

That wasn't the answer I expected. I tore down the steps angrily and screamed, "Get out of that bed and get ready for church. Whether you are Catholic or not, you are going to church with us."

My response scared me. I felt awful, but didn't apologize.

The following day, I called Dr. Smith expressing frustration for losing my temper. "She's the victim," I reasoned. "Talking to her about 'this new religion' would have been more civilized. I really blew it."

Dr. Smith asked, "How long was she angry at you?"

"For about an hour after we got home," I answered.

"Is that all? Did she say anything else to you?"

"No, everything seemed fine after that."

"Good. You did the right thing. Next week, you might need to go through it again. First of all, you are the parents and she lives in your home. She needs to know you have rules and that there are benefits for following them and consequences for breaking them. She may be angry for awhile, but she'll realize you have her best interest at heart. We'll talk about it when you come for your session this Thursday."

The light turned on. I knew why he was making Jan sit through those long, unresponsive sessions. It was as though the rule was to meet with Dr. Smith, but she could choose how to respond when she was there. Jan had her agency and she chose not to speak to him. But she was showing up for her appointments, and he claimed that was the most important thing and that progress was being made. We hoped so. The bill was mounting and our health insurance would not pay for it.

It was nearly Christmas. Jan and I spent two hours at the flower shop helping with the Christmas rush. Afterwards, we hurried to Grand Central to pick up a few last minute gifts, before picking up the girls from school.

Bob and I were hosting the first stop of a progressive dinner. It was late when we arrived home from the last stop for the dinner. The kitchen sink was full of dirty dishes. It was nearing one o'clock when I crawled into bed between cool cotton sheets and warm blankets. I had just begun to drift off when I was suddenly aware of a presence in the room. As I attempted to awaken and come to my senses, I heard a desperate plea.

"Mom, please . . . help me!" The words were choked with alarming emotion.

I opened my eyes to see Jan standing by my side. Startled, I sat up in bed and exclaimed, "Jan? Are you sick? What's the matter?"

She looked terrified. Sobbing, she responded in a mournful voice, "Oh Mom, I hurt so bad. I don't know what to do. Tell me what to do."

The cries I heard were not of physical pain, but the agony of a tortured mind. She sunk down to the floor. I reached out and cradled her head in my hands as she knelt next to me.

"Jan, honey, I'm here. Let me help you," I said desperately.

By this time, Bob had raised his head. "What's the matter? What's going on? Is Jan sick?" he questioned.

The crying was so painful, I felt frantic. Tears flooded down Jan's cheeks as she began to sob. "I don't know," she blurted out. "I just feel awful."

I tried pulling her up off her knees and into bed, but she resisted and sternly retaliated, "No! Leave me alone!"

"Jan, I want to help you. Just crawl in here and talk to me."

Bob quietly said, "I'll go sleep in the den. Jan, you stay here with your mother. Call me if I'm needed."

He slipped down the hall and I slid over to make room for Jan. She quickly crawled into bed and continued her deep convulsive sobs. Her small body trembled and heaved from the tremendous emotional outburst. Lying in the dark, I wondered what torment she had endured through the recent months of separation, let alone the experience of being torn from her family two years ago. She accepted my gentle pats on her tiny arm. Eventually, I wrapped my arms around her shaking form, clutching her until the sobs dissipated into tiny shivers.

She began to talk. She rehashed her feelings for Berchtold. They hadn't changed from two weeks ago—as much as I prayed for that miracle. She was missing him and afraid of what was going to happen to him. Jan was afraid for herself, unsure of her friends and how they felt about her. She wanted to return to Flintridge where she was accepted.

We talked for nearly an hour with my arms tightly around her.

I periodically brushed back tears—sometime hers, sometimes my own. Finally, exhaustion took over. As she began to relax, I thought of the heavy burdens she yet had to face. I peered at her small face lying on my pillow, and watched as she gradually slipped into a restful breathing cycle, and fell asleep.

The clock glared 3:15 A.M. I was wide awake. My mind wouldn't turn off. I kept thinking about the things Jan had said. Tears ran off my face and buried themselves in my pillow. I felt grossly inadequate in helping my little girl find peace of mind. Silently praying, I begged, *Please, grant me greater understanding. I hurt so much for her. I don't know how to help her.*

We were both exhausted in the morning. Knowing something had brought her into our room during the night, I prodded. "What frightened you last night, Jan?"

Her eyes glassy from lack of sleep, Jan said, "I don't know, but I hate my bedroom. I can't sleep there any longer."

"Okay, let's move you upstairs. You can sleep in Susan's trundle bed until we transform the den into your new bedroom. Will that help you sleep?"

A look of relief spread over her face; her big blue eyes danced with excitement. "That's great!" She dashed down the steps, loaded her arms with belongings, and delivered them to Susan's room.

My numb brain flashed, *You idiot! She tried telling you two weeks ago. Open up your mind to every word she says. You need to listen more carefully!* Jan never returned to sleep in her bedroom and never visited the room unless someone was with her.

Jan continued to keep space between herself and father. It was hard on him. He had always had a close relationship with his daughters, which included warm hugs and goodnight kisses, but now he realized she needed time. He would have to be patient and wait for her to invite a renewal of his fatherly affection.

With friends telephoning and making visits to our home, Jan's confidence was bolstered and she felt acceptance. Her friends in drill team encouraged her to come back and assured her that she was needed. We felt that our prayers had been answered as we observed her fitting back normally with her peer group. As we watched the interaction between them, we felt that Jan could return to her own junior high school after New Years. Flintridge was no longer an option.

"Dr. Smith said young people have the vibrancy to bounce back and throw off a lot of baggage," Bob reasoned. "I know Jan's dynamic spirit and she can do it. Our job is to keep her focused and positive."

The day following Christmas, George Shail called to express disappointment about a basket Jan had delivered to the county jail for Berchtold.

"Please, tell her she can't do that."

"What was in the basket? No file, I hope," I said jokingly, trying to hide my dismay.

He didn't think my comment was funny. "No, just a bunch of little nonsense items and notes. But criminy, doesn't she realize what kind of a jerk he is?"

"I wish she did, George. But Jan still thinks he's wonderful and continues to express love for him. Dr. Smith said this is a complicated matter which will take time, and we're dealing with it the best we can. I thought she understood there was to be no contact with him. We'll talk with her again."

We didn't want to add fuel to a flame we couldn't quench, but again we told her there was to be no contact. "I wanted B to know I still believe in him and he shouldn't give up," she said.

January 2, 1977

A day before the hearing, two sisters from Flintridge Academy arrived in Pocatello. They had been subpoenaed to appear as witnesses for the prosecution. Upon arrival, they telephoned asking for a visit with our family; they were most anxious to see Jan.

We graciously received them at our home and enjoyed their good humor and warmth. Jan particularly liked the fuss they made over her. Sister Maria and Sister Ramona extended greetings from many of the students and sisters from the school and many thanks for her thoughtful Christmas packages. The interaction was fun to observe.

Sister Maria admitted she had negative thoughts about us when Jan's true identity was discovered. "I believed Mr. Tobler, rather Mr. Berchtold, to be a perfectly wonderful man. I wouldn't accept the fact that he was not Janis's father and he'd been lying. I believed every word he said. I thought, Why would this lovely girl go with this fine man unless she had a terrible home life? I needed to meet you and apologize for my error."

"Believe me, it's understandable how you drew those conclusions. You needn't apologize. We believed a lot of things too. He's a master of deceit," Bob said.

Sister Ramona explained her position. "He was such a friendly, likeable person. We enjoyed having him come to visit because he made us all laugh and feel good. He always had a good story to tell. He used the office phone on several occasions to call President Ford. We thought they were close friends because he always addressed him as Jerry."

Feeling their embarrassment, we didn't comment.

"When the FBI told us who he was, I replied, 'You're wrong. It couldn't be him. You have the wrong man.' It took Sister Charlotte and those officers explaining what he had already done to convince me they had the right man," Sister Marie said sheepishly.

"We're so grateful to you for providing Jan a safe retreat," I said.

"I thought the worst. But you know, I had a strong premonition that Jan was in a private school and spent a lot of time researching and writing letters. I must admit, a Catholic school would be the last place I would have imagined."

Sister Ramona must have sensed my concern about Jan being indoctrinated with Catholicism as she explained a recent encounter: "I sat next to a Mormon on the plane today. I asked him a question about your religion and the fact that there are so many in Salt Lake City. He took the opportunity to not only answer my question, but gave me a great deal of information—in fact, more than I wanted. He finally asked if I wanted to have your missionaries visit me." She threw back her head and laughed heartily, causing us all to chuckle.

Sister Maria remarked, "I thought it odd when Janis first came that she never crossed herself when we prayed." Looking at Jan, she said, "Remember? You didn't do that, Janis." Jan nodded in agreement. "Her father, I mean Mr. Berchtold, said she was a very good Catholic. I thought maybe she was just out of practice."

"Shortly after Janis came to the Academy, I was passing through the chapel and found her sitting all alone," Sister Ramona said. "She was crying so I stopped to talk with her and asked if she wanted to talk. She began to sob and put her face into my robe. She said to me, 'I feel awful! I miss my family so much and I'm homesick.' She cried her heart out while I sat there patting her. The poor child. Of course, I thought she was grieving her mother's death and missing her father who was on assignment, so I cried too. There wasn't much I could do except offer my sympathy and keep her busy."

I became teary as I listened to the pathetic incident and was thankful Jan had felt a longing for home.

Sister Maria turned to Jan and asked, "How long did you intend to keep up this false pretense?"

Jan looked as if she had been slapped across the face and fled the room. We looked at one another uneasily.

"Oh dear. Maybe I shouldn't have said that, but Janis has to face the fact that she was living a lie," Sister Maria exclaimed.

I nodded at both the sisters. "We agree and are hopeful her appointment with a psychiatrist will help us understand what's going on. She won't talk about anything that has to do with Mr. Berchtold. She keeps telling us we won't understand."

"It may help you to know that Janis had become resistant to going with Mr. Berchtold the last few visits he made to the Academy," Sister Ramona said. "She preferred to stay at school with her friends and participate in the activities. I guess you know he's rather persuasive. I heard him tell Janis that he came a long way just to see her and he hoped he was more important than her friends. She didn't want to hurt his feelings so she would give in and go with him. I thought she was finally getting past her homesickness."

"The last weekend he was there, Janis gave him the school calendar of forthcoming events and told him to wait until Thanksgiving for his next visit," Sister Maria said. "He didn't seem too pleased when he left. I felt sorry for him because he made such an effort to do a lot of nice things for Janis when he came."

"Berchtold *would* be very unhappy if Jan put him off. He's the type of person who has to be in control. He becomes very disgruntled if things don't work out his way. We saw a lot of that, didn't we, Mary Ann?" Bob asked.

The sisters spent over an hour at our home and shared more of their experiences with Robert. Both were astounded at the roll of money he always flashed when paying for Jan's school fees.

Jan returned to the living room, quiet, and cold. However, it was impossible for her sullen demeanor to linger with these two delightful sisters recalling pleasant experiences they had with her at Flintridge. Soon Jan joined with them in relating some of their more comical fiascos. I had always imagined Catholic sisters to be somber and reserved, but these ladies changed my entire perception with their entertaining tales and good humor.

The time slipped away quickly and the sisters expressed thanks for our hospitality and wished us well at the hearing. They both were looking forward to seeing Mr. Berchtold in court and under oath. They expressed their disgust regarding his deceitful lies at the expense of "darling Janis" and the humiliation of their school.

Bob, serving as chauffeur and accompanied by Jan, returned the sisters to their motel. Their visit seemed to be a turning point for Jan. The positive notes and messages they presented Jan from faculty and friends telling how much she was loved, boosted her self-esteem. Jan recognized that she was still valued even though her Flintridge experience was marred by deceit.

January 3, 1977

The preliminary hearing ran four days, with several witnesses for both the prosecution and the defense. Jan's testimony was least damaging to Berchtold from the prosecution's list of witnesses. She claimed she left willingly and Berchtold did not kidnap her.

Berchtold's newest attorney filed a motion to dismiss the charge, asserting there was not sufficient probable cause to bind the defendant over for trial because of the total and complete lack of evidence from Jan's testimony. The judge refused, citing there was plenty of evidence from the police, FBI, Catholic sisters and us for him to face trial on a felony charge of first degree kidnapping. We were relieved to hear the decision, but Jan was upset. She didn't want a trial, hoping normality could somehow be restored in her tumultuous life. However, no matter what the trial might bring us, Robert needed to be punished by the law. Jan would not be a good witness.

Shopping at Albertsons had to stop since the County Jail was across the street. Through the open windows, a passerby could hear prisoners whistling or hollering for attention. Although Robert couldn't hurt us, it was eerie knowing he could be peering at us through the barred windows.

In the middle of January, Berchtold passed four handwritten letters to a former cellmate and asked him to deliver them personally to Jan. Instead of doing as instructed, the guy gave them to his girlfriend, telling her to see that Jan got them. She told her sister about the letters, who in turn disclosed the secret to their mother. The girl's mother confiscated the letters, reported the incident to the police and turned them over.

Two other letters were already in our possession; one that had been sent to Flintridge, and the second dropped in our mailbox with no postage. How many others reached Jan, we didn't know. Pete told us to safeguard the letters and present them as evidence when we went to trial.

The letters contained passages of undying love and devotion which an appropriate-age sweetheart or lover would cherish. But the object of this sick, depraved man's love was a young girl who remained his innocent victim.

Hi Darling,

I awoke this morning thinking of you as usual and loving you even more. I remembered you in Oliver and the night you cried when you sang "Where Is Love" especially for me. Honey, remember the song from Oliver "As Long As He Needs Me" and the meaning it had in the play. Please honey, sing it over and over and know I need your love more now than anything on this earth. Remember the movie we saw One Flew Over The Coo-Coo Nest. I have been placed in exactly those same circumstances. Only your love can save me. Evil forces would like nothing more than to destroy us and ruin everything. Please darling, don't fail me. Every great event on this earth has been met with evil. Christ himself had to suffer prison and death to accomplish his work. Each apostle was imprisoned then killed by man. Now they would do that to us. I can do no more than love you every minute of my life. This I can do easily. The rest is up to you. I know you love me to with the same love. We have endured so much. I am prepared to endure whatever comes because I look forward to the day all will be made right and beautiful. No matter how dark things look, it all has a purpose. It is you that taught me to believe. Honey, I do! I have so many wonderful memories of good times with you. I live with them daily, it brings you so close to me and gives me so much joy. I always look to the future and how marvelous it will be when the trial is over and there is just you and me, then the special someone who will be added. As soon as I can I will tell you all the wonderful things I have to tell you. Until then be brave do everything right and don't give up hope. I never will because thru it all there is you.

Forever -B-

Hi My Ephnot:

   Read then destroy!!! I love You!!!

   I remembered today our trip to Monterey as you drove along the coast hiway. It was so beautiful as the sunset set over the ocean. We would rise above the clouds, the golden sun turning the fluffy floor of clouds all shades of pink and gold. It was a horrible hiway but so beautiful to be with you and watch as you guided the car in and out of the cliffs. I love you so very, very much for all you mean to me. Honey I would like to have you answer some questions for me when you write. Did you get all your stuff back from California? The JVC, all your stuffed animals, bowling ball, etc. What did you do from the time you got back until you started school? Are they making you see a shrink? What is your life at home now? Have your parents improved any? Also I need to remind you of a few things. Remember rule number one. Be careful about any male relationships. Be careful in your contacts with the Church. I have joined the Catholic Church! I hope you still feel as close to the sisters as ever. Is it possible for you to attend the Catholic Church here? We have a time period now to get thru. It can't be more than sixteen months! What happens between now and then I don't know. Just have faith that after this period of testing then all will be made right again. Everything will be so great when we are together again. There is so much I want to do, motor bike riding, boating, hang gliding, snowmobiling, skiing. I want to travel all over the world with you and enjoy every country and people and adventure it has to offer. I want a beach house in California to go with the cabin in Jackson so we can have the best of summer and winter as we want to. Oh just being with you will be so wonderful. I dream of evenings by a glowing fire. You are curled up on a rug studying the script of a new movie they want you to do. I am working hard on another book. I look up from the typewriter to study the firelight dancing in your beautiful eyes. You smile and wink at me. That's all we need between us to know the world and more belongs to us because we have succeeded where no one else could have stood the test. We know our love was created for such a super special reason and because of this we are blessed above all men. I know we can do it honey. Believe and be brave.

Forever -B-

Hi Love,

I finally got the book Freckles from the library; your right it is great. I know when I first read it when I was ten, it was you I had in my heart as I lived that beautiful story. Honey read page 200 and know I know that is the way you feel and always will. I hope I can live to be worthy of that. I read your letters many times each day for strength. You always were the strongest one. When I get discouraged I always think what would Jan tell me to do. So I get busy with one of the things on the list you sent in the Christmas package and I always feel better. What would I do without you? Without your love? I LOVE YOU SO VERY

MUCH. *Have you heard from Zada? Did you know she is back at her old job. I got a letter from Sister Charlotte. She said to let you know everything is happening for our good and you are doing everything right. She said to tell you to have faith that by the time you are sixteen everything will be made right if we both do what we know is right!!! I work everyday to be more worthy of you and your love. Each night I pray for you and that all your hardships and heartaches will be made easier. Please write me honey. Either to our attorney or like the mailman will tell you. Life would be so much easier if I again could receive word from you. I love you so very, very much and live for the time we are together again. I live just for you.*

-B-

We only had knowledge of one letter Jan had written to Berchtold which the police intercepted:

Dearest B,

Hi! I know that your trying to send letters to me still but please don't. I'm afraid if you keep trying to send them it will get you into a whole bunch of trouble and I don't want that at all for you! So since I think its almost impossible for you to get your letters to me, don't do it. I don't want you to get in any trouble. I hope that you know it doesn't matter. Save your letters and give them to me later. I guess that our brain waves must be on the same frequency because I know how much you love me and how much you appreciate my letters. You don't have to tell me on paper. I take pleasant thoughts of you into my dreams every night and I know that you do too. Our thoughts are on the same path. I know that you love me and you know that I love you. Everything will work out, but don't get yourself in any more trouble. I know what your letters would say anyway.

I flunked my science test but I did ok on my Spanish one. I'm helping with the drill team and of "course" it's "improving"!! Thanks for trying. Know that I love you. Keep well for heavens sake. "Be Good." Keep Smiling.

Love, your Dolly

It was a relief to find her letter contained no startling news. Typically, it sounded like Jan. We didn't like what she wrote, but we could live with it. If we could only keep Berchtold away from her, surely she could be a teenager again and resume her normal life.

fire!

January 24, 1977

Slowly, and with much effort, we were attempting to recapture a normal routine in our home one day at a time. One evening we were in the midst of having family home evening (a weekly Mormon tradition) when the telephone rang. A male on the other end asked to speak with Mr. Broberg.

"I've got to run down to the store," Bob stated. "That was a guy from across the street from our store who said all the window lights are out. He just noticed they're off and thought it looked like smoke in the window."

"Hope everything's okay. Hurry back," I said grimacing.

Bob grabbed his parka and zipped it up. "I won't be long. We'll finish home evening when I get back. Save me some dessert. I hope it's something nice and hot; it's so cold tonight," he commented, dashing out the back door.

The rest of us continued our Scrabble game. Bob had been gone about fifteen minutes when I heard a siren. A wave of uneasiness swept over me as I thought the worst. It wasn't long before the phone rang. Picking up the receiver, Bob's frantic voice boomed out, "Our store is on fire!"

His words were inconceivable. I didn't want to believe it. "Bob?" I said, faintly.

"Fire engines are on the way! Don't come down. Stay there with the kids." In the distance, I could hear more sirens screeching out.

"Where are you?" I asked.

"Across the street, at the Loan Company. Honey, I have to go. There's a policeman wanting to talk to me. I need to leave right now. Fire engines are on the way!" he repeated.

The girls had come into the kitchen realizing something was wrong. Stunned, I blurted out, "Our store is on fire!"

Immediately, Jan became hysterical. "Oh no! It's my fault! I knew something would happen! It's my fault!" She was jumping around the room in a fury.

"Jan! Calm down. How could it be your fault? We don't even know what's going on."

Her gyrations continued as she ran into the dining room and the frenzy in her voice escalated.

Anxious, but uninformed, I began calling family. I couldn't tell them anything except what I heard from Bob. For twenty minutes, I kept telling the girls to be calm while I paced back and forth listening to one siren after another piercing the night air. Jan's fearful behavior persisted. Finally, I could no longer contain the suspense.

"Okay, get yourselves ready. Wear hats and gloves. Let's go see what's going on."

As I pulled out of our driveway, we could see pillars of smoke billowing into the crisp January night. I parked and we saw flames shooting from the building! It was bitter cold as we made our way towards the store. Water hoses, fire trucks, police vehicles and barriers filled the street. Firemen stopped us from proceeding farther.

Determined to get closer, I grabbed Susan's hand. "Come on, girls. Come this way," I cried out, pointing down an adjoining street. Jan and Karen followed as we ran down the block to find a different path towards the store. Circling the block, we ran to an alley which would lead us across the street from our store. Fire hoses were all over the place. In the dark, we were able to make it onto the street without interference. We nearly collided with Bob who was standing on the sidewalk, helplessly watching our business being consumed by flames. He appeared relieved to see us, but was grief stricken. I grabbed onto his arm, shaking my head, unable to speak.

"Well, Mary Ann, is this the final chapter?" he asked.

I didn't know what to say. We stood gaping at the inferno with our mouths open.

We huddled together and Bob remarked, "We're together and that's all that matters. Things have been worse."

"Do you know what happened?" I asked.

"Two employees at First Security Loan noticed the window lights were out at about 7:30 tonight. After looking at the store for a few minutes, they thought they saw smoke in the front windows. That's when they called me. Before I got here, they had already called the police. Two detectives investigated and discovered the back door was open with the doorknob and dead bolt laying on the ground. The smoke was so heavy they couldn't go in. They think someone broke into the store and set it on fire."

As we stood in the sub-degree temperature, the cold nipped at our fingers and toes. Bob motioned to the loan office in back of us. "They invited me to go in and watch from inside. Why don't you and the girls go in there? I'll come in a few minutes."

We retreated into the office to warm up, but I couldn't stay inside long, not without Bob. I again ventured into the cold night to stand near him while we watched tenants of adjoining businesses removing filing cabinets, desks and other items from their establishments in an valiant effort to save whatever they could.

Confusion prevailed, and many people were mulling around in the street. Curious onlookers stopped to ask questions. Among the observers was a young black man whose curiosity was so intense Bob was suspicious.

Pete Welsh appeared at the scene. Aghast at the destruction, he expressed sympathy.

"Berchtold's behind this," I said. "I don't know how, but I know he's the instigator."

Bob nodded in agreement and told Pete about the black man.

Pete acknowledged our accusation. "Go down to the police station in the morning and look at some mug shots. If you see that guy, we'll pull him in for questioning."

After withstanding the cold for nearly two hours, the plummeting temperature was too much to endure. I decided to take the girls home, but Bob felt compelled to stay.

It was near midnight when he returned, his mood somber. "The fire's still going, but the firemen think it's under control. There are so many hot spots, they expect to remain all night. The water has frozen around the building, making it hazardous for the men to walk anywhere without falling. One of them slipped on the ice, injured his back, and was taken to the hospital. The fire chief broke his hand. Those poor guys. What a night!"

"This sure leaves an empty feeling, huh?" I said.

"Oh, does it ever. But honey, there's no comparison to the way I feel about this and the total hopelessness I felt when Jan was gone. Then, when you left me . . ." he paused slightly, his voice cracking, "that was total devastation."

I squeezed his hand firmly and kissed his forehead, then reported, "There was quite a scene here after you called to report the fire. Jan went ballistic, blaming herself. Why do you think she did that?" I asked.

"I don't know!" Bob replied, shaking his head exasperated. "Which reminds me, you better call Dr. Smith tomorrow and cancel our appointment. No business, no money. Who knows when, or if, we can ever start over again. It makes me sick. I never thought of increasing our fire insurance. We barely finished the remodeling." He sounded defeated.

I gasped at the thought. "It's hard to think about anything right now, but we're not giving up. We'll find a way."

As we embraced, Bob's arms fell listlessly around me. He was emotionally drained.

Jan's Diary, January 24, 1977: I've got this sick feeling in my stomach. I'm so glad Dad wasn't in the store when it caught on fire. It's my fault this happened but I don't know what I did wrong. Maybe it's because B is in jail and everybody is against him or he put a message in the letters and I didn't get them. What can I do? I keep praying that B will get out of jail so we can get married. Things don't look very good right now and I'm scared to death.

The following day, Bob and I peered through a dozen pages of mug shots at the police station. It didn't take long for Bob to identify the inquisitive black man. George urged Bob to keep looking. He had to be certain. I hadn't paid enough attention to assist. My eyes were transfixed on the blaze. However, Bob had no doubt this was the man.

George and Pete looked at each other knowingly. "This guy was just released from jail a couple of days ago. He was in for burglary. He shared a cell with Berchtold. We'll bring him in for questioning," George said.

Lloyd Richard Lockhart was interrogated and confessed to the crime. He implicated an accomplice, Russell Mee, who also served time in the county jail with Berchtold. They were both brought in for questioning.

The two men told of Berchtold's hate toward the owner of the flower shop, and unraveled the plot. Berchtold had offered the men a handsome sum of money if they would torch the shop. Berchtold explained the layout of the flower shop, indicating the building was an older structure with creaky wooden steps. A room at the bottom of the stairs was full of boxes, paper and other flammable materials. Once that room was set on fire, the rest of the place would go like a match. He was hopeful the owner would go into the shop and be killed in the fire.

Berchtold led the men to believe he owned a cabin in Jackson Hole. After they completed their crime, he told them they could go there and hide out. At his release from jail, he would hire them to work for him in a new business venture, pay them $1,000 a month, give them an automobile, mobile home, and an unlimited expense account.

"This morning they went to the jail to give Berchtold details of the fire," George said. "Mee said Berchtold was so ecstatic with the news, he danced around his cell, laughing and clapping his hands like a little kid. He was going to get them their money in a few days."

The fire consumed nearly half a block of the downtown area. Eventually, eleven businesses had to relocate. Since the fire started in our store, our entire contents were a total loss.

Bob began searching for a new location to open shop. Ironically, next door to where we stood and watched our store burn, there was space available for rent.

Bob bought a floral knife and a few other basic supplies, and he purchased a used ice box from a grocery store. With the help of friends and family who rallied to help us paint, construct work tables, and set up a presentable shop, we were ready to open a week later. Fortunately, Bob had stored account information in an old, antiquated fireproof safe which fell through the floor into the basement and was recovered. Our business quickly re-opened, and we forged ahead in spite of Berchtold's attempt to destroy our livelihood.

I called Dr. Smith to cancel our appointment, and shared the devastating news. "We won't be continuing therapy. We have no funds to pay you. Please, be patient and we'll get you paid for past services."

"Mrs. Broberg, you can't quit coming," he said. "You need to see me more than ever. Don't worry about paying until you're back on your feet. I'm very concerned about Jan."

At his urging, we rescheduled our appointment.

We still owed Vern Jensen some money for the detective work he had done. Shortly after relocating, Vern came into the store and put a note in Bob's hand which read, "Paid in full!"

"Oh Vern, we want to finish our obligation to you," Bob insisted. "After all, you're the reason Jan is back. You'll get the rest of what is due you."

"You have paid me enough. Let me do this much to help you out."

A week later charges were filed against Berchtold for second-degree arson and first-degree burglary. That evening, he was found lying on his bed unable to be aroused. He was transported to the hospital for an examination. The doctor was summoned who had been treating Berchtold in jail for depression. He had prescribed a mild sleeping pill which was routinely given to Berchtold every night by a jailer. Evidently, he had either been saving the medication or had received drugs from visitors. He was treated for a minor overdose and returned to the county jail three days later. Until Berchtold had his trial, was convicted and removed from Pocatello, there would be no peace of mind for us.

Jan was shaken over the news. She kept asking if he was going to die.

"No, Jan," her father said. "He's just playing on everyone's sympathy. It's another one of his dramatic displays of being in control."

March, 1977

Spring was in the air. So far, the month of March had brought nothing earth shattering. Occasionally a caller would hang up when we answered the phone. "I guess Berchtold is checking on us to see if we have changed our phone number—or he's just trying to make us nervous," I said.

"Why don't we get a new phone number, Dad? Then he wouldn't call us anymore," Karen proposed.

"Honey, it wouldn't do any good. He can get anything he wants. I don't know how, but he can," Bob said.

We discussed changing to an unlisted number, but because our home phone was used for business purposes, it didn't make sense. To go underground and plead anonymity wasn't our way of living.

Midmorning, near the end of the month, the principal called with an urgent message. "Mrs. Broberg, I'm calling to inform you about two girls who were just in our office wanting Jan. They told our secretary that Jan's aunt was in a serious car accident. Supposedly, they had come to pick Jan up and transport her to the hospital. Mrs. LaMothe told the girls she needed to find out which class Jan was attending at that hour and would have her come to the office. The pair said they would wait outside in the car. Mrs. LaMothe told me and I felt I should see if you were home. I know from all the trouble you've had, this might be another problem."

"Oh, no! Where is Jan?" I asked.

"Still in class," he said.

"Thank heavens. There hasn't been an accident. Do you have any idea who they are?"

"Teenagers, high school age. They don't fit the appearance of your daughter's type of friends," Mr. Soderquist said.

"Keep Jan there. I'm coming."

By the time I arrived, I didn't see any occupied vehicles in the parking lot. In the office I found Jan with Mr. Soderquist.

"What's wrong, Mom?" Jan asked.

"We didn't tell her anything, Mrs. Broberg. I just asked her to come to the office." Sitting in his office, Mr. Soderquist repeated the incident for Jan's benefit. Ending the account, he said, "I looked out to see where they had gone. They were getting in a car with a guy who had his long hair pulled back into a ponytail. They sat out there for about five minutes and then drove off. I can call the police and describe the car."

"I wish you would," I said. "Jan, Aunt Carolyn has not been in an accident. Do you have any idea who they were or what they wanted?"

Jan appeared shaken. Her wide eyes and trembling lip conveyed fear. "No," she said.

"Do you want to come home with me?" I asked.

Uncertain, she looked at Mr. Soderquist.

"I don't see any problems if you stay. We'll alert the teachers. You'll be safe."

"It's okay, Mom. Are you going to pick me up after school?"

"I'll be here," I promised.

As soon as I arrived home, I called Bob.

"Is Berchtold ever going to give up?" he asked.

"I don't think so. Even though he is locked up, we aren't safe from this monster."

May 10, 1977

The defense had filed a motion asking for acquittal of Berchtold, due to "mental defect," which would eliminate the need for a trial. An evidentiary hearing would be held to determine if Berchtold was mentally insane and unable to stand trial.

Entering the court room, Bob and I recognized Berchtold's parents seated with a woman on a bench near the front. Surprisingly, the courtroom was nearly empty. I wondered if the news media was barred from attending, or had given up.

The Berchtolds turned to watch us enter. I nodded and murmured, "hello," but received no response. Mrs. Berchtold glared at me for a long time until I became very uncomfortable. I looked away and began conversing with Bob, but from the corner of my eye I could still see her staring. Berchtold was at the defense bench, busily turning pages of a manuscript. He avoided looking our way, but occasionally glanced at his parents, looking quite forlorn.

At 10:20 A.M., court hadn't begun. The prosecutor's assistant called us out to explain that Lockhart was refusing to testify against Berchtold. He and his accomplice, Russell Mee, had been transported from Boise Penitentiary as witnesses, but Lockhart feared for his life if he ratted on Berchtold. He was told by fellow inmates that others may retaliate against him when he returned due to the buddy system among prisoners, which demanded loyalty.

Mee was going to testify and reveal everything about the fire and his association with Berchtold. In exchange for his testimony, he would be granted immunity since he was an accessory and wasn't actually there when it started.

Returning to the courtroom, the judge entered and proceedings began. The first witness called was Richard Lockhart.

The attorney asked for the witness to state his name and address.

"I refuse to answer any questions on the fifth amendment," Lockhart said, with much anxiety in his voice.

The judge raised his eyebrows and said to the frightened black man, "You can tell us your name and address. That will not incriminate you."

The nervous soul turned anxiously to his attorney.

"Answer the question. It's okay," the attorney said.

He wiped his hand across his face as he blurted out," Richard Lockhart—Idaho State Prison."

He sank down in his chair and nervously tapped his fingers together waiting for the next question.

The prosecutor asked, "Mr. Lockhart, would you tell us the reason you are serving at the Idaho State Prison?"

Lockhart again stated, "I refuse to answer on the fifth amendment."

His attorney stood and addressed the judge. "Your Honor, my client feels that his life is in danger should he answer any further questions. I thereby recommend that Mr. Lockhart be excused from any further questioning in this hearing."

Judge Beebe replied, "Pursuant to the conditions stated in my chambers, I will comply. Mr. Petersen, do you have any objections?"

"No, Your Honor."

"You may step down and will be released back to the custody of those who brought you here," Judge Beebe said to the fidgety witness.

The young, attractive man almost jumped from his place on the stand to the floor. His darting black eyes displayed overwhelming relief at being dismissed from his uncomfortable seat. Lockhart was led from the courtroom area by his attorney. He passed our side of the hall and glanced at his brother. The young brother leaned over the bench and put out his hand in a gesture of concern. "Take it easy, Rich. See ya."

For a brief moment, Lockhart paused to acknowledge his brother's words of encouragement, slapped his brother's hand, and spoke softly, "Ya, man."

The second witness was called and stated his name and residence. "Russell Mee, Idaho State Prison."

"Where were you on the night of January 19, 1977?" Mr. Petersen asked.

"I was in the Bannock County Jail," Mee answered.

"Why were you there?" the prosecutor asked.

"I was serving time for burglary."

"Did you know Mr. Berchtold prior to your incarceration in the Bannock County Jail?"

"No, I had never met him until then."

Prosecutor Petersen asked, "Mr. Mee, would you explain for this court your knowledge of what took place prior to the night of January 24, 1977?"

"Well, Berchtold didn't like Broberg. He was very mad at him and said it was his fault that he was in jail."

"You mean Berchtold thought it was Broberg's fault that he was in jail?" Mr. Petersen asked.

"Ya, Berchtold said Broberg said lots of lies and he wanted to get even. He talked to us a lot about what he wanted to do to Broberg. He thought if he could run Broberg out of town, Broberg would go to Salt Lake City and then Berchtold had somebody who would take care of him."

"Take care of Broberg? What does that mean?"

"Beat him up, I guess," Mee replied.

"Why did he think Broberg would go to Salt Lake?" Petersen asked.

"He never said, but he thought if Broberg's business was destroyed, he wouldn't stay in Pocatello. Anyway, he came up with this plan. He said if we burned down Broberg's shop, he would make us partners in his business," Mee said.

"What kind of business?"

"He had a Fun Center in Jackson Hole, Wyoming. Ya know, all kinds of game machines and stuff. He said he needed people to go out and set up other Fun Centers. We'd get a motor home, $5,000, and an unlimited expense account. He has a place on an island where he wanted to set up the Huckleberry Fun Center, and it sounded like a great idea."

"And did you think he was telling you the truth?"

"Sure, man. He showed us pictures about where it was going to be built and had all the plans laid out. Man, we couldn't turn down that kind of offer and told him we would do it when we got out of jail. He drew us a floor plan of the building where Broberg had his flower shop. He said the building was very old and once a match was lit, it would go like a matchbox."

Mee stopped for a moment. Berchtold never looked at him while Mee was giving the account, but continued to study the manuscript on the table in front of him.

"He drew us a map and told us how to go in the back door and where the stairs go down to the basement. He said Broberg kept his wrapping paper and boxes in a room down there and the floors were all old boards. He said Broberg kept lots of money in the store. After the fire was over, we was to get some keys to a cabin in Jackson Hole where we could stay until things cooled off.

"When we both got out of jail, we met and decided to do it on Monday night. We drove downtown by the flower shop and it was still open. So, we decided to go get a beer. Lockhart left and told me he had to go see his wife and would be back to pick me up later. I waited for 'bout half an hour or maybe forty-five minutes 'fore he came back. When he came in, he said, 'I did it! I set the fire!' I asked why he did it without me and he said he jest decided to do it. He told me he had broken the lock on the back and tried to find the money, but didn't find nothing. He went downstairs and lit a match to a box of wrapping paper and all at once almost everything around caught on fire."

Mr. Petersen stopped Mee to ask him, "Then you were not there, Mr. Mee?"

"No, I wasn't, but I woulda' been if Lockhart had came back to get me," he answered.

"What did you do then?" Petersen asked.

"Lockhart said to come and watch the fireworks and we went downtown to watch the building burn."

"Did you see Mr. Berchtold after that?"

"Yes, we went over and told him the next day. We had to get the keys to the cabin from him."

"What did Mr. Berchtold do when you told him?"

Mee paused, trying to think. "He acted like someone would act when they were on the winning team of a ball game. He kind of went crazy. He giggled and danced around his cell, jumping up and down, clapping his hands. He jest kept laughing and saying over and over, 'This is jest great! I'd like to see Broberg now!'"

An objection was raised from the defending attorney. The judge overruled.

Mee concluded his testimony with a brief unemotional statement of being sorry for his part in the fire.

The defense attorney attacked Mee's character and credibility as a witness. He made a strong argument about Mee being a thief and a liar. Russell Mee stood his ground and never changed his account about the fire or Berchtold's plan when questioned thoroughly by the defense.

Dr. Crandall was the next witness and described caring for Berchtold's medical needs while at the Bannock County jail. He was questioned about Berchtold's overdose and suicide gesture. Dr. Crandall did not feel Berchtold was suicidal but was trying to gain sympathy.

A brief recess was called while the court awaited the arrival of a psychiatrist from State Hospital South who was one of two doctors that had done a psychiatric evaluation on Berchtold. Dr. Crandall returned to sit next to Bob and me.

I felt Mrs. Berchtold's cold icy stare once again. When she got up, I felt relieved. However, instead of leaving the courtroom, she walked over and in a high screeching voice said, "Mary Ann, do you remember when you and Gail came to see me and I told you to keep your daughter away from my Bob?"

"I remember coming to see you, but you never told me to keep Jan away from your son," I said.

She flew into a rage. Her eyes narrowed to small slits, her mouth forming a tight line. "Now don't you lie to me. I did too!" She struck out viciously.

I refuted her charge. "I'm not lying, Mrs. Berchtold."

She retorted wildly, "Look what you've done to him! It's you and Jan's fault!"

She was trembling with anger, her fists clenched tightly. I moved my body back trying to get out of her reach in case she decided to let loose. I was grateful Dr. Crandall was between us.

Bob said softly, "Don't say one word in return. She sounds just like her son."

I turned away, hoping she would leave. She stood there panting heavily. Her daughter came over and ushered her mother out of the court room.

Dr. Crandall turned to us and said, "Did you get the impression she was a little upset?" We chuckled very quietly.

Dr. Anderson's appearance brought court back into session. His evaluation of Berchtold was an eye opener.

"Mr. Berchtold is a sociopath. He has no guilt for anything that has happened and blames everyone else for his problems. He takes no responsibility. From the moment he laid eyes on Jan Broberg, he began scheming how he was going to have her. He has a criminal mind and has no remorse for what he has done."

Mr. Petersen asked, "Do you believe Mr. Berchtold is mentally ill?"

"Mr. Berchtold suffers from deep emotional problems and depression that can lead to temporary insanity. Yes, it is my opinion he is mentally ill."

"Do you believe Mr. Berchtold is a danger to society?" Mr. Petersen asked.

"I do. I feel Mr. Berchtold should be placed in a secure facility which will deal with his psychopathic personality."

"Do you believe Mr. Berchtold remains a threat to the Broberg family?"

"Yes. He has an aggressive impulsive disorder which may continue to endanger the lives of the Broberg family. His compulsive-obsessive behavior towards their daughter is extreme as has been demonstrated in the past two kidnappings. Miss Broberg is not safe from Berchtold and he is capable of taking her again should he have access to her."

"Do you feel it is in the best interest of Miss Broberg if Mr. Berchtold were placed in a locked facility?" Petersen questioned.

"I recommend placement in a state psychiatric hospital and that he be allowed to receive medical treatment, but it should be a locked facility," Dr. Anderson stated.

Following the testimony of Dr. Anderson, Bob and I were both called to testify. Bob expressed concern for his safety and well-being, bringing forth the events where Berchtold had threatened his life.

I told of Berchtold's plan to kill Bob and how he had pointed a loaded gun at him, but changed his mind. The defense attorney was on his feet continually voicing objections. Other events were pointed out about Berchtold's threats, but because they were considered hearsay, and no reports had been filed on him by law enforcement, they were not considered relevant to this hearing.

Jan was not subpoenaed to appear.

Mr. Petersen decided not to contest the mental defect in lieu of a trial. He felt Berchtold would be placed in secure confinement for a long period of time, which would serve us well and hasten his lockup.

Judge Beebe signed a commitment order to send Berchtold to the Idaho Security Medical Facility in Boise. He was expected to be taken there on June 27, 1977. We were ecstatic. It had been three years of hell, but at last, we were able to turn our lives in a new direction.

unraveling

We took on a whole new attitude about our approaching summer with Berchtold's transfer from Bannock County Jail to the Idaho Security Medical Facility in Boise. Other than a blurb in the newspaper, there was nothing eventful about his departure.

Completing junior high was a milestone for Jan. Watching her celebrate graduation festivities in her size-one dress, I became quite emotional and had to hide in the shadows so my tears wouldn't cause her embarrassment.

Drivers training began the following week. (In Idaho, fourteen-year-olds can get a daytime driver's license.) Soon, our spunky, tiny Jan, who could barely see over the steering wheel, began terrorizing other motorists, just like the rest of her peers. At last, she was in full swing with typical teen activities and, from our perspective, life was looking normal.

Dr. Smith discontinued our visits; Jan was still not ready to disclose the trauma she had experienced or discuss whether she had been sexually molested. He emphasized patience, believing that when she felt safe, she would talk. He coached me to look for signs that would indicate her willingness to disclose. With the perpe-trator out of her life, he expected her to transition back into her familiar surroundings quickly. Should there be a concern, Jan had earned top priority on his list of patients.

Jan expressed relief. Her complaints had persisted for several months about the tedious trips to Salt Lake, and she considered the visits a waste of our money.

Frequently, when the phone rang a caller would remain mute, but would stay on the line until we hung up. Although Robert was in a lockup facility, we blamed these annoying calls on him. On one occasion, Jan answered, and it became evident by the man-ner in which she was responding that this was not a friendly call. Determined Berchtold would not get to her again, I went to an extension and heard an unfamiliar female voice. When I raised the receiver, she hung up.

I questioned Jan. "I don't know who it was," she responded, appearing agitated.

"What did they want?" I asked.

"I don't know. It was a wrong number."

Her nervous behavior caused me to doubt the truth of her reply. "Jan, has Robert been trying to contact you?" I asked, trying not to be threatening.

"No. I told you and Dad I would let you know if he did."

"I know. I just have to be sure."

I called Mr. Petersen and related the incident. He was keeping a log of all unidentified calls.

Jan's Diary, August 29, 1977: It's been two months since B left and I haven't heard from anybody except that lady who called to tell me he's okay. She said don't worry because he is doing well and still thinks about me every day. Since he can't tell me, she is pass-ing his thoughts on. He said, "Tell her she is still my special angel and I love her with all my heart."

B used to worry that if he ever went to a mental hospital, the doctors would operate on him like they did Jack Nicholson in that movie. I miss B and no matter what happens, I love him. If he is trying to call me at home, I wish he wouldn't *because* he's going to get himself in a bunch of trouble.

In September, Jan, now fifteen, began her sophomore year at Pocatello High School. She complained about being so small and thought she deserved to look older than Susan. She was also concerned about her late maturation. "Why haven't I started having periods?" she asked me. "All my friends have. I must be some kind of dork."

"It will happen," I reassured her. "I didn't start until I was sixteen, and I was a little shrimp, too. It must be in your genes. Don't be so anxious."

Jan and her girlfriends attended a kickoff dance on the school's tennis courts to celebrate the beginning of school. Her excitement was refreshing as she burst into the house with an announcement.

"I met this cute guy who's Caroline's friend and he wants to take me to the homecoming dance. What am I going to tell him? I'm only fifteen and not old enough to date."

"Well, if it's a group date and with Caroline, we would consider letting you go," Bob said.

"But, Dad, I can't," Jan snapped back. "It isn't right."

"Okay. Just tell him you'll have to wait until you're sixteen," Bob said reinforcing her decision.

"That's not it at all. You don't understand!" Jan said as she fled the room.

Turning to me with a disgruntled look on his face, Bob said, "Women. I don't understand them and I live with a house full. Even the dogs are female."

"But it's a relief to see Jan enjoying attention from boys. She's always so standoffish when guys are around."

"What did I say that made her think I didn't understand?" Bob asked. "I was just agreeing with her."

"Oh, she's still trying to feel okay about herself. At least she's sharing feelings again," I said.

Jan ended up not going to the dance, but attended all other homecoming activities with friends and said she had a marvelous time.

The temporary tranquillity of our lives was brought to an abrupt halt at the end of September when we heard Berchtold could be released right away. The news was harrowing.

We met with the prosecutor, Mr. Petersen, who was more than distressed; he was angry. "This is nothing short of ludicrous. An order of release is being filed in District Court. It's only been three months."

"How could this happen?" Bob questioned. "I thought we had years before he was out terrorizing us again."

"Can you believe he's been declared not to be dangerous to himself and others by two psychiatrists? How absurd." Mr. Petersen growled.

"What can we do to stop it?" I asked.

"Write letters to your Congressmen—Health and Welfare, too. We'll do what we can from our office to stop it. I'm appealing to Judge Beebe requesting Dr. Anderson reexamine him. After all, the Court relied upon his expertise when they declared Berchtold had a mental illness. That guy is not ready to be let out on the street."

It was appalling that two experts found him to be perfectly well and in need of no further care. The prosecutor stated to the press, "If the Court is now willing to rely upon the opinion of staff members from the Department of Health and Welfare, surely it would be incumbent upon that person or persons to read and consider the evidence adduced at the hearing, whereby the Court found Berchtold to be both mentally ill and dangerous."

The prosecutor emphasized, "Mr. Berchtold is continuing to contact Miss Broberg, either himself or through a third party, which indicates he has not changed." Petersen's bold statement included, "I am convinced that there will be bloodshed if Berchtold is released and allowed to return to this community."

Letters were sent to several influential individuals and agencies in an effort to stop his release. An editorial appeared in the local newspaper which felt the criteria of mental defect was being manipulated by defense attorneys for accused criminals:

> The game consists of convincing the psychiatrist and jury that you were crazy when you (created the crime); then you're home free. Unfortunately, there are too many persons taking advantage of that tactic—at the expense of our legal system. Mr. Berchtold, who was acquitted on a charge of kidnapping a Pocatello youth by reason of mental defect, has been deemed sane following mental evaluation by the Idaho Department of Health and Welfare, and the department now recommends that he be freed.

In spite of efforts to block Berchtold's release, a Court order was signed by a Sixth Judicial District Court Judge:

> In this cause, the defendant, Robert E. Berchtold was acquitted on the grounds of mental illness and committed to the custody of the Director of Health and Welfare. On October 13, 1977 . . . a report, including psychiatric evaluations, requesting the discharge of Robert E. Berchtold from the custody of the Department of Health and Welfare upon the grounds that Berchtold may be discharged or released on condition without danger to himself or to others;

And the court being satisfied by the report . . . such conditions being reasonably necessary and required to control the pedophilia or pedophilia tendencies, existing or heretofore manifested, relative to Jan Broberg, a female minor, and conduct related thereto and directed toward said female minor and her parents, it is:

Hereby ordered that Robert E. Berchtold be conditionally released from the custody of the Department of Health and Welfare upon the conditions that said Robert E. Berchtold not voluntarily be physically present during the next three (3) years in Bannock County, Idaho so long as Jan Broberg or her parents or any of them are residents therein.

There was nothing for us to do except live with the order and pray he would stay away. Jan had nothing to say. We were not able to detect her feelings. Discussing the conditions of his release, we pled with her to tell us if he tried to see or contact her in any way.

We became extremely cautious about where our children went, and wanted to know every detail of their time away from us. Our involvement at every activity our children participated in, whether it be school, church, or community, was considered by some to be extreme.

Jan's Diary, November 30, 1977: Today I got a note at school to call a number after school. I about dropped dead when I heard B's voice. B had gotten released from the hospital and needed to see me, but he can't come into Pocatello so I had to work something out, then drive out to Fort Hall. I had play practice tonight so I told Blenda I was sick. I almost got lost since it's been so long since B took me out there. When I saw him, he looked good and was very happy. He told me a little bit about being in the hospital and he had quite a time convincing them that he wasn't crazy.

B asked if I was still doing everything I was supposed to and not going out with any guys. Of course I am, but I hadn't heard from "Z" for a long time. B said since I'm following the plan, they don't need to make contact. Time was short because he didn't want to get caught so he'll get in touch with me later and we can figure out the plan. Nobody can find out about our meeting or he'll get sent back to Boise. He's not supposed to see me until I'm 18. Right now, I hate my life.

The year since Jan's return was full of high emotions which often ran amuck while Jan struggled with herself. She often felt discouraged, out of place with peers, or hurt when she thought others were whispering about her. Most concerning were her incidents of becoming preoccupied, and our inability to engage her in conversation. However, she only allowed herself brief intervals of depression before her list of projects overshadowed her secrets. Overall, she was making remarkable strides.

Jan's sophomore year found her excelling scholastically while she also participated in drill team and a variety of organizations, with particular emphasis in music and drama. She was involved in every project and play offered by the Drama or Music Department.

Jan heard about a summer workshop at Brigham Young University for high school youth. She expressed excitement about going as she waved the application in front of us. "I'll learn everything about acting and we get to do costumes, design sets, lighting, all kinds of productions. It really sounds cool."

Housing would be in a girls dorm where each attendee had to adhere to strict rules. Participants were not allowed to go anywhere without a chaperon or to leave campus during their stay. Travel to local theatrical productions would be in closely supervised buses. The environment appeared safe.

I watched Bob's eyebrows raise while he savored her enthusiasm. Turning to me, he smiled and winked. "There's no question about it. You're going. Just call us collect every few days so we know you're okay."

"Please," Jan begged, "don't tell anyone about what's happened. I don't want them to think I'm some weirdo."

Prior to her departure, a teenage boy called our home asking to speak with Jan. I told him she wasn't home, but if he would leave his number I would have her call him. It didn't sound like a local call. The boy identified himself as a friend and said he would call back.

I enlisted Karen's help, asking her to take the call if the boy called back and try to find out who he was. At first, Karen refused, but after explaining the importance of Jan's safety, she reluctantly accepted. "You and Jan sound so much alike, the caller will assume it is her. If it's Berchtold, I need to know so we can report him," I said. "It's imperative that he doesn't interrupt Jan's life again."

A couple of hours later, the phone rang. Karen said "Hello." After a few brief moments, she looked surprised and handed me the phone. I listened to a high-pitched, falsetto voice who was babbling something strange that didn't make sense. With no response on our end, the caller hung up.

Relating the incident to Jan, she was furious. "Don't anyone ever do that again!"

"Well, Jan. It wasn't any big deal. Probably some kid sitting home bored."

I concluded she was so out of sorts only because she felt her privacy was invaded.

Jan was into the third week of the workshop in Provo, Utah, when our dog, Tiffy, went into convulsions. We rushed her to the vet and found she had been poisoned. There was no guarantee the dog would make it. Tiff had been such a wonderful comfort to all the girls during the worst of times; to lose her would be a hard blow. Karen and Susan were in tears. Two days later, the report was encouraging; although shaky on her legs, the dog would survive. Later in the morning, Tiff's puppy was found in the front yard having convulsions. Rushing her to the vet, it was confirmed. She had been poisoned too.

Jan called home, per instructions, on the day of Bandit's poisoning. "Oh no!" she shrieked. Her outburst was reminiscent of the night the store burned. "Mom, who did it? How did it happen?"

"I don't know. I saw two girls walk by the house the day of Tiff's poisoning. One was carrying a paper sack. I don't know. I doubt it was them, but it's sure strange. Both dogs, but at different times."

Jan was bawling. "Oh, I just feel like . . . I don't know. If they die . . . They can't die, Mom! Should I come home?"

"Jan, the vet said Tiff is doing better. I think she'll come home tomorrow. It's too early to tell about Bandit."

Jan wanted to know details, so I handed Karen the phone and she explained every excruciating movement of the dog's convulsions to her sister, who was nearly hysterical. Jan's affection for the dogs was strong, but this was beyond sorrow. It was a cry of helplessness. We felt that this unexplainable emotion from Jan needed to be scrutinized.

"Bob, something's wrong. Jan's overreacting. She's too emotional about this," I said. "I know she doesn't want us talking about her past, but I think somebody needs to know about Berchtold. What if he knows she's there?"

We made an appointment with a dorm counselor and workshop director and drove the following day to the campus. They informed us the young participants were kept busy and always chaperoned on outings. During the day there were short periods of free time, but students were not allowed off campus. Generally, the students went in groups to the student union for meals. Jan appeared to have lots of friends and wasn't a loner. The counselor assured us there had been no suspicious persons sighted.

I explained that Berchtold was not a suspicious person; he would fit naturally into any setting. His power over our daughter was frightening. Not certain the counselor shared our concern regarding Jan's vulnerability, we asked all adult leaders be informed and asked to watch Jan very carefully. Also, we requested that they keep Jan's past from her peers since she was extremely sensitive and didn't want the stigma of being known as "that girl."

Jan would celebrate her sixteenth birthday at the workshop. With permission, we bought party decorations and ordered birthday goodies to be delivered to her dorm for a gala event. Assured that her birthday would be a fun surprise, we apprehensively returned home.

When I called the day after her birthday, a counselor reported, "The birthday was a huge success, except Jan was certainly emotional."

Not knowing what Berchtold meant in his letter about *having time* before she turned sixteen, we suspected there was a reason.

August 11, 1978

Caroline came to stay overnight after Jan returned. Jan, in a jubilant voice, told the girls all about the conference.

"Oh, this cute guy from California said he was in love with me," Jan giggled. "You guys saw what he did when we were getting ready to leave; he knelt down on the hot pavement in front of all my family, took my hand like he was proposing, and said how much he would miss me. Then he said, 'please grow up and wait for me.' He was really dramatic."

Laughter erupted from the girls.

"These drama people are more than I can take," Bob said as he picked up the newspaper and headed for the patio to enjoy the beautiful August evening.

Karen, Caroline, and Jan retreated to the basement where they could talk privately without parent comments or big ears. Caroline asked as they headed downstairs, "What do you think of your bedroom since David and Karen changed it?"

"Looks good. I like it, but I'm still not going to sleep in there. Yuck!"

Listening to her comment, I wondered if anything would change her opinion about the room. It seemed odd that after this long, she still wouldn't reclaim it.

During Jan's absence, Karen and her cousin David had decided to change the room by hanging new posters, introducing new colors, even taking the wallpaper off the walls. Karen longed to have Jan's company again in the basement.

Determined, they approached me with some ideas and asked for my input. I offered to buy a can of paint so they could change the inset dresser panels to a bold bright blue. I told them I was doubtful it would make any difference because Jan disliked the room intensely. Feeling strongly about the alterations, however, they followed through with their plans. Caroline came over to observe their labors and contribute her comments. They were all excited when they finished the project. But after all that valiant effort, hearing Jan's comments had to be deflating.

■ ■ ■

Upon Caroline's arrival, the three girls retreated to the basement for privacy and girl talk. Caroline had plenty of information to dispense about her activities over the past five weeks that Jan had been gone.

Eventually, the trio wandered from Karen's room into Jan's newly decorated bedroom. Jan plopped down on her bed while Caroline laid across the hanging love seat. Karen pushed Caroline's feet over and crawled onto the bench with her.

"Ah! Will this hold both of us?" Caroline asked.

"Of course! Don't get excited. We're just fine," Karen reassured.

"You can come over here if you want to," Jan said.

Finally, the girls were settled. "Okay Jan, now you've heard everything I know, tell me about this guy who made the big scene. Did he really propose?" Caroline asked.

Jan giggled. "Curtis? Oh my gosh, he was crazy. He kept us laughing all the time."

"Was he your boyfriend?"

"Heavens, no. A group of us kind of hung around together. Ya' know how it is."

"Yeah, I know," Caroline said. "Karen said there were lots of cute guys."

Jan nodded her head in agreement.

"Did Curtis have cute buns?" Caroline asked.

"Caroline!" Laughter erupted from the three teens. "Sure. He was okay . . . but Jeremy was really the cutest. One day he bought me ice cream at the Student Union."

"Oooooh!" Karen and Caroline chorused.

"Oh, he wasn't my boyfriend or anything like that," Jan said. "He was 'Billy' in the play. Do you remember him, Karen?"

Karen was playing with the cushion zipper of the hanging chair, opening and closing it." Yeah, he was cute," she said. "Ya' gonna write him?"

"Maybe . . . I don't know. He wants to go back to the workshop next year, so I might see him if I go too."

Karen was zipping the blue cover on the cushion closed when the zipper became stuck. She spied a piece of paper wedged alongside the foam cushion and pulled it out. "I really thought Curtis would be a blast. He's the one I'd go after."

Jan chuckled. "Well, he was fun and definitely crazy."

Conversation among the girls went from one event to another. Caroline's update on her latest boyfriend brought raised eyebrows from Karen.

"Of course my parents are having a fit about me dating Ricky. Dad says, 'That kid doesn't seem to have much sense. Can't you find somebody better?'"

Laughing, Jan said, "Your Dad's never liked any of your boyfriends, Caroline."

"Jan, what's this?" Karen asked, holding up the crumpled piece of paper she had pulled from the cushion. "Who's Zada?"

"Zada?" Caroline said, laughing.

Jan sat up with a startled look, the color draining from her face. "What did you say?"

"This note. I found it in here," she said, pointing to the cushion. "It says . . . 'call this number and Zada will. . .'"

Jan was on her feet, screaming at Karen. "Give me that!"

Karen held her hand above Jan's reach and continued reading, ignoring Jan's protests, '. . . will tell you what's next. There's still time!' Time? For what?" Karen asked.

Frantically, Jan attempted to grab the paper from Karen's hand. With one final lunge, Jan grabbed the paper, shrieking at the top of her voice, and shredded it into small bits.

Caroline shouted, "Jan, what's wrong with you? You're acting crazy! Karen, stop it!"

"Tell her, Caroline. Tell her what we found!" Karen hollered.

"When we were working on your room, David found some notes B wrote to you, but we took them away from him and now I've got them!" Caroline exclaimed.

Jan stared with disbelief at Caroline. "What? Did you read them?" she shouted.

"Yeah! And now you've got to tell us what's going on."

"You aren't supposed to . . ." Jan never finished the sentence, but stood in complete silence. Life drained from her body as she moved her head slowly, mechanically. She became transfixed on some item sitting on her dresser.

"Jan, what's wrong?" Caroline asked.

Jan continued staring at the dresser.

Karen snapped at her. "Come on, Jan. Quit it!"

Jan's head moved slowly toward Karen. The blank expression on her face was strange. Her eyes became fixed, as though she were in a trance.

Within a few moments, her persona changed dramatically as she started talking incoherently and began brushing her arms frantically, like she was trying to brush something off her body. Her tongue thickened. She was forming words, but they were jumbled and strange. Without warning, Jan's knees buckled under her and she fell to the floor.

Karen thought Jan was staging a scene, which she had done before as a way to tease her sisters. She was quite an actress. Jan's face was buried in the carpet, and her piteous groan became a painful wail. Her body was still and she began hyperventilating. They were afraid she was going to pass out.

Caroline and Karen glanced at each other wide-eyed, then stared at Jan while she continued the mournful cries.

When the moans turned to gagging, Caroline scolded, "If you're going to throw up, go to the bathroom, for heavens sake!" As the contortions continued, Caroline cried out, "Karen, something's wrong. Jan's sick! Get your mom!"

Ignoring Caroline's plea, Karen stood over her sister's contorted body demanding that she "get up and stop it!" Jan continued to groan as she rocked her body from side to side pulling at the carpet with her fists. She continued to babble incoherently. "Jan, quit acting this way and tell us what's wrong!" Karen said, annoyed.

The gyrations began again as Jan's eyes widened and she sat up. She stared into space and began mumbling undecipherable words. Again, she started brushing off the imaginary creatures which were crawling on her body. "Get them off!" she cried out and again fell into a heap on the floor, mourning painfully as she pulled at the carpet.

"Oh! You can't," Jan groaned, "you can't know about this."

Caroline knelt down by Jan. "Jan, you're scaring me to death. What's wrong?"

Jan's response was another wail, her face ashen.

"I'm going to get Mom!" Karen reported.

"No! Karen! Don't, please don't," Jan cried out, "You're . . ."

Again her speech was garbled.

"You're not making sense. Tell us what's wrong!"

Jan laid in a helpless stupor on the floor, her face glistening with per-spiration, her skin cold and clammy. She continued to paw at the floor, and her awful moaning persisted. Jan was always dramatic, but Karen had never seen her sister act so strange.

"We need to do something," Karen announced, realizing things were getting out of hand.

Caroline clutched Karen's arm as she stared at Jan's feeble form. "What's wrong with her?"

Karen shrugged her shoulders. "I don't know, but that's B's writing," she said, looking at the bits of paper strewn around the floor.

Whimpers emerged from Jan's shaking, trembling body. With Karen and Caroline hovering over her, Jan slowly began to relax from her astound-ing trance. She let go of the carpet, pulling her body into fetal position. Outrageous sobs burst from the small frame. Four years of agony were being expelled, and once she found an outlet, her sobs seemed unstoppable. Berch-told's carefully planned secret had been discovered. She didn't know what to do, and her sobs were gut-wrenching.

They had no knowledge of what had caused Jan's unexpected outburst, but Caroline encircled her emotional friend in her arms and Karen patted her sister's limp hands, both offering silent comfort.

■ ■ ■

It didn't surprise us that the girls were up late talking. But around one-thirty in the morning, Bob heard a commotion coming from the basement. He got out of bed, and walked to the top of the stairs. "Are you girls ever going to turn it off?" he asked.

Karen stuck her head out the door and responded, "Sorry, Dad. We'll try to be quiet." The door closed quietly but we could still hear loud whispering.

"It's late," Bob stated loudly. "You kids need to get to sleep." Within a couple of minutes, Bob was back in bed.

■ ■ ■

When Karen heard her father's voice from the top of the stairs, she had looked at Caroline and said, "I don't think Dad should come down here right now."

So Karen opened the door and spoke to her father, closed the door, then whispered to Caroline, "Let's get Jan out of here."

Although Jan was able to walk on her own, the two girls assisted her to the family room. For short periods of time she seemed to be getting a grip, then would revert to her previous condition—crying, gasping, and scratching her head, arms, and lower torso.

Karen and Caroline whispered to each other: Had Jan seen something in the room that scared her? They both had looked around carefully, but seen nothing unusual. The duo decided to wait out the ordeal until Jan could give them a sensible explanation.

Gradually, Jan's energy began to return. Between trying to speak and choking back sobs, she took a deep breath and said, "Okay, here goes!" There was a long pause. "I have to tell somebody, but I can't. You don't get it. This will affect all of you. You're in danger. They might be listening," she whispered as her eyes darted around the room.

"What are you talking about?" Karen asked.

Finally, she blurted out, "I'm going to die! I failed!"

"Jan, you're not going to die," Caroline stated boldly.

Bawling, Jan repeated, "I'm going to die."

"Why are you saying that?" Karen said.

"She said so!" Jan cried out.

"Who said?" Karen asked.

"That person! Zada!" Jan shrieked, her body trembling.

"She told you were going to die?" Caroline said.

Jan exploded. "Yes!" She began rubbing her arms again. "You're not supposed to know!"

"Know what?" Karen asked. "That you're going to die?

"About me having a baby!" Jan exclaimed holding her hand to her mouth as tears gushed down her face.

"What!" Karen's mouth flew open as she stared at her sister in shock.

"You're going to have a baby?" Caroline questioned in disbelief.

"No . . . I mean I'm supposed to . . . to help them!" The words spewing from Jan sounded desperate, but didn't make any sense.

"Help who?"

"People from this other world!" she blubbered, scratching her arms furiously.

The girls stared at each other.

"Jan, have you gone goofy?" Caroline asked. "You're talking nonsense."

"You've got to stop acting crazy and tell us what you're talking about," Karen declared.

"Awful things! I can't!" Jan's voice wavered between sobs.

"Like what?"

"Bad things to both of you!" Jan cried out.

Karen and Caroline looked at each other in disbelief. Prodding Jan to tell them about Zada, the girls' demeanor softened as they felt Jan's fear. In a trembling voice, Jan began recounting the traumatic experience of her past.

Recalling the horrid account of awakening in the motor home with her arms and feet strapped, Jan's body quivered and goose bumps appeared on her arms, making the hair stand on end. Karen and Caroline looked at each other in wonderment. With great emotion and long pauses, she related her encounter with Zada and Zethra, reliving each horrid episode. Relating each event brought her renewed terror. Only prodding from Karen and Caroline persuaded her to continue.

Dumfounded, the two girls listened carefully to the incredible story. Though it had been nearly four years, Jan's memory remained vivid. Frequently, Jan stopped and would go through the peculiar antics of rubbing her skin and moaning before being comforted by her listeners. Concluding her unbelievable ordeal, the girls stared at Jan.

"Whew. It's so weird!" Caroline stated.

Jan only nodded.

"And you believed they were real . . . these people from another world?" Karen asked, doubting her sister could actually think such a thing.

Jan murmured emotionally, "They were real."

"What did they mean when they said you would cease to exist?" Caroline asked. "I don't get it?"

"They told me I wouldn't have a spirit. If my mission failed, I would be nothing. My spiritual body would be gone, just disappear, evaporate, and I wouldn't exist in the next life."

"Did you always believe they were real?"

"Yes, there's so many of them," Jan replied, frustrated.

"Who are they?" Karen prodded.

"I don't know. Just a bunch of people that call me or I've had to go meet them," she responded anxiously.

"Why?"

"Because I had to. I'd go on my bike—to Ross Park, down by the railroad tracks, once to the train station, to a trailer park that was a long way out on Yellowstone, when it was raining really hard. I'd get so scared." Jan wept.

"Are they real people? I mean, what do they look like?" Caroline asked.

Jan nodded her head. "They're just like us."

"Maybe that's who they really are," Caroline said. "You know what I mean?"

Jan shrugged her shoulders and looked perplexed. "Do you remember the homecoming dance? I wasn't supposed to go anywhere with guys unless they said so. You were so mad at me because I wouldn't go, so your parents said you couldn't go either."

"Yeah. My parents think you're so levelheaded," Caroline said, laughing.

"Caroline, this isn't funny," Karen reprimanded.

Jan's voice was quivering. "Caroline, something bad is supposed to happen to you."

"Me? You're kidding! What?"

"A bad disease . . ." Jan's voice drifted off as she began thinking about her failed assignment.

Caroline nudged Jan, bringing her back to the present.

With trembling voice, Jan said, "Sometimes I hoped I'd die or get killed! Then it would all be over."

"Oh, Jan, you didn't!" Caroline responded.

"It's so awful." Jan broke into sobs. "But I kept thinking about Susan. What if they took Susan?" Jan burst into another episode of crying and groaning as she thought about her little sister. She clawed and pulled at her skin.

"Don't do that," Caroline said, grabbing Jan's hands. "This is sick."

Karen jumped up and brought a roll of toilet paper from the bathroom, handing it to Jan since the tissue box had been emptied. Jan blew her nose, and sniffled while she continued, "When nothing happened after the dance, I started thinking everything might be okay. B was in prison so I couldn't marry him, so the plan wasn't working like they said. But then he got out and told me it was going to happen. Then the dogs were poisoned and I knew they'd seen me with Jeremy. I was in bad trouble."

Looking anxiously at her sister, Jan's voice rang with alarm. "Karen, if you went blind, it would've been my fault."

"Why?" Karen asked.

"They said! Look at all the things that happened," Jan replied. "All the time I'm afraid somebody's going to give me a note or something. I got lots of messages at school until B went to prison. Before he got out, I got a note from the school office to call a long distance number. I knew it was a message from one of them."

"Did you call?" Caroline asked.

"I had to." Jan shuddered, then blew her nose. "The lady told me I needed to meet B and make a plan when he got out, but he couldn't meet me in Pocatello because he'd get thrown back in prison. So, I had to drive out on the Indian Reservation and meet him. I went to play practice, but I told them I was really sick, then I went to see him. He knew I was scared and felt bad. He said I should stay in school. This summer we were supposed to work something out."

"What's going to happen now?"

"I don't know? But what if they take Susan?" Jan asked, alarmed.

"You're going to tell. You have to," Karen said.

"No matter what these people say, you're not supposed to marry B," Karen remarked.

"But they told me I had to!" Jan declared.

"Karen and me think something else is going on," Caroline said firmly. *"I mean . . . you said once that B really loves you and . . . well . . . you know . . . you and me talked about sex and other stuff . . . uh . . . has he done bad things to you?"* Caroline asked.

Jan's face dropped.

Caroline's position as her best friend became an advantage. They didn't keep secrets. Curious, she asked Jan pointed questions about the relationship between them. With Caroline's assertiveness, Jan disclosed small bits of information regarding Berchtold's sexual advances toward her. As Caroline sought deeper explanations about the abuse, Jan protected her dignity by disassociating herself from the molested child.

"When it first happened, they were on a trip together. She was very frightened, but B said he would take care of her. He loved her so much that he promised he would do everything he could to save her."

Through the long difficult night of confession, Jan revealed that the molestation had continued over a three-year period.

"B was only doing what he was told because she had to try and get prepared for the baby and he had to protect her from other people who wanted to hurt her. Since nobody understood, it was really hard for both of them."

Caroline asked for details about the molestation. Jan was specific. The information Jan revealed was pitiful. The sinister crime had left deep wounds. Karen, who maintained the position as a silent listener, was shocked and pained as she tried to imagine the horrible defilement of her sister. Karen couldn't understand why Jan was not recognizing herself as the victim.

"Did he ever try to do it, for real?" Caroline probed.

"Yeah, but she was too little. He didn't want to hurt her."

Contemplating the admissions from Jan, Caroline tried to make sense out of everything she had heard. Jan continued expressing details concerning her admitted abuse.

"This little girl was supposed to be free from any impurities, you know, like not having periods."

"Girls have to have periods to have babies," Caroline exclaimed.

"That's why this little girl was so special, because she could fulfill the plan."

"But it's not possible."

"They said not to worry and it would happen when it was supposed to."

"You mean getting pregnant?" Caroline asked. "Is that why you've been so worried?"

Unwilling to share more insight, Jan shut down and refused to reveal anymore details.

Caroline stared at her dearest friend for a long time before she spoke. "Jan, this has all been one big fat lie . . . "

Jan's eyes filled with tears again. In one last effort to make them understand her mission, she tried to explain. Quietly the two girls listened while Jan dug at her arms again. "They said their planet was sterile and all the young men had died. They only had women, children and old men left. I was chosen to have a special child that would save their planet. I want to be a mom, anyway, someday. I don't want to die. I just want to go on with my life."

Caroline put her head back on the couch without responding. The silence brought welcome relief to the subdued troupe. Karen thought Caroline's interrogation had ended until she asked, "When was the last time you saw B?"

Yawning, Jan quietly said, "A long time ago." After a brief pause, she said, "He called me before I went to the workshop. I was supposed to call him when I got there. He wanted to see me and talk about stuff."

"Oh, now that's scary."

"I wrote him a letter, but didn't mail it. It's in my suitcase."

"I want to see it," Karen said, jumping up. Running to Jan's room, she picked up the suitcase and returned, handing it to her sister. Jan rummaged *through her unpacked bag and pulled out an envelope. Karen took it from Jan. It was addressed to Robert Berchtold. It read:*

Dear B,

Sorry that I can't be with you. I wish I could be. Please have a nice week. I'll try to be able to call you while I'm here. I love you. Please remember this all the time. I really long to be with you. I love you more and more every day!

Smile all the time because I love you. So keep smiling today and always. Be happy because we are going to make it no matter how hard the road may be. So keep in mind I'll always love you no matter what happens. I think you are Grrrreat.

I'll do my part and anything I can to help you. I love you so much that I couldn't show you. XOXOXOXO

I'm having a great time. Maybe I'll call you if I get the chance!
Love, Your Dolly Jan

After reading the note, Caroline asked, "Jan, remember when I'd come over and you would leave? You wouldn't tell Karen and me where you'd gone. When you got back, you were like a . . . "

Karen interrupted and said, "You acted like a zombie."

"Karen and me used to talk about it and get so mad because you wouldn't tell us, but you always had this strange look on your face."

"Before you left for the workshop, you left on your bike and came back with a new necklace. We knew it was from B. You can't hide it anymore," Karen spurted out. "B did all of this."

Jan put her head down and didn't answer.

"You've gotta make it stop," Caroline remarked.

"But B didn't know," Jan replied, defending him. "They told me stuff that B didn't even know. That box was everywhere. It would just show up, like magic, in my bedroom—there were no chords, it just talked to me! I didn't dare touch it because it had some kind of power and I might die. It scared me to death."

Her eyes darted fearfully. The troubled look on her sister's face made Karen feel extremely sad. Why didn't she see that B had done this to her?

Drained from Jan's overwhelming disclosure, Karen had all she could take. The high emotions of the night were evidenced in blood shot and puffy eyes. "You guys, it's almost four o'clock."

"You can't tell anybody about this," *Jan said pathetically.*

"Oh sure. So what are we supposed to do? Let B come and get you?" *Caroline said.*

"Mom and Dad have to know," *Karen said, emphatically.*

Caroline urged. "Jan, you've gotta tell them."

"I just don't want people to think I'm crazy. They might lock me up like B and do bad things like what happened to him."

"Your parents won't let that happen," *Caroline said.*

"What if they make me go back to Dr. Smith and he thinks I'm crazy?" *Jan asked.*

Caroline and Karen silently glared at Jan.

Finally conceding, Jan said. "Okay, I'll tell them."

"Are ya' going to tell them about the bad things he did to you?" *Caroline asked.*

"I don't know."

"That would be awful. I'd never tell my parents," *Caroline said.*

Exhausted, Karen pulled a blanket onto the carpeted floor and wearily rolled up in it while Caroline spread out in the large overstuffed chair. Jan stayed on the couch. Sleep did not come easily since they could not turn off their disturbing thoughts; they slept restlessly.

at last we understand!

Jan's thoughts, feelings, and dreams were a jumble that morning as she drifted in and out of a restless sleep. She was so relieved that Caroline and Karen finally knew, but felt such apprehension about telling her parents. She had told and had-n't died; but she was still so confused about what was real and what was not real. Her tired, feverish mind bounced from one thought to another: Wow! I told Caroline and Karen about "Z" and they believed me. But I'm afraid Mom and Dad will think I'm crazy or just making it up. They will be so mad at me for not telling them before. I've wondered for a long time about "Z" because one time when one of them talked to me, I was so scared that I ran out of my bedroom and B was standing in the hall. It scared me so bad I thought I would faint. He said they had talked to him earlier and he knew they were going to tell me some things. He came over to see if I was okay because he knew how they frightened me. I don't know how he got in the house. He wasn't supposed to be here. Even if Zada and Zethra aren't real, who are all the other people that call me and leave me notes? "Z" told me they were part of the plan. I can't be sure about any of this. I just know I'm going crazy and can't stand to do it anymore. Karen and Caroline are right, Mom and Dad need to know. If I die, they have to protect Susan from them. I don't believe them that Dad is not my real dad. I'm praying that I can do this and he will understand. He has to. It's all true.

The whir of the lawn mower going past the window aroused the sleeping trio all too soon.

Caroline stretched and yawned. "It's too early. I need more sleep." She groaned, pulling the blanket over her head. For the next fifteen minutes, the girls shifted positions, hoping they could miraculously fall back to sleep.

Eventually Karen said, "Are you awake, Jan?"

"Uh huh," she grunted.

"Did last night really happen, or was it just a bad dream?" Caroline inquired.

Receiving no response from Jan, Karen and Caroline discussed how they would get her to disclose her bizarre past to her mom and dad. Unable to reach a sensible conclusion, they urged Jan to get up. After tossing around several suggestions, Caroline finally insisted that she just go upstairs and tell her parents.

Jan nervously bit her fingernails. "I can't," she said uneasily.

Annoyed, Karen brushed past her and made her way toward the staircase. "Then I'll tell them."

"Okay! I'll go!" Jan blurted out, irritated. "Just give me five more minutes. I've got a splitting headache."

Caroline and Karen attempted to pump Jan full of confidence by offering support. Did she want them to go with her? Would it be easier if one of them told? Still trying to recover from her difficult confession of the past night, Jan felt trapped. Knowing her parents needed to hear it from her, she finally conceded and began her climb up the steps.

Jan decided it would be easier to tell her dad first. His patience over the past year had been remarkable; he had never questioned why she had been so emotional or impulsive. All these months, she stayed a safe distance from him. For a time, she really believed he was not her father.

Her heart began to pound furiously against her chest. Standing at the back door, she paused.

Only Karen and Caroline's presence at the foot of the stairs caused her to keep going. Making certain Jan carried through, they watched until she was on the patio and addressed her father.

■ ■ ■

That morning, Bob had left for work early as I went out for my morning jog. On my return, the house was quiet; only Susan was up, eating a bowl of cereal. "I can't go down and watch TV because the girls are in there sleeping," Susan said.

"You can use the TV in my bedroom," I offered. "The girls didn't sleep much last night. Guess we should let them sleep in."

Bob returned from work later in the morning to mow the lawn. After he finished the job, he settled in a lawn chair on the patio to cool off. I needed to snap the mess of beans Bob had brought from Grandma's garden; I took them and joined him on the patio. It was good to inhale the warm summer air.

"The girls must have been up half the night," I said to Bob. "It's nearly noon and they're still sleeping."

"They were on some kind of marathon last night. I didn't think they would ever go to sleep," Bob commented as he put his head back and closed his eyes.

"Oh, Jan's been riding high night and day over her new friends and the workshop."

I felt a sense of peaceful satisfaction as I watched squirrels jump from one tree to another. I continued to snap beans and toss the ends onto the lawn. I was blessing counting when Jan appeared at the patio door, ghostly white and trembling.

"Jan, what's the matter?" I asked in alarm.

"Dad, can I talk to you?" she said in a quivering, soft voice.

I nodded my head at Bob and quickly left them alone and went into the house.

Over an hour later, Bob came in the house, wide-eyed, pale, and perspiring.

He swallowed hard and said breathlessly, "You have to come and hear what Jan has been telling me. You won't believe it! Berchtold was trying to persuade Jan to leave the workshop with him, but that's only one small part of it. You won't believe what Jan's been through. It's so awful!"

We returned to the patio. Jan was seated at the picnic table looking pale and forlorn; her eyes were red and swollen. Bob asked me to listen and let Jan tell me what she had just related to him. I sat across from her as she began disclosing her unbelievable story. I listened flabbergasted as she told of awakening in the motor home and hearing a strange alien voice. In detail, she described the message of being a chosen and special spirit that was to help these unknown visitors populate their world.

"From the minute I heard her voice, I believed what she said. Her name was Zada and she was from another world. The other person was Zethra."

Trying to be a good listener and avoid asking questions, I nodded and swallowed hard.

Jan's voice quivered as she related the afflictions which would accompany her inability or decision not to follow the plan. How could she allow her sisters to be harmed, or her dad? Although she never knew how her life would end, she knew she would be destroyed if she told. To think about placing Susan in the same circumstances was unthinkable.

"When Brother B told me what they did to him, he was really scared and didn't know what to do. B was afraid of those people . . .

you know, *the aliens.* They told him he was supposed to take me to Mexico. He didn't know what would happen to us if things didn't work out right. I heard their voices a lot when I was in the motor home. Sometimes B was with me and other times I was alone. They kept repeating over and over what I had to do and told me I was chosen to be the mother of a special child."

Bob and I avoided each other's gaze as we concentrated on Jan. Her voice shook, there was a noticeable tremor of her body, and she continually pulled and scratched at her skin. Obviously traumatized, she repeated how important it was for her to fulfill her mission and not fail.

I wanted to rush around the table and hold her close, but dared not interrupt her accounting of this grotesque story.

"Do you still believe these people are out there and are going to make you do these things?" Bob quizzed.

Jan shrugged her shoulders. "I don't know. Remember when I went with my friends to the sophomore party at the tennis courts? I wasn't supposed to have any male relationships, but I danced with a boy and nothing happened. But when the dogs were poisoned, I knew one of them saw me go to the Wilkinson Center with a boy. I just don't know who they are and I'm scared."

"How many times have these people contacted you?" I asked.

Jan shook her head slowly. "A lot. Maybe a hundred times. Sister Charlotte was always watching me when I was at Flintridge, and I was afraid I'd do something wrong. She's supposed to be one of *them* and I was scared of her."

"Jan, I know for a fact these aliens are not real," her father said. "We know Berchtold planned and schemed all of this so he could control you. You may not believe it now, but you will."

Solemnly, Jan stared into space, squinting her eyes, trying not to cry, but mirroring back doubt about her father's statement. She wiped her nose with a wad of toilet paper.

Firmly, Bob stated, "Berchtold has been manipulating your life, lying to you, scaring you out of your wits. He will continue to do anything he can because he only wants one thing and that is you, my precious daughter. Don't let him win."

Jan's eyes looked hurt and sad. She pursed her lips and sobbed desperately.

"Does he frighten you?" I asked.

Jan nodded and blubbered, "I don't want him or these people to do anything to any of us. I just want them to leave us alone."

The relief of hearing her statement caused my heart to leap. I could no longer hold back the tears. Confidently, I retorted, "The first step is for all of us to stay away from him and his whole family."

Bob added, "We want to protect you, and we will, no matter what the cost."

The more she willingly revealed, the more vigorously we questioned her. Finally Jan heaved a sigh. She looked exhausted.

"Okay. That's enough, honey," Bob announced.

"I've been scared for so long," Jan said sniffling. "I still think something is going to happen."

Her desperate eyes made my heart ache.

Bob's extended his arms in invitation, and Jan folded into them and sobbed mightily. As he tenderly held his firstborn and comforted her, tears rolled down his face. It had been a long time since he had the privilege of showering her with affection. Seeing Jan in her dad's arms comforted me as well. After several minutes, Jan stood up and in a quiet whisper said, "Thanks, Dad. I love you."

"I love you too," he replied.

I embraced Jan and acknowledged the lonely burden she had carried for so long. "I'm so sorry. I can't begin to realize what you have gone through. Anytime you feel nervous or scared, talk to us. We can't help you if we don't know." She nodded her head in agreement.

"I can't believe I told you," she whispered. She headed towards the patio door, then turned around with a perplexed look and implored, "I've been scared for so long. You don't have to talk to anybody about this, do you?"

"Not right now. We'll discuss it later," Bob assured her before she went inside.

After a few moments of studying Bob's anxious gaze, I said, "Jan's a bright girl. She's smarter than this. How could she believe it all and not figure out Berchtold was behind it?"

"Why not? We fell prey to his criminal mind, and we are adults. I think Jan has just scratched the surface telling us what happened." Bob groaned. "I can't imagine what kind of damage he's caused her."

"I could kill the creep," I growled.

"I think that's my line," Bob mused.

We fell into a companionable silence, both of us trying to digest the unimaginable circumstances Jan had just revealed. The great mystery of her behavior and attitude was finally solved. How different things had looked from her perspective than from ours! I was touched to know that concern for the safety of our family had been her prime motivation for her continued connection with Berchtold. Her belief that her family would be harmed if she did not comply with her instructions from "the aliens" had kept her in bondage to him and we had been in bondage to our ignorance. The threat that Jan would cease to exist if she told must have been the hardest thing a child could live with. Now that she knew that was a lie, perhaps she could grapple with the rest.

I smiled as the image of Jan in her father's arms came back into my mind. The truth would make us all free. Jan was finally home—really home—again.

epilogue: sorting it out, moving ahead

It was hard for Jan to pinpoint the time when she finally knew for sure there were no aliens, no other planet. Thankfully, within a few months she finally recognized Berchtold as the deviant mind behind every painful event that had happened. Jan admitted she had believed for years that the aliens were real because she heard their voices so often, and it seemed she heard them everywhere. She became suspicious of Berchtold only once when he appeared shortly after she heard an "alien" message and knew everything she had just been told. To cover up he had said that a similar message had been given to him. There was just enough deviance in his scheme to keep her mind totally confused.

After we got Jan back the first time and I took a stand against Berchtold, he had to find a way to contact Jan that I wouldn't know about. He had apparently hired strangers to deliver messages to her. Each iniquitous contact either gave Jan specific instructions or an affirmation that confirmed everything was going as planned and she would be told what to do at a later date. Unable to free herself from Berchtold's psychological maneuvering, Jan had resigned herself to follow the controlling authority.

With so many strangers interfering in her life, confusion abounded. She admitted being really frightened of Berchtold after the fire, but dared not incriminate him because of fear of retribution. Mostly because Jan had feared for her life and the fate of family members, Robert's deceptions had continued to work. Upon Berchtold's release from the Idaho Medical State Facility, sporadic contact continued to enslave Jan until she revealed the secrets of her past.

Over the next few days, I persistently quizzed Jan over matters that had been bothersome, and Jan's response to our questions brought us small increments of insight into her pitiful plight. However, her anxiety escalated whenever we asked for clarification in regard to any of her experiences, and we realized she needed professional help. Dr. Smith had conducted several tests and found Jan mentally stable, and she was not on medication. Consequently, an out-of-state child psychiatrist who was our friend advised us to take her to a psychologist or therapist instead of a psychiatrist.

Jan agreed to meet with a local counselor, but was concerned that anyone who knew her story would consider her crazy. She was promised that any admissions would remain confidential. However, finding the right counselor that suited Jan's willingness to express her past was not successful. Life at home continued with little disruption once Jan chose to counsel with us regularly.

The Secret Agony of Sexual Abuse

Although we knew that Jan's innocence had been robbed, she refused to talk about the abuse. We speculated Berchtold's marriage demand was his coverup for sexual molestation, and his only hope for copulation without child sexual abuse charges. But the year was 1978, and sexual abuse of children remained a quiet and personal issue. Few convictions against perpetrators were accomplished.

Most children didn't talk with parents or adults about sexual matters in those days, and ours were no exception. The counselor told us that children rarely disclose sex crimes committed against them, but keep them hidden because of shame, guilt and demoralization. Many become non-trusting of adults in general.

We were encouraged when we learned that victims are generally more willing to disclose after they realize they are not responsible for the abuse. However, we were warned that they don't necessarily do so. Often, children carry guilt in regard to the crimes committed against them into adulthood until they finally internalize the fact that they had little or no control to stop the abuse. Many child victims remain embarrassed about their victimization and reject any thought of disclosing what they perceive as shameful secrets. For whatever reason, Jan chose to remain mute regarding her sexual victimization. We were disappointed, because her refusal diminished any hope of bringing justice against Berchtold.

Parents' Dilemma

Bob and I found it difficult to deal with our feelings of guilt, anger, resentment and shock. It was not only Jan who had been manipulated and brainwashed; we had as well. In the beginning of our relationship with Berchtold, we were so enraptured by him that we overlooked warning signs: He spent inordinate amounts of time with our daughters. He gave gifts which were often lavish, made visits at bedtime, and initiated excessive activities which involved them. His focus on Jan should have been a red flag, especially when he asked her to work part time at his furniture business when she was underage. The fact that he was fun-loving, witty, charismatic, a big kid at heart, and a dad himself, overshadowed his underlying condition. A trusting relationship well established between our families, and my absolute belief that Berchtold would never do anything to hurt my children, gave him privileged ground. We suffered great remorse for being blinded to Berchtold's long-term goal which caused our daughter to be unjustly demoralized. Parents are supposed to protect their children and we let the unthinkable occur.

The Healing Journey Is Often Lonely

Our entire family faced the challenge of trying to recover from those crisis-laden years. Each handled their personal healing independently. Bob soon closed the door on the past and refused to discuss any aspect of the trauma. He was not alone in feeling that solution best. Many family members and friends felt our ordeal had intruded on their personal lives long enough and they were tired of dealing with questions from outsiders and tired of the whole ordeal. Trying to appease their feelings, I too felt compelled to stop discussing my feelings and move on.

To keep my emotional afflictions private, self-inspection became a priority. I turned towards educating myself on the problems that nearly destroyed my family. I read where survivors of horrendous experiences found comfort by writing about their trials. Writing the story brought me satisfaction. I went back to school and graduated with a Social Work degree. My studies and work in this field made me recognize that the comfortable, protected life I had lived before Berchtold came on the scene was no longer viable in our unkind, and often brutal society.

It appeared Karen and Susan escaped unscathed. Only years later, feelings emerged that connected their anger and consternation to the grim ordeal. At the time, we didn't realize that each family member was a victim. We gave so much attention to Jan, while her sisters kept their feelings hidden. We didn't realize that Karen had been saddled with detailed knowledge of Jan's sexual abuse. She kept her thoughts and emotions to herself since the ordeal seemed closed to discussion. It was unfair. Family counseling could have been a great healer and benefitted all, but because no one ever suggested it, we didn't think it necessary.

The Continuing Berchtold Story

The only interruptions over the ensuing years where Berchtold became the suspect, were in the form of long distance phone calls with the caller refusing to speak but remaining on the line until we hung up.

That was, until 1984. Thanksgiving had barely past when I answered the phone and a friendly voice asked what I was doing. After a few minutes of conversation with the caller, he laughed and said, "I can't believe you don't know who this is." Panic engulfed my entire body as I recognized the frivolity of Berchtold's voice. Cheerfully, he explained the phone call was not for himself, but for his son, Jimmy who wanted to make contact with Karen. I hung up mortified.

A year later, while all three daughters were attending college and living together, Jan was called to the phone and spoke with an unnamed caller who didn't hesitate to discuss personal events regarding her recent life.

Unable to put a face with the voice, she made an accounting about a personal matter before realizing she was speaking with Berchtold. Shocked, she made frantic gyrations for Karen to pick up an extension and listen in. Berchtold had some personal belongings of Jan's and wanted to return them. Asking if he could see her, she said, "I don't think so." He gave her a Salt Lake address and told her he worked for a large auto dealer. Didn't she want to retrieve a home movie from her performance of *Amahl and the Night Visitors?* Unprepared to challenge him, she made no commitment and hung up.

Frantic, she and Karen called home. Fearful he might interrupt her life again, we insisted she and her sisters take protective measures by staying in the company of others whenever possible, never going home alone, keeping doors locked, and carrying a protective repellent. Alerting campus police offered some protection, but most importantly, we were all aware that Berchtold could show up anywhere, unexpectedly.

Within the month came the following message:

Dear Jan:

As I told you on the phone, I am engaged to be married in June. I had my attorney check in Mexico to see if you and I are still married, since your mother agreed to take care of this and apparently did not, we are still legally married.

I have filed for divorce and you will probably be required to attend a hearing. My attorney will notify you of the time and place. Since we haven't been together since the night on the reservation in Pocatello in 1977 there shouldn't be any problems getting a quick divorce.

Thanks, B

Receiving no response, he mailed a second letter two months later, obviously determined:

Dear Jan,

The reason you haven't heard from anyone is that I changed my mind about any plans for marriage. I am convinced that everyone is allowed one love per life time, I have had mine. If there is ever anything you need or if you just need someone, let me know. I will always be here for you.

All my love, B

Would Jan ever find relief from the Berchtold plague? Professionals have determined that personalities of his type never shoulder the responsibility of their devious crimes. Furthermore, there's no cure for a pedophile. In some cases, treatment can be successful as long as the addict stays away from his addiction—children.

Even though Jan was no longer a child and should be considered free from her molester, Berchtold also had an obsessive-compulsive disorder and she was apparently still his target.

Credible sources have provided information regarding Berchtold over the years: In 1986 he was arrested for two counts of rape of a child in the state of Utah. He pled guilty to one count and was sentenced by the Third District Court of Salt Lake City, Utah to one year in the Salt Lake City Jail in September 1987. Following his release, he was placed on probation and moved to Nevada in 1989. Robert Berchtold should be listed on every state's registry as a sex offender. More recently, a reliable party stated that Berchtold became a drifter, and having difficulties with employment, moved from one western state to another. He suffered a severe heart attack and nearly died. The party stated that Berchtold claimed responsibility for "ruining" the lives of two families. In that interview, Berchtold also stated he had watched Jan in various TV movies and was surprised she looked so beautiful and capable since he thought she would end up in a mental hospital.

A Family of Survivors and Thrivers

In spite of what Berchtold thought he accomplished, the Broberg family survived. Our family unit became stronger than ever. We still believe that truth will prevail and justice will be administered whether it be today, in the future, or in the hereafter. This gives us satisfaction to press forward with peace of mind. Enduring what seemed impossible odds has proven "and this too shall pass." Our girls are exquisite examples of the resilience of the human spirit.

Jan's Life

Over the years, flashbacks of Jan's horrific ordeal have been a challenge for her. She has acknowledged that the affect of brainwashing and sexual abuse changed her life forever. Although she remains angry over her stolen innocence, her focus has always been on self-improvement and a positive attitude. She counsels with trusted friends, family, or a professional, if the burden becomes overwhelming. Her opinion is that brainwashing can be overcome in a matter of time. Unfortunately, child sexual abuse leaves deep scars on the mind.

Jan chose to keep her sexual abuse secret until she was twenty-three years old. She found disclosure of the nature of Berchtold's sexual crimes therapeutic, but expressed bitter hostility toward him. One psychologist told her, "It's healthy for you to be angry. You need to scream and holler and call him whatever names you feel he deserves because of the misery he has caused you and your family. And it's okay to hate him—at least for now."

By the time Jan chose to reveal the crime, however, the statute of limitations had passed and it was impossible to bring legal charges against Mr. Berchtold.

Determined not to become an emotional cripple, Jan ignored her sexual victimization by pouring an intense amount of energy into school studies, music and drama. She was elected Senior Class President, addressed her class at graduation as valedictorian, and received a scholarship to Brigham Young University where she studied dramatic arts, music, and dance.

Jan's love of and talent for music and drama has been a sustaining force. During college, she was heavily involved in dramatic productions and also performed as a member of *The Young Ambassadors*, a performing song and dance group that tours throughout the United States and foreign countries. She interrupted her college studies to serve an eighteen-month mission for The Church of Jesus Christ of Latter-day Saints, which took her to Guatemala City, Guatemala.

Jan married Duke Tanner and spent three years in Orlando, Florida where they performed as vocalists, dancers, and entertainers at Disney World. After the birth of their son, Austen, Jan opened a Performing Arts Studio for children and teens. Later, she returned to BYU, graduating *summa cum laude* in Cinematic Arts and Theater. Fluent in Spanish, Jan taught kindergarten to

Spanish-speaking students in Southern California while perfecting her own acting skills. Jan loves to teach and direct. She directed and coached new actors to success for Cine Paris Film Productions in Los Angeles, has taught music and dance to special needs children, and recently directed and taught drama at Tuacahn High School for the Performing Arts in St. George, Utah.

Life continues to bring its challenges and rewards. Jan's indomitable spirit has survived divorce, single and step-parenthood. She and her son, Austen Tanner, along with her husband, Larry H. Felt, and his four daughters, McKenzi, Tess, Melissa, and Faith, are generating a new, creative, family circle. She has enjoyed continued success as an accomplished actress in film, television, and live theater. Jan is also a popular speaker. Her humor, warmth, and exuberance for life inspires youth, adults, and professionals at conferences throughout the Western States.

Karen's Life

Karen was also a member of *The Young Ambassadors* and graduated from BYU in premed. Her plans for medical school were put on hold because marriage took precedence and she is now the mother of five exuberant children: Eric, Allison, Dane, Nathan, and Paige. Karen tutors students in math and science, is a talented and published writer and singer who creates and produces musical and dramatic presentations for community and church events. Karen is a strong advocate for families and a member of United Families International, an organization that focuses on issues to preserve the family. She has served as a delegate from Arizona to the United Nations World Summit for Children where she has lobbied on issues that threaten moral values and supports issues that are vital to maintaining traditional family values.

Susan's Life

Susan graduated with a degree in Chinese language and Asian

Studies after completing a church mission to Taiwan. Following the tradition of her sisters, she was a member of *The Young Ambassadors* and *The Lamanite Generation*. She excelled at her responsibility of designing, creating, and building costumes for the performers. Susan returned to the Orient after graduation where she taught English to Chinese students at an Aviation University in Tianjin, China. Following her year abroad, she entered law school at Brigham Young University. She was elected Student Body Law President, addressed her graduating class and received a Juris Doctorate degree. Susan is a practicing attorney in the state of California. She is also very involved in community and church service.

Bob's Life

Bob continued to dedicate his professional life to the floral business and has been revered as a "master of design." Always active in the State organization, he has served as president of the Idaho State Florist Association and chaired several programs and conventions over the years. An active member of Rotary and Chamber of Commerce, he has been recognized in the community for many acts of service. His personal life has been dedicated to church service and his family. With humor and compassion for others, his contribution to creating a pleasant and positive home environment has been the center of his life. As grandchildren came into our lives, Bob found a new enthusiasm to further enhance his joy of living. He is considered by his children as the "grand master of grandparenthood."

Silver Linings

The Chinese symbol for crisis is danger plus opportunity. I believe that all my daughters were strengthened and motivated to achieve by the traumas of our lives. I am overjoyed that our crisis became an opportunity to benefit others. I will close with an example in my own life:

During the 1996 Idaho State Legislative session, I responded to a phone call from Elaine Hofman with a surge of excitement. She proposed that I lend a voice in favor of a missing children's center. Elaine was serving her third term as a member of the House of Representatives and was hoping to secure passage of a bill to authorize the establishment of a state-level clearing center for missing and exploited children. Only two other states besides Idaho were lacking a clearinghouse.

Elaine asked, "Mary Ann, would you be willing to address the Legislature as the mother of a missing child? Ernest Allen, president of the National Center for Missing and Exploited Children, will be here to testify. Your testimony could be the emotional support we need."

I thought back to the critical situation of twenty years past. The memory of our inability to do anything except report it to the law stung fiercely. I felt pain for parents whose missing children appeared in local news reports while they despaired over the fate of their beloved child.

Preparing a brief statement was no easy assignment, but I worked diligently to give an insightful plea. Several persons would testify, both in favor and against the bill. This was the third year they had sought approval for the bill. The first two times the bill had not even made it out of committee and onto the floor.

When I appeared at the State Capitol, the House Education Committee room was packed with supporters, news media, and opposition. I felt extremely nervous as I approached the podium. After I had delivered the first few sentences of my speech, my voice cracked and my eyes blurred with tears. After apologizing and gaining control, I continued my prepared testimony.

Mr. Chairman; Members of the Committee;
    Thank you for allowing me to be in this hearing today and offer my personal testimony.

Have any of you experienced the trauma of losing your young child, if only for a matter of minutes, in a supermarket or department store, even your neighborhood? Remember that overwhelming panic which consumed you until your little one was found? Now imagine feeling that way for days, weeks, even months. It was the most helpless experience of my life.

My young daughter was abducted twice by a person we had considered a "best friend" leaving a permanent lump in my throat and a large knot piercing my gut for the duration of those two horrific abductions. The FBI and other law enforcement agencies were extremely capable and supportive. We felt they gave us their finest service. Yet, they had no leads as to where the kidnapper had taken our child. After several days, the only hope we were given was the assumption that the perpetrator would eventually slip up. After five grueling weeks, her discovery was made when he called a family member and the phone call was traced to Mexico.

The second episode resulted in a horrendous three and a half months of fear and despair. Because there was no evidence that her previous kidnapper was involved, she was listed as a runaway which removed the Federal Bureau of Investigation from involvement. We were informed runaways were not actively sought by law enforcement officers. However, local police and the FBI had reason to believe that this man was involved in her disappearance and they didn't abandoned us. One detective from the police department spent personal time, beyond his work hours, investigating leads, as did our local FBI agent. Finally, a phone call made to us from our abducted daughter, assisted the law to concentrate their efforts in a certain area of the country which eventually led to her recovery and the arrest of her captor. He had placed her in a private school under an assumed name with the faculty unaware of his deception.

How can a family actively seek for their child when personal finances are limited? Where do they turn beyond those committed servants of law enforcement? Friends and relatives rallied to help us, but they asked, "where should we go beyond Pocatello and how do we distribute information?" Willingly they tried, but efforts proved fruitless. It was an impossible task.

This tragedy happened over twenty years ago. How fortunate that resources have progressed—beyond what limitations we had available—with the formation of the National Center for Missing and Exploited Children. As I hear or read about children who have been located in other states through the assistance of this organization, I applaud enthusiastically. With every child that is found, the hearts of thousands rejoice. The abduction or exploitation of any child affects not only the parents, but all of those within the community, and I dare say, the nation.

With advanced technologies readily at our fingertips which will provide technical assistance to law enforcement and support to families, it is beyond my understanding why our grand state has not been on the front line long before now, cheering and pushing for the establishment of an Idaho Missing Person's Clearinghouse. As a mother who experienced the traumatic emotions of a missing child, I beg you, give the children and families of Idaho the support of this organization. Thank you.

After the hearing was over, Mr. Allen grabbed my hand and squeezed it firmly. "If they didn't hear anything else, they heard you. Believe me, what you shared made a difference. We were all touched. I would be amazed if they turned this down. Thank you for sharing your personal story with us."

A news conference followed the hearing. Numerous reporters seeking further information, sought out "the lady whose child was missing" and bombarded me with questions.

One asked if I could explain why I broke down during my testimony. Responding I said, "First of all, I've never forgotten the pain, and second, the relief of finding my child is indescribable. It stirs my emotions every time I think about it."

The Bill passed the House with overwhelming support and a short time later, passed the Senate, allowing a three-year funding source for the establishment of a clearinghouse. The Idaho Missing Persons Center continues today with glowing reports of its success. The Idaho Clearinghouse offers valuable leads in locating missing persons and provides a link to all other forty-nine state Clearinghouses and the National Center for Missing and Exploited Children. To know I had a small part in that is gratifying beyond words.

AFTERWORD

The special friendship between the Brobergs and the Berchtolds, including their strong religious connections, worked against
Jan from the outset. Even when the criminal was caught, some
members of their church begged the Brobergs to forgive the criminal and show him mercy. They didn't want him locked up because
his children deserved to have their father at home. One might
wonder what those sympathetic church members might feel if it
was *their* daughter who was drugged, hands and feet strapped in
the darkness of Robert Berchtold's specially created prison cell,
and then brainwashed and sexually assaulted for months.

I realize the mid-1970's were not particularly enlightened years
for anybody on this subject. However, the Brobergs made every
mistake in the book, with the very best of intentions. The first mistake was not calling the police immediately, regardless of the reason for Jan's absence, be it an accident or misunderstanding. She
was a twelve-year-old who should have been home on time. Their
first job as parents was to protect their daughter, not create imaginary alibis for their "best friend." Waiting to call authorities is
mind-boggling to me as a judge and parent of three children. Sadly,
as you have learned, she might have been rescued in the first few
days had they but picked up the phone. Frankly, the adult pride of
Mrs. Berchtold and the Brobergs' sympathy for her allowed this illegal and immoral catastrophe to occur.

Robert Berchtold, as you have read, was eventually taken into
custody in Mexico. And, as is often true in battered women cases

as well, his loyal but naïve wife posted his bail. (By the way, it does not surprise me that Mrs. Berchtold posted her deserting, criminal husband's bond. This is quite common in the battered women cases I see. Their loyalty and dependency trumps reality and common sense.)

This led to the Broberg's second mistake. Upon Robert's release from jail, they should have immediately applied to a local court for a protective or restraining order, some type of injunction keeping this criminal from having any contact with Jan whatsoever.

Their third mistake was in not hiring a *competent* lawyer immediately! The lawyer might not only have assisted with all of the foregoing legal actions, but might have gone back to the criminal court asking it to enter a "no contact order" with Jan as a condition of the criminal's bond. A lawyer would have prepared the Brobergs for the hearing process as well. Mrs. Broberg made an excellent defense witness for the man who kidnapped her daughter.

Their fourth mistake was not immediately getting a competent psychological counselor for Jan and, perhaps, her own lawyer. No adult seemed to protect the child's needs or interests. The poor child didn't even know she was a victim of the crime of kidnapping!

Their fifth mistake was continuing a relationship with the Berchtold family. It was a tactical mistake that a good lawyer would have advised against. What would change in the world if the families stayed apart until the criminal matter was concluded? Their continued relationship benefited only one person, Robert Berchtold.

The sixth mistake was the meeting between Mrs. Broberg, the victim/child, and the criminal! As a judge, lawyer and father, I find that unfathomable. Again, their lawyer would not have allowed that trap. Any first year law student would know the criminal would use the very fact of that meeting to diminish the prosecution's case. This guy was still manipulating, and Mary Ann was the willing marionette. Imagine allowing this criminal pedophile close enough to kiss her daughter on the forehead the day he was battling for clemency.

The seventh mistake was in meeting with the criminal's defense lawyer. Criminal trials are adversary proceedings. Each side, the prosecution and the defense, are obligated to oppose each other; one on behalf of the state, and usually the victim; the other, the defense lawyer, whose sole duty is to defend. That is, to get Robert Berchtold off, or at least out of prison. In terms of the best interest of the child, such meetings are never, never, never for that purpose.

The eighth mistake was not detaining Jan when she was boarding the plane. As I read that part of the book I felt like screaming, "Tackle her, damn it, she is your child, she is a minor, and she does not have your permission to board an airplane. Stop her!"

The ninth mistake was in not forcing the authorities to take action after the second kidnapping when they had solid evidence that the criminal again had control of their minor child. Choosing "confidentiality" over the reality of a quiet investigation is highly questionable, especially when practically every state has a law against the impairment of the health or morals of a child.

Mistake number ten: had the police become involved, they might have trailed the criminal upon his release from jail. Instead, the Brobergs became the police and did the investigation. Not surprisingly, they weren't any better in the police profession than they were in the legal profession.

Mistake number eleven belongs to the law enforcement community. Mrs. Broberg was given a gun to put in her purse for her meeting with the criminal. Why weren't undercover police in the area? Her protection was her younger brother Randy. His qualifications for the safety stake out? He was a postal employee! Quite a perplexing inaction.

In spite of all Jan's emotional and sexual involvement, and the absolute misery it inflicted upon her wonderful family, one must feel relieved that there is a happy ending to this story. I suppose the book has educated us, but beyond that, it brings a message of hope to all who have ever been sexually abused or maltreated. As you know now, pedophiles are not one-time offenders.

I met Jan for dinner the night before we were both to speak at a conference on child abuse. She sent me a draft of her mother's book to read. I offered to write the foreword and an epilogue. After reading the book, I said, "Jan, I am not so sure you want me to do this since your family made every mistake in the book." She said, "We're beyond that, Charlie, go ahead and write."

I then asked Jan, who is about as attractive and intelligent a person as one might meet, "How did you make a comeback after all of that?" She said, "Because of the absolute love and support of my family the first twelve years in my life, and a bit of good counseling along the way."

Ironically, in the end, it was what the Brobergs did right for Jan that won the day: they loved her.

-Judge Charles Gill

About the Judge:

Connecticut Superior Court Judge Charles D. Gill is a tireless advocate for the rights of children. In 1988, he co-founded the National Task Force for Children's Constitutional Rights. He is a nationally recognized expert on children's issues and an advisor on children's issues for major radio and television network news programs, including CNN, Good Morning America, Nightline, and 20/20. He is a consultant to the U.S. Department of Justice, Office of Juvenile Justice. The Honorable Charles Gill has testified in Congress in behalf of children and delivered a speech to members of the United Nations General Assembly on the need to include children in their Constitutions. Judge Gill has been a lawyer for forty years and has served as a judge for the past twenty years. He is married to Joan Reynolds Gill, a pediatric nurse, and they are the parents of three children: Charles Gill Jr., James Reynolds Gill, and Kasey Marie Gill.